The Prophet Elijah in the Development of Judaism

THE LITTMAN LIBRARY OF JEWISH CIVILIZATION

EDITORS

David Goldstein
Louis Jacobs
Lionel Kochan

This Library is dedicated
to the memory of
JOSEPH AARON LITTMAN

The Prophet Elijah in the Development of Judaism

A Depth-Psychological Study

AHARON WIENER

ROUTLEDGE & KEGAN PAUL
LONDON, HENLEY AND BOSTON

First published in 1978
by Routledge & Kegan Paul Ltd
39 Store Street,
London WC1E 7DD;
Broadway House,
Newtown Road,
Henley-on-Thames,
Oxon RG9 1EN and
9 Park Street,
Boston, Mass. 02108, USA
Set in Bembo 12pt 1pt leaded
and printed in Great Britain by
The Camelot Press Ltd, Southampton

British Library Cataloguing in Publication Data

Weiner, Aharon

The prophet Elijah in the development of Judaism.
– (The Littman library of Jewish civilization).
1. Elijah, the Prophet 2. Bible. Old Testament
I. Title   II.   Series

77-30442

Distributed by Oxford University Press
ISBN 0 19 710010 4

*To my beloved wife and children
and in memory of my teacher Erich Neumann*

Contents

Abbreviations

BT   Babylonian Talmud
JT   Jerusalem Talmud
M.   Midrash
M. r. Midrash Rabbah
M. z. Midrash Zutta
R.   Rabbi (before a name)

Passages from the Old Testament are generally taken from *The Holy Scriptures* of the Jewish Publication Society; the transliteration is in accordance with the *Encyclopedia Judaica* (Jerusalem, 1971).

Introduction and Acknowledgments

The depth psychology inaugurated by Freud and the layers of the collective unconscious uncovered by Jung and his school have given a new direction to the exploration of *homo religiosus* and religions. Earlier William James in his detailed book, *The Varieties of Religious Experience*, repeatedly mentioned the existence of a 'subliminal consciousness' and 'subconscious activity', and in his conclusion wrote about the striking influence of 'the subconscious self' upon religion.[1] Rudolf Otto, too, in his impressive *The Idea of the Holy*, spoke of the 'wholly other' and of the numinous 'feeling penetrating the consciousness as superrational element'.[2]

These intimations were followed by specified observation and evaluation of the psychodynamic processes which may be the basis of man's general numinous and specific religious experiences as well as of his working them through by reflections and expressing them by actions. Combined with the usual anthropological, mythological, historical and sociological methods of research, they formed a new synoptic view and threw a new light on the sources, essence and meaning of man's religiousness.

These depth psychologically directed investigations were concerned in the beginning with the reactions of human groups to the 'wholly other', not neglecting the personalities of their leaders, the sorcerers, medicine men, shamans, etc., or later the founders of institutional religions, their priests, prophets and other spiritual guides. Thus the psychological development of *homo religiosus* as individual, his personal transformations and that of his image of

God were analysed, and at the same time the reciprocal relationship between the religious experiences of the individual and the official religions were illuminated. Furthermore the various religious themes such as divine incarnation in man, redemption, resurrection, and their mutual relations were clarified.

It became obvious that, dissociated by his consciousness and self-awareness from his oneness with the universe, man had to strive for a new experience of unity within himself, with nature and his fellow-men.[3] Gradually he becomes aware of a 'higher part of himself', which, according to James, is 'conterminous and continuous with a More of the same quality which is operative in the universe outside of him',[4] and Otto paraphrased the deepest and most fundamental element in religiousness as the experience of the *mysterium tremendum et fascinans*.[5]

The findings of anthropologists, ethnologists and biologists such as Robert Marett, Robert Lowie and Julian Huxley confirmed that the response of primitive man to this extraordinary 'wholly other' was the source of religion.

Apparently it was man's need to 'cover' or at least to mitigate the *tremendum*—the dreadful, sometimes even the demonic—which brought him to devotion and worship, expressed by sacrifices and magic rituals, at first primitive and crude—ancestor worship, animism, totemism—but gradually refined by myths, symbols, ideas and doctrines. The fascinating aspect of the numinous came more and more to the foreground,[6] giving rise to ecstasy, either in the 'I—Thou' relation[7] of love to a personal god, or in true mystical experiences.[8]

Thus the depth psychologically directed researches seem to have brought about the proof that the 'holy', religiousness in its broad sense, is an intrinsic factor of human existence, 'a reality itself', as James called it,[9] or an '*a priori* category' as it was named by Otto.[10] Paul Tillich defines faith as 'the state of being ultimately concerned', and says: 'Faith as an act of the total personality is not imaginable without participation of the unconscious elements in the personality structure', and 'man is driven towards faith by the awareness of the infinite, to which he belongs but which he does not own like a possession.'[11] Henri Bergson, while formulating a clear definition of 'static religion', interprets 'dynamic religion' by a fascinating description of the true mystic's experience,[12] and Gordon Allport concludes from his psychological research of religion that man's religion 'is the ultimate attempt to enlarge and complete his personality by finding the supreme context in which he rightly belongs.'[13]

Furthermore it became obvious that the manifold differences of religious experiences by human groups and individuals, as well as those of the various myths, motifs, symbols and conceptions emerging from them, can be traced to a relatively small number of distinct patterns. The apparently great variations are dependent upon historical, geographical, environmental and especially social factors.

Many authors, such as Sigmund Freud, C. G. Jung, Ernest Jones, Otto Rank, Theodor Reik, Erich Neumann, Erich Fromm, Géza Róheim, Joseph Campbell, James Hillman, Siegmund Hurwitz, Josef Jashuvi, Rivka Schaerf-Kluger, Josef Rudin and Gustav Dreyfuss, have published significant depth-psychological studies in this field.

My present study is concerned with the prophet Elijah as he appears in the biblical record and to throw light on his out-standing personality by depth-psychological interpretation. I shall, moreover, investigate the absorption and modification of the biblical portrait of Elijah in the course of Jewish history—in so far as it is reflected in Jewish literature over about 2,500 years—and find out in what sense and to what extent the various concep-tions of the Elijah-figure may have influenced the development of Judaism from biblical times up to our own days.

Finally, I shall attempt to demonstrate, against the national and temporal historical and cultural background, the universal mean-ing of the Elijah-figure, and thus point out the more or less corres-ponding religious attitude of Jews and of mankind generally.

My examination is based throughout on the Masoretic, tradi-tional text of the Bible. I am not taking into consideration the results of those biblical researches which, on the basis of philo-logical examination of the text and study of the sources and of archeological finds, attempt to separate historic facts from legend.

For it is obvious that it was Elijah as he is described in the biblical text who impressed and influenced the Jews, collectively and individually. However, the biblical representation of Elijah, as champion of patriarchal monotheism against the paganism of his time, still essentially matriarchal, requires special consideration of its mythological and historical aspects.

In the chapters about Elijah from the Aggadic, Kabbalist and Hasidic viewpoints, I mention especially, cite and interpret, out of the abundant material available, those opinions and expressions which—to judge from their frequent, albeit variable, appearance in the texts—are typical of the basic attitude of each of these spiritual approaches towards his personality. From among different views I emphasise only those which, in connection with Elijah, stress religious attitudes previously only intimated in Judaism.

The interpretations of Jewish Bible exegetes and the opinions of Jewish philosophers are mentioned, mostly in notes, only in so far as they amplify variations in the Aggadic view.

I would like to express my indebtedness to Mrs A. Jaffé of Zürich for her many suggestions and advice which have been of valuable help. I also wish to thank my friend Isaak Lange of Zürich, Professor G. Scholem and Rabbi A. Steinsalz, both of Jerusalem, for several valid remarks respectively in the Aggadic, Kabbalistic and Hasidic fields. I am grateful to our daughter-in-law Nechama Cohn for her help in connection with chapter VIII.

The first draft of this study, written in German, was translated into English by Mrs Karen Gershon-Trop. This translation proved to be a very helpful basis for the final version of the book. I want to thank Mrs C. J. Raab for her excellent conscientious work as Academic Editor, and I am most grateful to Mr L. T. S. Littman and to Rabbi Dr David Goldstein for their proof-reading.

Above all I am deeply indebted to my wife for her close companionship and indefatigable help in all stages of shaping my study and its conclusions into the final form of this book.

The Biblical Record of the Prophet Elijah from the Viewpoints of History, Mythology, Religion and Depth Psychology

The Bible (Kings I and II) describes the life and activities of the prophet Elijah. In addition, there is a brief reference to him in Chronicles and a significant mention in the Book of Malachi.[1]

Bible scholars agree that Elijah was a historical person who lived about 920–850 BCE and that the biblical account of him, as the Books of Kings generally, was composed or edited about 100–150 years later.[2] Unlike the later prophets, no prophetic speeches by Elijah have been handed down, neither is any continuous biographical account of him provided. His appearance is rather an organic, although fragmentary, part of the story of the Jewish people in the days of its kings. This is in accordance with the basic attitude of the Bible, which is predominantly the history of the Jewish religion.

The stories of the first human beings, the patriarchs, the slavery in Egypt, the exodus, the wanderings in the desert, the conquest of the Promised Land, the period of the Judges and the establishment of the kingdom and its development are all represented in the biblical account almost exclusively from the religious point of view, as is the reciprocal relationship between the Israelites and their God. Its positive aspect is the belief in the *one* transcendent God and the conscious dependence of the chosen people on his rule; its negative aspect, disregard of his commandments or complete apostasy from him.

The creation, with which the Bible begins, postulates one God for the world and all mankind, whose will alone rules everything which he has created. The life of the first human beings in Paradise is portrayed in the light of a primary, undifferentiated monotheism, through which God, mankind and the world are united in a *participation mystique*.[3] Through his awakening consciousness, prehistoric man rises from this to become historic man, confronted with the divine as totally different on which, fearfully, he feels himself to be dependent and with which he seeks to establish a relationship.

The godhead in the Bible is not an abstract idea—not a philosophical concept. Its existence and its essence is revealed in its actions. The God of the Bible is omnipotent. He is not dependent upon any superior destiny and has no personal history reflected in myth. He can be identified with neither celestial bodies nor natural phenomena. Everything has been created by him and is dependent upon his will.[4] His rule is restricted solely by human disobedience, which he permits with certain limitations. He is experienced metaphorically and personally as creator and ruler of the world, father of mankind, king and lawgiver.

He thus reveals himself to the first human beings (later especially to the progenitors of the Jewish people) as the one who guides their personal destiny and as partner in a covenant which he makes with them and their descendants as those whom he has chosen. Later, they become his chosen people through experiencing the God of their fathers and through their fateful dependence on the fulfilment of this covenant.

In this chosen group, too, it is primarily the individual who is granted an immediate experience of God—as happens generally when human civilisation, i.e. the development of the human consciousness, has reached the stage of organising and gradually centring the individual ego. He experiences the revelation of the divine will, may become his messenger and so the mediator between God and his group and, through its recognition of his mission, its leader.

Being the chosen and the emissaries of the godhead is intrinsic to Israelite prophets. In this they differ from the *mana*-personages of pre-literate peoples, who are distinguished by ecstasy, divination and visionary and healing powers. Although in the early history of the Israelites such mantic prophets do make their appearance, unless they are under the influence of the inspired prophets, they do not bear divine tidings to the collective, but essentially counsel and help the individual.[5] To the extent to which these true prophets show mantic abilities, they serve above all to confirm their true mission. The central task of the prophet is to receive God's word and to proclaim it to the people. Thus Moses is summoned at the burning bush, against his will, to bring to the descendants of the patriarchs, the children of Israel —who were thereby declared to be a people—the message of the Divine: 'I am that I am.'[6] Through God's commandment to him and through his personality, humbly aware of his mission, he becomes the leader and liberator of the people, and through the revelation on Horeb (Mount Sinai) becomes the mouthpiece of God and the teacher of his Law. He renews the covenant made by God with the Israelites through their fathers, and strives to keep alive the faith in the transcendent God who directs the destiny of man and ensures the observance of his revealed will. He fights continually against the inclination of the people to lapse into nature worship and fetishism.

A close examination of the accounts in the biblical Books of Judges and of Kings reveals that the monotheistic faith of the people remained essentially alive and effective uninterruptedly from the days of Moses. The tendency to idolatry which appears over and over again until the Babylonian exile does not seem to have been in general a real turning towards the divinities of nature with their mythological all-too-human way of life. It was pre-dominantly more a matter of a relatively superficial acceptance and practice of pagan forms of worship. In the beginning this occurred under the influence of the Egyptians and the tribes which the Israelites encountered in the desert. Later, after the conquest of

Canaan, some of the provincial population of Israel fell under the influence of the remnants of the pagan cults which had persisted there. They were inclined to worship the Baalim, the local fertility gods—personifications of the natural forces but with no control over them—and to practise the associated rites, which were mostly of a sexual character.[7] Frequently, apparently, the fusion of the local Baalim into one single regional deity led to a presumptive identification with the God of Israel.

At the same time, for political, cultural or personal reasons, the Israelite rulers allowed the religious cults of their neighbours to be practised in their own country. Thus did Solomon, out of consideration for his non-Israelite wives, and also Jeroboam, to demonstrate the religious independence of the region belonging to the tribes of Israel ruled by him from the sanctuary in Jerusalem belonging to Judea.

But again and again emissaries from God appeared, following the example of Moses, who once more preached God's word to the people and endeavoured to restore the purity of the monotheistic cult. They appeared as prophets, judges, Nazirites or martial heroes. At times they became the counsellors of the leaders of the people or, when necessary, admonished and fought them in opposition; at times they themselves became the leaders of the people. Always they emphasised above all that the national existence of the Israelites depended upon their accomplishing the divine will (e.g., Judg. 6: 7–10; II Sam. 24: 11–13). Thus mostly only individuals or relatively small groups lapsed into out and out idolatry. Below the thin layer of pagan rites and forms of worship the monotheistic faith remained alive in the people as a whole.

A significant change occurred when the dynasty of Omri began to rule the kingdom of Israel (about 880 BCE). Omri, politically far more capable and active than his predecessors, made a pact with the neighbouring Sidon-Tyre (Phoenicia). This was sealed by his son and successor Ahab through his marriage to Jezebel, the daughter of Ethbaal, king of Sidon and a priest of Astarte.[8] Jezebel was not satisfied with remaining personally faithful to her native cult of Baal and Astarte at the court of the Israelite king. She summoned a group of priest-prophets of Baal and Astarte to be permanent court officials and endeavoured with their help to spread the Phoenician cult among the Israelites.

Ahab himself did not break faith completely with the God of Israel. His children bore names which refer to God. But at the same time he tolerated the service of Baal—partly out of political considerations, partly because of his personal dependence upon Jezebel. He even prayed to Baal himself, built him a temple of his own in the newly founded capital Samaria and erected beside the altar an *ashera*, the wooden pole dedicated to the goddess Astarte[9] whose cult was connected with sexual licence and with magic.[10]

This was the first time in the history of the Israelites that the worship of an alien god was explicitly sanctioned side by side with the cult of the God of Israel and accorded equal status. That they were completely different made a fusion of the two religions unlikely. The one acknowledged a universal God, whose far-reaching religious and moral demands affected the life of the individual and also that of the people as a whole; combined with this was the natural simplicity of the Israelite pastoral and peasant tradition. Integral to the other were worship of the divinities of nature, connected with fetishism and sexual licence, and also a ruthless political and economic striving for power and a more polished civilisation which did not recognise any moral obligations.

The co-existence of these religions was bound in time to lead to a confrontation. The Israelite prophets saw and understood the critical situation, the threat to the survival of their religion, but they felt powerless to oppose the efforts of the royal house. Those who attempted to fight against the danger of a syncretic development were cruelly persecuted by Jezebel's underlings and supporters. The attitude of the people as a whole towards these events was inconsistent or indifferent. The biblical record of the appearance of the prophet Elijah opens against this background.

The first mention of Elijah in the Bible occurs immediately after a short historic account of King Ahab's rule, especially of his idolatry. Nevertheless, the editor presents the prophet as appearing unintroduced before the king with the surprising words: 'As the

Lord, the God of Israel, liveth, before whom I stand, there shall not be dew nor rain these years, but according to my word' (I Kings 17: 1–3). Then immediately, at God's command, he flees into the desert.

Sudden entrances and disappearances of this sort are peculiar to Elijah, and are known and feared, as is mentioned later (I Kings 18: 12). Elijah is neither a 'prophet of the cult', connected with a sanctuary, nor, like many of his predecessors, subject to the royal court and at its disposal, nor has he a constant home where people can seek him out. He wanders from place to place, appearing suddenly 'here and now' when a divine call commands him or when he believes of his own accord that he must represent God and act on his behalf. He appears as 'a hairy man, and girt with a girdle of leather' (II Kings 1: 8), resembling a nomadic shepherd or an archaic figure of the time when the Israelites were wandering in the wilderness. His simplicity, naturalness and spontaneity are in sharp contrast to the polished manners of the royal house. They also constitute a warning to large sections of the population, who are attracted by religious and cultural assimilation to their pagan surroundings.

Nothing is said about Elijah's family history. As to his origins, he is merely designated in the Hebrew text as 'Eliyahu Ha-Tishbi' ('Elijah the Tishbite' (I Kings 17: 1)) 'mi-Toshave Gilead' ('mi' meaning 'of' or 'from'). Gilead is a province east of the River Jordan. Instead of 'Toshave', the Septuagint and Josephus read 'Tishbe',[11] which some scholars identify as El Istib in Gilead, and others as Jabesh-Gilead in the Jordan valley. But the expression 'mi-Toshave Gilead' may linguistically also mean 'of the settlers of Gilead', suggesting that Elijah was not a native of the area but had been living there temporarily.[12] This leads some researchers to suppose that Elijah belonged to the sect of the Rechabites, who were living in southern Palestine as nomadic shepherds and had always been distinguished by their special fervour for the God of Israel and by their simple, almost ascetic way of life. Others assume that Elijah originally belonged to a small group of prophets persisting and active in Judea and Israel.

No matter whether he was an individualist from the beginning

or a member of a group who grew beyond it, from his first appearance Elijah is already the 'Great Individual'. This is expressed in
his words: 'As the Lord, the God of Israel, liveth, before whom I
stand'. These words may refer less to his having an explicit vocation as a prophet than to his firm conviction that he had to undertake the obligation to fight for God's cause. In any case, the
'standing before God' signifies that he is neither exclusively one of
the ecstatic prophets possessed by the Divine, as, for instance,
Saul, nor a prophet who receives visions or dreams. From the
wording of the prophecy made to Ahab concerning the lack of
rain it is not apparent whether Elijah is here transmitting an
explicit divine decision, or on his own responsibility stating what
he knows or supposes to be the divine will.

Only later does the story of Elijah show that, like Moses and the
later prophets of the Bible, he became capable of holding a dialogue with God, and also that, on impulse and over-zealously, he
frequently goes beyond the direct revelation and command and
intervenes decisively of his own accord.

The name 'Elijah' in any case indicates that he has been chosen:
'Eli-yahu'—'My God is YHV'. YHV are the first three letters of
the tetragram, the name once used by God to reveal himself to
Moses out of the burning bush.*

The absence of rain, prophesied by Elijah in a few pithy words
to King Ahab, is mentioned earlier in the Torah (Deut. 11:16–17)
as the customary punishment for idolatry, for the apostasy of the
Israelites, and is clearly closely related to this sin. The Baal who
was worshipped in the Near East and at this time also by the
Israelites was above all a fertility god, whose annual death and
resurrection personified the regular cycle of nature and also
guaranteed the occurrence of the rainy season. The belief that the
worship of Baal guaranteed the normal cycle of nature was shaken
by Elijah's prophecy that the life-giving rain would not come for

---

* The name of a person in the Bible is mostly a significant reference to the
character of its bearer, and represents his nature. This applies especially to the
numerous proper names including the first two or three letters of the tetragram. The anonymously appearing Elijah, whose father's house and whose
tribe are unknown and about whose family life nothing whatever is revealed,
is matched with a name which expresses his vocation[13]

an indefinite period. Baal, dependent upon fate, was confronted with the living God of the Israelites. In the world ruled by him, man's actions did not only determine his own fate but also the fertility of the soil.

The valley of the Cherith (I Kings 17: 2–5), in which Elijah hid according to the divine command after his prophecy to Ahab, was presumably in the Aramaic region ruled by Damascus. It is assumed that Ahab will see Elijah not merely as the prophet of the divine decision, but will hold him personally responsible for the threatened punishment and persecute him.

The region to which Elijah flees did not belong to the Israelites, but was also subject to the power of their God; it also suffers a drought. Although Elijah is miraculously provided by ravens with bread and meat in the mornings and evenings, he too shares the misfortune of the water-shortage when the brook eventually dries up. Then he receives a summons to go to Zarephath, a town in Sidon, from where Queen Jezebel came. Although it is also suffering drought and famine, a poor widow sheltered and fed him. In this way Elijah comes into direct contact with the simple, non-Israelite pagan population. He promises the widow that she shall lack neither flour nor oil while the famine lasts. In humble faith she passes the test imposed upon her by Elijah, to share with him the supposedly last frugal meal which she had prepared for herself and her son. When, later, her son dies and she regards this as a punishment for her sins, Elijah reproaches God. Then he endeavours to resuscitate the child, and succeeds (I Kings 17: 8–22).

The miracle of the inexhaustible barrel of flour and the cruse of oil is a reward to the widow for having faith; her son is resuscitated as a sign that her sins are forgiven. Neither miracle is of a magic nature: the first occurs at a direct divine command,* and the resuscitation consists of a method which resembles one used

---

* Bronner (op. cit., pp. 84–5; 139–40) shows by means of the Ugarite mythology of the gods that Elijah's miracles primarily demonstrate that all the power ascribed to Baal, especially control over fire and water (rain) is entirely dependent upon the will of the universal Israelite God. She draws attention to the fact that Baal was also venerated as the giver of oil and corn. Elijah's miracle of oil and flour and his promise that these would last until the reappearance of the rains therefore show that in the country of Baal-worship, too, the God honoured by the Israelites is the only giver of oil and corn[14]

nowadays for this very purpose: in the biblical text it is symbolic
—accompanied by prayer, Elijah's breath pours life into the dead
boy (I Kings 17: 23–4).

This episode in Zarephath demonstrates the attitude of biblical
monotheism that the God of the Israelites rules the fate of all mankind, including that of the non-Israelite nations, without at the
same time demanding that they should acknowledge and worship
him (see p. 34 and n. 62).

After the rainless period has lasted for about three years, Elijah,
following God's command, prophesies its imminent end to the
king in order to demonstrate that the life-saving rain will be made
to fall by the God of the Israelites and not by Baal. Elijah's
encounter with Ahab shows his assurance and his sense of superiority over the monarch because he is conscious of his prophetic
mission. This is given particular emphasis by being contrasted
with the timidity of the royal vizier who is also present. He also
believes in God and has secretly saved a large number of true
prophets from being persecuted by the royal house. But he is
afraid that the stormy unheralded appearance and disappearance
of the prophet, with which he is already familiar, will arouse the
king's anger. By contrast, Elijah has no doubts. He answers the
king's rough greeting fearlessly in the same manner. Then he
demands that the people and the prophets of Baal be summoned
to Mount Carmel (I Kings 18: 1–20). Under the forceful impression
made by Elijah, Ahab carries out this command without demur.

After the conquest of Canaan by the Israelites, the Carmel range
was the boundary between them and the Phoenicians. It had consequently a fluctuating population and was subject to frequent
border shifts. In former times it had been a place of pagan worship;
later, presumably at the time of David, an altar to YH was also
erected there. The Carmel region was therefore especially suited
to Jezebel's endeavours to encourage and spread the cult of her
native Sidonian god among the Israelites.[15]

Baal-Melkart, who was at this time worshipped in Phoenicia
and Canaan, was derived from the Baal of the Ugarite pantheon, a
son of the mother-goddess Astarte and the great El whom he later
dethroned. Originally predominantly of a chthonic character,

Baal-Melkart later assumed the aspects of the weather god as well as of the rain god Baal-Hadad, and also the solar traits of the Baal-Shaman. Baal's consort Anath, later considered to be equal to Astarte, was the goddess of love and fertility but also of war and destruction. Baal was swallowed up by his brother Mot, the god of aridity and death, and had to dwell in the underworld together with rain, clouds and other retinue. Anath mourned her brother and husband, killed Mot and freed Baal, so that rain and fertility might again come to the earth. This mythological occurrence then became an annual ritual event within the framework of the cult. The periodic disappearance of the fertility god into the under-world, or his death, led to the withering of the vegetation and the infertility of animals until the female deity resurrected her lost lover and their union brought about a new cycle of vegetable and animal life.[16]

In response to Elijah's demand, the king summons the people and the prophets of Baal and Astarte to Carmel. Elijah appears before them as one against all, as Noah and Abraham before him, and as after him Isaiah and Jeremiah. He calls upon the people: 'How long halt ye between two opinions? if the Lord be God, follow Him; but if Baal, follow him.' The people answer with silence, which signifies not assent but indecision. Then Elijah suggests that they submit to divine judgment: the priests are to sacrifice a bullock to Baal and Elijah himself one to the God of Israel, without putting fire to the altar. Each shall then call upon his god, and the god who accepts the sacrifice by sending fire down to it from heaven shall be acknowledged by the people as the only true God (I Kings 18: 20 ff.).

The general symbolism of animal sacrifice, its development from 'feeding and propitiating the gods' to the 'sacrifice of the human ego' to the godhead by means of identification with the sacrificial animal by the man offering it, cannot be examined in detail here. This development essentially expresses the changing relationship of man to the Divine. The exclusive fear of the tyran-nical godhead and the attempt to pacify it are eventually replaced by the experience of meaningful divine guidance and the striving to submit to it, and also the intimation that the Divine has need of the human, which later finds expression in the Aggadah and Jewish mysticism (see pp. 77, 106).

The contest between Elijah and the pagan priests is not concerned with which divinity it may be possible to influence favourably through propitiation or sacrifice to send the desired rain; Elijah has been assured of rain beforehand, even if it is retrospectively interpreted as a consequence of the return of the Israelites to God. Rather, the god who reveals himself through sending down fire to consume the sacrifice is to be acknowledged as the only one. Not a gift from him is to be evoked, but his revelation.

In paganism, fire is either worshipped as divine in itself or as one of the divine attributes, especially of the sun god, as within the framework of the cult of Baal. The Israelite and other highly developed religions regard it as one of the divine aspects, as an expression of the numinous—positively, as purification, enlightenment through the spirit, or as energy to maintain life; but also negatively as the demonic, that which consumes and destroys. God reveals himself to Moses, the individual, through the burning bush, and on the burning Horeb to the Israelites. But in both instances the fire may also consume, so that Moses hides his face and the people shrink from it. Elijah's contest on Mount Carmel is concerned not with a direct revelation of the godhead but with an indirect one: the consuming of the sacrifice through fire which is sent by God instead of through the flames normally lit by the hand of man. There are corresponding examples in the Israelite cult. At the consecration of the tabernacle in the desert (Lev. 9: 24), as well as that of the temple of Solomon (II Chr. 7: 1), the sacrifice was consumed by fire from heaven. The same happened with the sacrifice offered by David (I Chr. 21: 26) as a sign of God's favourable answer to him. This is also the significance of the fire which decided the contest on Mount Carmel.[17]

Elijah is confident and calm. He knows that the God of the Israelites is the only God and will once again manifest his omnipotence. Having this certainty, he is aware neither that he is taking matters into his own hands on Mount Carmel, nor that his personal fate depends upon the result of God's judgment which he invokes, as it was customary for the one defeated by the judgment of God to be killed by the victor. Confronted with an undecided people and a king who is prepared to compromise, he acts resolutely: with blunt ironic words he mocks the priests of Baal who are praying for a sign, saying that their god may be pre-occupied, thus impelling them to greater ecstasy and to self-mutilation.

When it becomes perfectly clear that the priests of Baal have been unsuccessful, Elijah acts with calm resolution. He asks the people to come closer to him and builds an altar out of twelve stones, which represents the unity of the twelve tribes of Jacob through their belief in the One God.[18] The narrator here recalls that after his struggle with the angel (Gen. 32: 28–9), Jacob's name was changed to 'Israel' ('God's fighter'). He quotes verbally the confirmation of this change of name before Jacob's return to Canaan (Gen. 35: 10). The patriarch who struggled with the Divine here appears in the figure of Elijah the fighter for God, before the people who have lapsed into idolatry.

In order to make the expected miracle appear even greater, Elijah has water poured over the sacrifice and around the altar.[19] Then he prays to the God of his fathers to reveal himself and so lead his people back to their faith in him and at the same time confirm his own prophetic mission: 'Hear me, O Lord, hear me, that this people may know that Thou, Lord, art God, for Thou didst turn their heart backward.' Then God's fire descended and consumed the sacrifice together with the wood, the stones, the dust and the water in the trench. The people saw it and fell on their faces, exclaiming: 'The Lord, He is God; the Lord, He is God' (I Kings 18: 37–9).

Elijah does not content himself with this decisive victory. His fervour seems to have been fanned into ecstasy and he asks the people to kill the priests of Baal, who spread idolatry among the Israelites and persecuted the true prophets of God.* Elijah then expects the rain to set in at once. He can already hear its murmur.

---

* R. Isaac Arama, the important Bible exegete and religious philosopher (c. 1450), refers in detail to the fact that in killing the prophets of Baal Elijah had exceeded his competence as a prophet[20]

He squats down, puts his head on his knees in humble expectation and sends his servant out seven times, until he sees a raincloud rising from the sea. Then when the downpour starts, he becomes ecstatic. Exulting in his triumph that the divine revelation has taken place and his mission has been confirmed, he runs as herald before the chariot of King Ahab to the gate of his palace (I Kings 18: 40–6).

But before long Elijah's victory turns into defeat. The politically shrewd king had accepted the divine judgment which had taken place before his eyes and seemed to be prepared to acknowledge the God of Israel as the only one. Not so Jezebel, who considered her native land and its cult far superior to the primitive kingdom of Israel. For years she had striven to drive out the Israelite faith in favour of the worship of Baal, and had believed that she had almost succeeded. Now she is made extremely angry by the defeat, and especially by the murder of the prophets of Baal who were under her protection, and she is not prepared to acknowledge the hated zealot and his invisible God. She accepts Elijah's challenge, threatening him with persecution and death (I Kings 19: 1–3).

Elijah knows that where Jezebel is concerned Ahab is weak and powerless and that, as her pliant tool, he will not protect him. He fears for his life and also suspects that the people, in spite of the revelation which they have received, will not remain faithful to the God of Israel. He has made a passionate effort and now sees himself as a failure. Completely disheartened, he flees from the kingdom of Israel to neighbouring Judea, where he would be safe from Jezebel's persecution. But, alone and in despair, he wanders on—into the desert.

He wishes for death. 'Now, O Lord, take away my life.' Finall y, completely exhausted, he falls asleep under a *rotem* tree (*Retama roetum*=broom). Then an angel appears, wakes him and hands him a cake and a drink of water. When Elijah goes back to sleep, he is again aroused: 'Arise and eat; because you have a long way to go.' He wanders still further into the empty desert, strengthened and accompanied by the newly-awakened realisation of his sole and direct dependence upon God, upon the God of Israel who,

13

unlike Baal, is not restricted to dwelling in a certain place but goes with him, as he once guided his people on its journey through the wilderness. After forty days and nights he reaches Horeb, where Moses first received God's word—the mountain on which God then revealed himself in thunder and lightning to his people delivered from Egypt, spoke to them and renewed with them his covenant with their forefathers. There Elijah hopes to receive divine guidance (I Kings 19: 5-8).

He enters the cave in the mountain, intending to spend the night. There the word of God comes to him, directly now, not through an angelic messenger. Like an exhortation, he hears the question: 'What doest thou here, Elijah?' His answer is a complaint, but at the same time also an accusation: 'I have been very jealous for the Lord God of hosts: for the children of Israel have forsaken thy covenant . . . I only am left.' Then he receives the command: 'Go forth, and stand upon the mount.' At the mouth of the cave he now experiences a revelation manifested by complete extremes. A strong wind, an earthquake, fire, the inescapable forces of nature at God's command, appear as its precursors. Then the Divine itself reveals itself to him 'in the small voice of silence'. He is profoundly moved by it. Without words, the silence speaks to him.

The Hebrew words '*kol demamah dakkah*' are usually taken to mean 'gentle breeze' or 'quiet voice', occasionally also 'shrill whistling'. They are accordingly interpreted either as a spiritualisation of Elijah's image of God, as a lesser theophany, in which the Divine is hardly perceptible, or as an expression of the demonic aspect of God. However, the literal translation of the text, 'small voice of silence', expresses as a *coincidentia oppositorum* the *mysterium tremendum et fascinans* of Elijah's theophany.* Elijah covers his face, comes out of the cave into the open, and then the word of God comes to him.† God's case is not lost. It does not

* The Talmud regards the '*kol demamah dakkah*' as 'soundless stillness', and illustrates this with a sensitive paable[21]

† Note the parallel that the 'revelation in speech' begins only after Elijah has, through veiling his face like Moses at the burning bush, appeased the *tremendum* and comes out of the cave unharmed. But his paradoxical individual experience of God at Horeb contrasts with the unequivocal revelation to the collective on Mount Carmel

depend upon Elijah alone. It cannot be lost. There will always be a remnant of the faithful among the Israelites. At the moment, no further impetuous human intervention is required. The struggle is adjourned and it will not be Elijah who will be called upon to resume it when the time is ripe. He is instructed to anoint new kings over Syria and Israel to continue the fight, and to name the young Elisha, the son of a peasant, as his successor. Elijah turns back—no longer driven by the spirit, as before, but led by it and towards it.[22]

When Elijah first meets Elisha on the way to Damascus, he throws him his prophet's cloak. This is the test to show whether Elisha is ready to follow God and to become Elijah's pupil. He may have been chosen by God, but he must first prove himself. In contrast to Elijah, the nomadic wanderer in the desert, Elisha is the child of a rooted culture. He accepts with his eyes open the summons to follow Elijah and leaves his home and his parents after bidding them good-bye (I Kings 19: 19–21). Elijah's instructions to anoint kings in Damascus and Israel, who would one day resume the fight on behalf of God, are carried out not by him but, later, by Elisha.[23]

In both the biblical accounts concerning Elijah which follow, he appears as acting directly on God's behalf: he receives the command and carries it out. Now it is not only a matter of acknowledging God, but above all of ensuring equal rights to the ordinary man and to the king: Ahab covets the vineyard of Naboth, his subject and neighbour. With Ahab's knowledge, Jezebel causes false accusations to be brought against Naboth and, with the help of false witnesses, has him condemned to death and his property confiscated. Then, at God's command, Elijah appears, and confronts Ahab with the words: 'Hast thou killed, and also taken possession?', and prophesies that he and Jezebel will before long die a cruel death and that their royal house will cease to exist (I Kings 21).

The social justice demanded of the Israelites by God contrasts with the absolute power of the ancient oriental despots represented by Jezebel. Here as well Elijah's real opponent is not Ahab—his conscience revives when Elijah appears and he repents of his crime—but the tyrannical intriguer Jezebel. Ahab's punishment is deferred because of his change of heart, but Jezebel's fate is sealed.

In the story of Ahaziah, Ahab's son and successor who, when ill, appealed for help to the god Baal-zebub, Elijah is also essentially the bearer of a divine message. He first prophesies to King Ahaziah's messenger, who is on his way to the temple of Baal, that the king's approaching death is to be regarded as a punishment for his apostasy. When the first two captains, who recognise the prophet, disregard him and give him curt orders, Elijah's passionate fighting spirit comes once more to the fore. He brings upon them God's punishment of death by burning.[24] At God's behest, Elijah follows the third captain to be sent, who approaches him respectfully, to deliver in person his message to the king (II Kings 1: 1–16).

Then follows the description of Elijah's ascent to heaven (II Kings 2: 1–18). The author of the account assumes that the fact as such is known, but goes into a description of the details. There is something mysterious about Elijah's final days and hours. God's fighter, once so zealous, now appears very calm and self possessed. Knowing that his end is imminent, he takes the 'way home' which is his, chosen for him by God. He travels towards the River Jordan, via places in the country hallowed by history, in which God has revealed himself to his people—Gilgal, Bethel, Jericho (Josh. 4, 5, 6; Gen. 12: 8, 28: 19). He, the Great Individual, who has always appeared only sporadically, unexpectedly, now goes from place to place; no longer alone, followed everywhere by the local prophet-disciples. They venerate him with awe as their great master—they also have a presentiment that this is his last journey.

Elijah's only immediate companion is Elisha, his personal pupil and his successor chosen by God. They both know but do not speak about what is before them. The disciple wants to remain close to the person of his spiritual friend and guide until the last moment, but the master feels that he has to be alone on his last journey. Three times he sends Elisha back, but is finally overwhelmed by his love and loyalty and gives in. Still together, they cross the Jordan, which rolls back before the prophet's cloak. Elijah has returned to his native ground, his starting-point. He now offers to grant Elisha a wish, and Elisha asks for 'a double portion of Elijah's spirit'. This wording seems to allude to the traditional Jewish right of succession, which allocates a double portion of the paternal estate to the first-born (Deut. 21: 17). This signifies the rebirth of the father in the son. Elisha accordingly wants Elijah to appoint him his immediate successor, but Elijah cannot agree. That he was told at Horeb of Elisha's succession, and the casting of his prophet's cloak upon him, mean to Elijah no more than that Elisha has been chosen as his pupil; the summons to prophecy must come directly from God. Elijah's answer: 'if thou see me when I am taken from thee', is to be understood condition-ally. Elisha's ability to see Elijah's ascent to heaven would prove his competence to be his successor. They continue their dialogue as they go on together after crossing the Jordan, while the rest of the disciples remain on the other bank. Finally, a chariot of fire with horses of fire separate master and disciple and Elijah goes up to heaven in a whirlwind.[25]

Elisha sees his master ascending to heaven and exclaims: 'My father, my father, the chariots of Israel and the horsemen there-of!'[26] According to Elijah's words, this signifies that Elisha has been chosen. Because of this, and at the same time as a symbol of mourning, he tears his own cloak and takes instead the prophet's cloak which has fallen from Elijah. With it he performs a miracle, as his master did: he divides the Jordan with the words: 'Where is the Lord, the God of Elijah?' and crosses back to the other side.

The disciples who remained on the bank saw this miracle and said: 'The spirit of Elijah doth rest on Elisha.' Nevertheless, they do not understand Elijah's disappearance. They had surmised that he would be taken from them for ever but, as they did not see the ascent, they cannot understand what has happened. They assume that his body has been carried away by the whirlwind and is still on earth for them to find, and search for three days, but in vain (II Kings 2: 15–18).

Thus the record of Elijah in the Books of Kings ends with his sudden disappearance inexplicable to those around him, just as it opened with his unheralded, spontaneous, threatening appearance.

The circle seems to close about this figure of the Great Individual seized by the whirlwind of the spirit. Even his contemporaries, used to miraculous and strange happenings, saw him as an archaic, mysterious, numinous figure, always moved—indeed at times ecstatically enthralled—by the God of Israel, the creator and master of the world, who demands unconditional obedience of his chosen people. On him, his spiritual father, Elijah's zeal is totally concentrated. He sees his God making uncompromising demands, and so he himself does not compromise in his fight for him, while the Israelites equate him with the transitory and local idols of the neighbouring nations. And just as the simple people, thoughtlessly imitating the inhabitants of the conquered land, are backed by a weak king seeking to compromise, so he is backed and dominated by Queen Jezebel. She is Elijah's real opponent.

The description of the struggle between the queen and Elijah on behalf of their deities plainly reveals in its strong emphasis the anthropological and depth-psychological aspects which form the basis of the confrontation between Israel's faith and paganism. The characters and actions of the two opponents are determined by their religious attitudes. Collective and individual confrontation intermingle.

In the history of religion, Baal, worshipped in Asia Minor and the Near East as early as the matriarchal age, was originally above all a young fertility deity—like Adonis, Tammuz and Osiris. He is the son of the great mother-goddess Astarte and his fate depends upon her alone. She herself, like Aphrodite and the other mother-goddesses, shows in relation to her son both her positive aspect as the origin of all life—as conceiving, carrying, giving birth, lovingly caring, nourishing and healing—and also her negative aspect—as dominating, greedy, castrating, devouring, burying. Her symbols correspond to this ambivalence: vessel, womb, maternal animal, earth, cave—but also grave, abyss, sea bottom, dragon, chaos.

The beloved and at the same time dominated divine son represents, psychologically, to some extent the male aspects of the divinity preponderantly experienced as female. Only gradually there develops in contrast to the mother-goddess an independent male image of God, which characterises the patriarchal age. In mythology, the separation of the male divinity from the great mother-goddess is represented by the hero's victorious fight with the dragon, and also by his night sea voyage to liberty from the west to the east in the belly of the sea monster. This latter mythologem is the basis of the prophet Jonah's transformation recorded in the Bible. But while in the mythologem the hero frees himself by killing the monster, Jonah is freed through his prayer to the father-God.[27]

In sexual symbolism, the young man fascinated by the Great Mother, passive, castrated by incest or killed, then becomes the man who overcomes his fear, who conquers the terrible, dominating side of the female and unites with her creative one. With this he becomes the hero, the equal of the deities.

Mythology, anthropology and depth psychology have become aware that the mythologems which arise in every culture originate in the collective unconscious of mankind and represent its content.

From the psychological point of view, the Great Mother in her unconscious naturalness symbolises the matrix of the human consciousness regarded in contrast to her as male. It is born of it, fed by it, but in its dependence upon it is also constantly threatened with aggression and destruction and therefore forced to fight for its independence. This ambivalent aspect of the mother is, interestingly enough, expressed in that the Hebrew word 'womb' is 'reḥem'—the singular form of 'raḥamim' (compassion) —but that in the Talmud the womb is also called 'kever' (grave).[28]

Erich Neumann shows in detail the philogenetic and ontogenetic development of the human consciousness,[29] the centring of the ego and the structure and the function of the various psychic factors by means of the myths concerning the creation, the divinities and heroes.

The heroic fight is accordingly seen by depth psychology as the archetypal pattern of human psychic development. Every successful encounter and confrontation of the ego with his personal and above all with the collective unconscious leads to the extension of the consciousness and to reorientation, and can activate the creative in man. Every evasion of the fight-constellation means psychic and spiritual paralysis; every defeat means regression into the unconscious. A complete and constant victory in the psychic process, like the victory of the mythological hero, is not possible for everyone. Only some succeed not only in assimilating their individual unconscious but also in coming to terms with the contents of the collective unconscious revealed to them, and in controlling the emotions released by them. Through this, their ego is freed from compulsion, undergoes a transformation, and follows the 'Self', the psychic 'centre', the individual psychic potential striving for realisation.

Both in the history of religion and in the individual, the progressive development of the human consciousness corresponds to the development of man's image of God and its transformations. The image of God of which man gradually *becomes conscious* consists at first predominantly of male-active traits; the female-natural aspects of God at first remain unconscious.

In the time of Elijah, the world of the divinities of the Canaanite and Phoenician peoples was largely patriarchal, although matriarchy had not yet been entirely overcome. Although Baal-Melkart has the independent male character traits of the storm and sun god, at the same time (as the young fertility god) he has still to submit to the fate determined for him by the mother-goddess Astarte.[30] By contrast, the God of Israel had been acknowledged for generations as omnipotent and unique, the spirit present always and everywhere, personified as father, king, lawgiver and judge, making direct demands on man. Accordingly, the 'living God' signified, for the Canaanite, the deity who, having died, returns to life; for the Israelite, the eternal God who out of his own living existence creates life.[31]

The opposition of the two divinities Astarte and YH corresponds to the opposition of their human exponents. Jezebel identifies unconsciously with the mother-goddess Astarte; at the same time she appears to be psychically dependent on her royal and priestly father. She fights jealously and ruthlessly for her young fertility god Baal against the invisible God of Israel who is incomprehensible to her. With the help of her followers, the priests whom she transplanted to Israel from her native country, she persecutes and murders his prophets in order to supplant his cult by the sole worship of Baal and Astarte. She entirely dominates her royal consort Ahab, her mortal 'son-lover', just as Astarte dominates the young Baal. At her command, he encourages the spread of paganism throughout the country. Yielding to her insatiable greed for power, he himself becomes a despot who allows his subjects to be robbed and murdered.

Only towards Elijah is Jezebel unsure of herself. She despises the uncultivated, nomad-like wandering prophet, but at the same time fears and hates him as the only power opposing her and her deity.[32] She wants to kill him, but by overtly threatening him with death gives him the opportunity to escape. Rationally this might be explained by saying that she wanted only to prevent his further influence over the people, not to turn him into a martyr in their eyes by murdering him.

From the psychological point of view, one may suspect a blunder because she was unconsciously afraid that the God of Elijah would take his revenge on her. Even after Elijah's return to the royal court and his prediction of the death which God had decreed for her as a punishment for the crime which she had plotted, she does not dare to persecute him. She is rendered incapable of action by the presentiment that in the end she and her idols will be defeated by the hated sinister prophet and his invisible God.

Elijah, without family and friends, consciously lives only for the God of his fathers, who claims his chosen people as a whole and also individually. Seized by the dynamic of the ruaḥ, the whirlwind of his God, he is inspired; he confidently appears at the right moment and intervenes significantly in the course of events. But far more frequently he is seized ecstatically and carried away by the overwhelming spirit of God. His fanatic fight for him, on the assumption that he is the only one who has remained faithful (I Kings 18: 22; 19: 10), makes him fight his own people. His love for mankind is repressed. It comes forth only once, in his prayer for the widow's dead child. His autocratic summoning of the judgment of God, his challenging prayer for confirmation and also his later breakdown in the desert show his disposition and his vain attempt to surpass his human limitations.

In psychological terms this implies inflation, identification with the divine. But at the same time, the harsh ascetic demands which Elijah makes on himself, and his blind merciless fanaticism, indicate a psychic insecurity which has to be covered up. It arises from his vacillation between his female-unconscious possession by the divine and his male-conscious knowledge of his God. The attempt to escape the conflict makes his image of God one-sided, super-male, zealously demanding. He refuses to acknowledge the benevolent-motherly aspect of God, and so represses his insecurity and, at the same time, his love for his people. His own insecurity, his shadow,* seems to be projected onto the weak-willed Ahab. Accordingly, they accuse each other of 'troubling Israel' (I Kings 18: 17–18), and Elijah fights Ahab when he worships Baal-Astarte and submits to Jezebel-Astarte, but ecstatically hastens ahead of him when he returns to the God of the fathers, and forgives him when he repents of his crime against Naboth. The young and the mature man in Elijah wrestle with each other. The repression of his insecurity frees Elijah from fear so that he provokes the divine confirmation. He does not realise that, in accordance with the custom of the times, his defeat in the contest on Mount Carmel would undoubtedly have meant his own murder by the priests of Baal. Thus he succeeds for the moment in defeating Baal and Astarte.

The ensuing massacre of the pagan priests which he brings about can be interpreted mythologically as the conquest of the male-aggressive aspects of the mother-goddess. In the personal-human realm it seems unjustifiably cruel, especially as he has already been victorious, even if it represents a reprisal for the murder of the Israelite prophets by Jezebel's priests of Baal. The victory for the father-God which Elijah has gained by his zeal

---

* The 'shadow' symbolises psychologically the sum of the emotions and tendencies not admitted to consciousness, as well as the still undeveloped psychic functions[33]

does not make him aware of his benevolent aspect and accordingly he represses the female component of his own soul.

Characteristic of Elijah's lack of balance is also that—in complete contrast to his authoritarian behaviour during the contest and to his outrage—he immediately afterwards in a humble meditative position awaits the expected rain, and when it begins to fall he impetuously runs ahead of the king's chariot.[34]

When the presumed victory turns into a defeat and the queen wants to take her bloody revenge on him, Elijah's inflation collapses. Jezebel's words: 'I make . . . thy life as the life of one of them by tomorrow about this time' awaken guilt feelings in him and make him, previously fearless, suddenly fear for his life; they undermine his trust in God.

In despair, he flees, and does not remain in the inhabited country of Judea. He wanders on, into the desert. In its monotony, uniformity, lifelessness, it corresponds to his depressed mood, the longing for the dissolution of his ego. He sees not only his fight but his whole life as a complete failure. His words: 'I am not better than my fathers' express his realisation of his presumption: apparently he has never been the individual guided by the spirit-father; he was and is a simple mortal like everyone else; he had been mistaken about his mission. He longs for his death: 'It is enough; now, O Lord, take away my life'.

Thus Elijah escapes Jezebel's revenge but, from a mythological point of view, falls victim to the 'devouring mother-goddess' whom she personifies, i.e. to the passive incest mentioned above; from a psychological point of view, to the regression into the unconscious.

His flight is in reality a flight from the necessity to change himself and his image of God.

Thus the struggle of the male-consciousness for its independence from the female-unconscious takes place on three corresponding levels. The image of God as the spirit-father with his heroic son created by him in his likeness confronts the image of the great chthonic mother-goddess with her 'son-lover'. The personal champions of the deities who identify with them—on the one hand Elijah, on the other Jezebel and Ahab—fight each other bitterly in the external world. And each is himself caught in the conflict between the male-conscious and the female-unconscious currents of his own inner psychical world.

Symbolically, the desert in which Elijah's psychic breakdown occurs is not merely a lonely and deserted place. It is also a place of isolation from the external world, of withdrawal-into-oneself, where man depends only upon the Divine to be able to hear the call of his internal world. When Hagar flees from Abraham's house and also later, when she is driven away from there with her son, she receives a divine promise in the desert. The children of Israel delivered from Egypt experienced the great revelation in the Sinai desert. And the prophet Isaiah exclaims: 'Make plain in the desert a highway for our God' (Isa. 40: 3).

That Elijah lay down and slept in the desert signifies first the impulse to return to the unconscious; but his ego is not completely extinguished. The desired 'sleep of the dead' takes place under the broom tree, the roots of which can be turned into smouldering coals by the heat of the desert sun:* a symbol of the life force of the spirit reawakening after being near to extinction.

The angel who awakens Elijah and hands him a cake and a drink of water, and so rekindles the dying spark of his soul, can, from a psychological point of view, be regarded as the positive, nourishing, reviving aspect of the female. It appears here as divine messenger, representing the female aspect of the godhead. The perceiving of this aspect, which has hitherto been concealed from him, grants Elijah an extended image of God and reactivates his libido inhibited by his unconscious.

The rousing of Elijah from the 'sleep of the dead' is later followed by his being roused from a healing sleep through the angel who reappears. Although it does not appear in explicitly female shape, it can be regarded psychologically as the 'anima', the female component of the soul originating in the Great Mother, inspiring him, leading him through the depth of the unconscious

* Talmudic and Aggadic literature repeatedly mention that embers from the roots of the broom tree, the trunk and roots of which are used as fuel by the Bedouin, continue to glow for an extraordinarily long time even after they have apparently gone out[35]

to find his own way.*[36] She 'touched him, and said: "Arise and eat; because the journey is too great for thee" . . . And he arose . . . and went in the strength of that meal forty days and forty nights unto Horeb the mount of God.'[37]

His goal is not the institutional national sanctuary in Jerusalem which was in existence at that time. He seeks the expected divine guidance at the mountain from which the Divine had revealed itself to his forefathers.

For the forefathers delivered from Egypt received the revelation not in the Promised Land but on the way, in the desert: it does not depend upon the possession of the Promised Land. God speaks from the mountain towering above the desert into the sky, on which his spirit becomes manifest,[38] while the children of Israel stood 'on the nether part of the mount'. The revelation of the Lord was a 'descending' to his people, and the decalogue was proclaimed to the collective which shrank from the numinous.

But Elijah first enters the cave in the mountain; he 'lodged there' for the night, and 'the word of the Lord came to him'. He goes by choice into the cave—symbol of the womb and of the unconscious—but not, as when he lay down in the desert, wishing for death, in order to give up his ego. He wants to spend the night in the cave so as to awake feeling renewed. Psychologically, therefore, this is an instance of active introversion, in contrast to the regression of the sleep in the desert.

Active introversion is the attempt to direct psychic energy consciously into the depth. A successful confrontation of the ego with the images of the collective unconscious ascending from the depth leads to a considerable influx of the libido and the possibility of directing it consciously. Indian Yoga is based on this, and so is C. G. Jung's 'active imagination' practised under suitable circumstances in present-day psychotherapy. The relationship of active introversion to the creative process of the artist is dealt with by Otto Rank.[39]

He is in the cave in the mountain, the sheltering cave; the

---

* C. G. Jung remarks (*The Archetypes and the Collective Unconscious*, p. 29): 'the anima can appear also as an angel of light, a psychopomp who points the way to the highest meaning'

female aspect of God is united with the male, the female within the male. This corresponds to the awakening of Elijah's own female-receptive psychic component and enables him to enter into the relationship of dialogue with the God of Israel experienced as male. Now he is not addressed by an angel, but by the Divine within himself, which calls him to account. His ego is steadfast. He asks for the meaning of his failure.

In reply, God calls him out of the sheltering cave to its entrance, in the same way as he put Moses in the cleft of the rock (Exod. 33: 22).

The Hebrew word for a cleft in the rock, *nikrat ha-zur*, is composed of the words *'nikrah'* ('cleft') and *'zur'* ('rock'). The root of the word *'zur'* is synonymous with the root of the word *'yazor'* ('to transform creatively'). The cleft in the rock as well as the entrance to the cave symbolises the place of birth, of being created anew. The later revelations to Moses in the sanctuary in the desert also usually took place at its 'entrance'. The Aggadists frequently describe Elijah as standing 'at the threshold'.

In this borderline situation—psychologically, the encounter of the ego with the deeper layers of unconscious—Elijah hears 'the small voice of silence'. He realises that the elementary, creative and destructive forces of nature in themselves are not God. They are his precursors, symbols and tools of his dynamic effect upon the world and upon the fate of the individual. God himself cannot be comprehended by the human senses; but in the nothingness of silence his word becomes audible.

Elijah encounters the numinous, and his first immediate response is to conceal his face: awed, humble, ceasing to be aware of his surroundings; suspending also his own psychic activity, all his senses, in order to hear the divine voice within. Psychologically, this phenomenon differs from active introversion by the complete passivity of the ego. It becomes femininely receptive to the 'Self', which reveals itself to it.[40]

His consciousness is extended. His experience of God is transformed. He begins to realise that even in his wilful actions he was, like storm and fire, a tool in the hand of God. His activity was, so to speak, embraced within the divine will. He had been assigned

26

a place in the course of his people's history devised by God. Now, after the revelation which transformed him, he had to cease to serve only the collective and had to complete his own spiritual development.

Thus through his psychic crises, his supposed failure, Elijah reaches renewal.[41] Psychologically, his introverted psychic function becomes conscious and activated; through this, his ego becomes aware of the Self which embraces and directs it, and begins to submit to it consciously.

This also transforms his attitude to his fellow-men. He becomes tolerant and emerges from his solitude, thus to become the friend of Elisha assigned to him as his pupil. On their shared journey—for Elijah the journey home, the way, as he has become aware, to his God—the relationship between Elijah and Elisha grows so close that they seem to have common roots and yet at the same time each must respond for himself to the divine will (see pp. 16–17).

The disciples who have remained faithful venerate Elijah as their master. They, too, accompany him from place to place, but remain, in accordance with the stage of their own development, on the near side of the River Jordan. With Elisha alone Elijah crosses the river.

Passing across the river itself signifies Elijah's transcendence. Then follows the parting from his last human companion through the chariot of fire with horses of fire and his ascent to heaven, expressing the transcendence of his terrestrial existence.

The chariot of fire, or of the sun drawn by animals, mostly horses, appears frequently in mythology. In Greek myth the sun god or the sun itself travels its daily orbit in a chariot drawn by horses.[42] As the sons of the patriarchal-divine prototype of the hero, kings devoted to the cult of the sun travel in the morning towards the sun with specially consecrated chariots and horses.[43] The Bible (II Kings 23: 11) reports this also of Jewish kings. In many myths, the hero travels in a four-in-hand to his adventures or ascends to heaven in fire after struggling successfully with the chthonic powers.[44]

The relations between the sun-hero symbolism, the human

experience of God and the endeavour of the individual to transcend his terrestrial limitations can be grasped—like all symbolism —intuitively without being entirely open to rational explanation. It may be said that the light and fire of the sun symbolise the omniscience as well as the creative, preserving and destructive omnipotence of the godhead. The light of the sun and its youthful daily renewed activity are reflected in the human hero, in the extension of his consciousness, his enlightenment, in his constantly revived courage and valiant energy. The struggle of the warrior with his external enemies corresponds to man's inner conflict with his inhibitions, with the evil within him and with the limitations of his ego. The trials and wanderings of the mythic hero, his contests with monsters and natural catastrophes, his defeats and his final victory, are projections of the individual's quest for the realisation of his psychic potential and the conquest of his egocentricity. The setting and renewed rising of the sun symbolise the possibility of human transformation and psychic rebirth.

The hero ready to act and eager to overcome obstacles is accordingly the heroic human being in quest of his completion. His ascent to heaven is the end of his terrestrial existence.

The Bible, appreciating the meaning of the mythologems and transforming them in accordance with monotheism, gives expression to the symbolism of the sun hero in the Psalm of David (Ps. 19: 2–8):

> The heavens declare the glory of God, And the firmament
> showeth His handiwork; Day unto day uttereth speech, And night
> unto night revealeth knowledge; There is no speech, there are no
> words, Neither is their voice heard. Their line is gone out through
> all the earth, and their words to the end of the world. In them
> hath He set a tent for the sun, Which is as a bridegroom coming
> out of his chamber, And rejoiceth as a strong man to run his
> course. His going forth is from the end of the heaven, And his
> circuit unto the ends of it; and there is nothing hid from the heat
> thereof. The [Torah (instruction)[45]] of the Lord is perfect,
> restoring the soul; The testimony of the Lord is sure, making
> wise the simple.

On the basis of his thorough researches into religion and

mythology, Mircea Eliade concludes: 'In whatever religious context you find them [ascents to heaven], whatever sort of values is placed upon them . . . they always signify a transcending of the human and a penetration into higher cosmic levels.'[46]

Ancient Indian symbolism regards the chariot as the body of the hero, the horses as his dynamic; the driver himself is his spirit.*[47]

Elijah is borne up by horses and chariot in fire and whirlwind. He had experienced his God on earth as fire and whirlwind, fought for him in fire and whirlwind. Both are ambivalent, creative, as well as destructive. Now, in the hand of a higher power, fire and whirlwind become for him regenerative forces transforming the soul and the body as he ascends.

This description of the biblical Elijah-figure and its historical and religious background requires a summary. In the Books of Kings Elijah represents the figure of the 'Great Hero' as it still exists in the imagination of all peoples and religions—though with variations due to historical, geographical and sociological differences. For example, Otto Rank,[49] Carl Kerényi,[50] C. G. Jung,[51] Erich Neumann,[52] Joseph L. Henderson,[53] Géza Róheim,[54] and especially Joseph Campbell,[55] are, on the basis of their anthropological, mythological and depth-psychological findings, largely in agreement regarding the fundamental characteristics of the hero's fate: his uncertain origins, his being chosen and disassociation from his surroundings, his initiation tests, trials and adventures, his transformation, his return into the world.

A comparison of the historical Elijah portrayed in the Bible with the mythical hero accords with the conception mentioned above, that the mythical images of the collective unconscious have an archetypal character and may accordingly find their living expression in the striving and fate of human beings.

In his introduction to A. S. Rappoport, *Myth and Legend of*

---

* The far more differentiated vision of the *Merkavah*, the divine chariot, of the prophet Ezekiel (Ezek. 1) can be similarly interpreted. Presumably it concerns the image of the dynamic of the divine emanation perceived by the human soul and its immanence in the terrestrial—human world. The quaternity of the wheels and the various animal figures symbolise mutually opposed human impulses and functions which, in their unification, bear God's throne, in fact constitute it. On it is enthroned the *adam kadmon*, the image of God who is incarnate in the perfect man, his likeness.[48]

Ancient Israel, Raphael Patai, the renowned anthropologist, mythologist and biblical scholar, writes:

> For as Walter Otto so correctly discerned, the most original and genuine myth, wherever and however it appears is true. More than that: it is not merely true next to other truths, but is *the* truth, because it brings to light not only that which is temporarily right, or for the time being just and proper, but the existence of things as image, as the form of all forms, the Divine. If this be so, we have all reason to approach with respect also the actual contents of the myths.

To this quotation Patai adds: 'When properly understood . . . the myth reveals itself as a highly potent force which, even centuries or millenia after it was fixed in written form, can still exert its spiritual influence and thereby mold the destinies of both individuals and human groups'. And in a critical survey of the different interpretations of the myths, Patai says in his own book: 'When a historical event is transformed into myth it loses a lot in accuracy and in detail . . . However, at the same time it gains immeasurably in longevity, in continuous effectiveness and in cultural potency.[56]

In its historical books, the Bible generally portrays primarily the relationship of the people as a whole to their God. It therefore emphasises in its representation of the individual personalities their activity and its effectiveness on the religious development of the people. Their individual internal and external experiences are portrayed not continuously but sporadically, episodically, in so far as individual and collective religious experiences are interwoven. This interweaving exists with Elijah, as has been shown, inasmuch as the psychic experience of Elijah, the Great Individual in advance of his time, displays the transformation process of which the collective is about to approach only the threshold.

The Bible throws no light on Elijah's origins and his early life. He emerges from obscurity as one who feels that he has been chosen, as indicated at his first appearance by his words: 'God . . . before whom I stand'. Although he lives apart from the world around him, he is at the same time responsible for it, appears in it when the moment seems to be ripe, and acts on its behalf. His trials and adventures are: his wilfulness on the occasion of the drought, his first flight and miraculous preservation, his encounter with the pagan widow, the resuscitation of her dead boy, his confrontation with the king, his challenge of the divine judgment with which he endangers himself, his victory over the priests of Baal, his flight from Jezebel's threatened revenge, his psychic breakdown in the desert, the regaining of his strength and his being overwhelmed by the revelation. These are the main phases of his struggle against the devouring Great Mother represented in person by the queen, collectively by the cult of Baal-Astarte. His struggle against her is at the same time a struggle on behalf of the divine father which takes place in almost all its stages with his help.

Elijah's transformation, beginning with his journey through the desert to the mountain of God, reaches its climax there in his numinous experience of the revelation of the godhead in whom all opposites are reconciled. He begins to be aware of the Divine which dwells within himself, and lets himself be guided by it. Thus he matures towards his transcendence. The hero ascending to heaven in the unity of his body and spirit is the human being who has realised his likeness to God in his own individuality.

The hero's ascent in itself says nothing about his further fate. He may, like Hercules,[57] in the end be transformed into a deity among other deities. Or, in the more highly developed religions, he may take on a certain divine character like Enoch or become part of the godhead like Jesus or, like Buddha, return to earth transformed into the figure of Boddhisatva to influence his fellow-men.

The Books of Kings merely describe Elijah's ascent, and provide no further information. The exclamation of Elisha, the only witness: 'My father, my father, the chariot of Israel, and the horsemen thereof', seems to indicate that the ascent was to him the divine acknowledgment of his master as 'Israel's hero'. This understanding is a definite proof of Elisha's own prophetic vocation.

The crossing of the Jordan by Elijah signifies for him that the way is open for his transcendence. For Elisha, returning to his fellow-men, the crossing signifies the awakening from his numinous experience.

Elijah's cloak, which Elisha inherited, is here not only (as the cloak generally) the *persona* of the wearer, his appearance to the outside world; through being passed on, it also symbolises the spiritual heritage which passes from the master to the pupil and makes him a prophet.[58]

In the subsequent chapters of II Kings, Elijah is several times mentioned as Elisha's master and protector. Elisha's miraculous deeds frequently resemble his. Just as he has, like Elijah, rolled back the Jordan, so he later resuscitates the dead child of his benefactress and continues to refill the widow's oil-jars. Elijah's 'inheritance' becomes apparent in his pupil. On the occasion of an attack by hostile troops, Elisha has a vision of a fiery chariot and horses protecting him and his surroundings (II Kings 6: 17).

There is a surprising mention of Elijah (II Chr. 21: 12–15), to some extent a parallel of that in the books of Kings, as a source of the history of the Jewish kings before the Babylonian exile. King Joram, who is related to the house of Ahab, receives a letter from Elijah which threatens him with death as a punishment for the murders he has committed and for his apostasy. But it is apparent from the biblical context that several years have by this time gone by since Elijah's ascent and that Elisha is at that period a prophet in his own right. According to Bible scholars, the editor of the book regarded it as entirely natural that, after Elijah's inexplicable disappearance and the fact that his body was nowhere to be found, he should continue to be capable of intervening in the course of history.[59] Jewish traditional exegetes add the psychologically interesting commentary that this letter was dictated by Elijah to one of his disciples in a vision.[60]

A further most significant mention of Elijah in the Bible occurs in the closing passages (3 : 23–4) of Malachi, the last of the Jewish prophets, who lived at the beginning of the fifth century, about a hundred years after the return of the Israelites from the Babylonian exile and the rebuilding of the Temple in Jerusalem—about four hundred years after Elijah.

The first few generations after the return from exile did not see the realisation of the hopes which the religious-cultural and national restoration had aroused in the earlier prophets and

probably also in the elite of the people. There had been no
intensification of religiousness: even the priests and leaders had
remained unaware of the fateful dependence of the individual and
the people on God and on obedience to him. Religious and
national unity were endangered by the increase in mixed marriages with pagan neighbours. The moral and social attitude of the
people offended in the grossest manner against the demands made
by Moses and the prophets—even formal worship in the Temple
was not observed faithfully (Mal. 1 and 2).

Malachi eloquently describes this situation, condemning the
religious and moral lapses by the people and the priests with
reference to the covenant made with God through Moses and
Aaron. Then he proclaims (3: 1ff.): 'Behold, I send My messenger,
and he prepares the way before Me: and the Lord, whom ye seek,
will suddenly come to His temple; and the messenger of the
covenant, whom ye delight in, behold, he cometh, saith the Lord
of hosts. But who may abide the day of his coming?' The prophet
then describes the day of judgment: those found guilty shall be
punished with death by burning, the faithful shall be rewarded
with the healing rays of the sun (3: 19-20). And the prophet calls
for repentance, and ends with the words: *Remember ye the law of
Moses My servant, which I commanded unto him in Horeb for all
Israel, even statutes and ordinances. Behold, I will send you Elijah the
prophet before the coming of the great and terrible day of the Lord. And
he shall turn the heart of the fathers to the children, and the heart of the
children to their fathers; lest I come and smite the land with utter
destruction.*[61]

The day of judgment prophesied by Malachi is not the apocalyptic Last Judgment 'at the end of days' prophesied by Isaiah and
Micah before him, but a judgment that will concern the Jewish
people exclusively.

Malachi, like his prophetic predecessors (e.g. Mic. 4: 2-5),
perceives in the God of the Israelites the universal godhead, just
as the Torah presents him as the creator of the world and master
of the entire history of humanity. Malachi, too, condemns
paganism as such, but demands faithful worship of the one God
only from his own, the Jewish people. The toleration of idolatry

33

by other peoples until their acknowledgment of God 'at the end of days' is expressed by Malachi in the words: 'For from the rising of the sun even unto the going down of the same My name is great among the nations; and in every place offerings are presented unto My name, even pure oblations; for My name is great among the nations...' (Mal. 1: 11, also Mic. 4: 5). And Rashi comments on this verse: 'Our rabbis said that it is because they [the nations] call Him the God of Gods. Even the idol-worshippers know that One God is above them all, and everywhere even the heathen pay Him homage.'[62]

Behind these words lies the knowledge, then still vague, but which later became increasingly clear, that inherent in pagan idolatry is a gradually advancing search, unconscious to begin with, for the 'Great Only One', which was to reach its goal only in the distant future.

God's covenant with the Jewish people was made with the patriarchs and renewed after the revelation on Horeb; collectively and individually they face God's continual demands and are accountable to him. The covenant expresses the personal aspect of God which is predominant in the Bible, the dialogue between God and the Israelites. 'The angel of the covenant' appears repeatedly in the Bible as watching over its fulfilment. It accompanies the people in their historical development, warns against alliances with pagan peoples and their gods, threatens punishment for breaking the covenant and carries it out unless repentance follows (Judg. 2: 1–5). The angel appointed after the revelation on Horeb, of whom God says: 'My name is in him', who is to lead the Israelites on their journey through the desert (Exod. 23: 20–3), has to be regarded also as the guarantor of the covenant renewed through Moses. Therefore Malachi prophesies that the angel of the covenant will appear on the Day of Judgment.*

* The Hebrew term *malakh* (angel) means 'a messenger' generally, *sensu strictiori* 'a divine messenger'; a figure or voice perceptible to man which conveys God's word to him.[63] Sometimes, in a similar sense, prophets (in Malachi also the ideal priest) are called 'angels'. The name of the prophet 'Malachi' is equally presumably not his proper name but an indication that he is a messenger, or a reference to God's messenger whose coming he foretells (3: 1–4)

One may understand the warning to keep the Torah which has been given to Moses. What is unexpected is Malachi's prophecy of Elijah's return—about four centuries after the end of his existence on earth. It can be explained by the obvious assumption that his contemporaries did not consider Elijah to have died in the conventional sense. His overwhelming intervention in the course of history by means of sporadic unexpected appearances had not merely kept him alive in the heart of the people but had aroused and maintained for generations the belief in his possible return and his renewed activity on behalf of his people.

Elijah's return intended by God is now proclaimed prophetically by Malachi (3: 23–4). It is to occur before the coming of 'the great and terrible day of the Lord'. The day is designated as 'great' because on it God will return to his sanctuary; at the same time it is 'terrible' because of the judgment which threatens the sinners. It is now Elijah's task to move fathers and children to repentance in order to save the country and the people from complete annihilation.

The Hebrew word *al* in the prophecy of Elijah's return quoted above (p. 33), *ve-heshiv lev avot al banim* and *ve-lev banim al avotam*, generally means 'upon' but also frequently 'together with'. Accordingly, the meaning here is that he will turn (to God) the heart of the fathers together with the children and the heart of the children together with the parents. The word *al* is, however, used in the Bible repeatedly also in the sense of '*el*' ('to'). According to this, the meaning would be that Elijah leads fathers and sons back towards each other. This could refer to the reconciliation between the generations about whom Malachi complains.* But as this is only one of the many transgressions of the people mentioned by the prophet because of which judgment is threatened, the first explanation, also less questionable linguistically, is probably to be preferred.

According to the simple wording of Malachi 3: 1–2 quoted

---

* This is the more usual interpretation of both Gentile and Jewish exegetes. Rashi, following an earlier tradition, interprets this last verse of Malachi as follows: that there will be fathers who will lead back their sons to God, and sons who will lead their fathers to God, and thus peace will come to the world.[64] Redak says explicitly that '*al*' means 'with'

above, and in the view of most scholarly exegetes, the messenger preparing the way for God, the angel of the covenant who sits in judgment and the prophet Elijah mentioned at the end of the chapter are regarded as three different messengers of God. Many consider the proclamation of Elijah's return to be not merely the conclusion of Malachi's prophecies, but as an epilogue to the books of the prophets as a whole.[65] Its position in the ultimate verses of the books emphasises its particular significance.

But most of the Jewish traditional commentators identify both the messenger preparing the way and also the angel of the covenant with Elijah. This is not inconsistent with the wording of the text. It seems to be obvious that the mention in verse 1 of the messenger who is to prepare the way for God refers to Elijah who, according to verse 23, will lead the people back to God. The identification of the angel of the covenant with Elijah is equally understandable. In the time of Ahab he was indeed the champion of the covenant (I Kings 19: 10, 14) and had led the people back to it, albeit only temporarily. Moreover, God predicted to Elijah that there would be a trial of the apostates and that only a small faithful remnant of Israelites would be left (I Kings 21: 18), as Malachi now also prophesies (3: 16–17). He is therefore in post-biblical Aggadic literature explicitly designated as the angel of the covenant. Elijah's function of judging and punishing and also exhorting and saving is not contradictory within the context of Malachi's prophetic speech. His ambivalence and its harmonisation are later particularly emphasised by the Aggadists, and the Jewish exegetes of the Book of Malachi followed suit (see pp. 75–7, 177–8).

But, no matter what his listeners thought of the details of the events prophesied by Malachi or how they were later interpreted, of the greatest importance are his last unequivocal words. They are to be regarded as the final prophetic appeal to Israel before the day of judgment: they prophesy the return of Elijah, the 'hero of Israel', after his transcendence. Sent by the God of Israel, he returns not—or not only—as accuser and judge, but able to effect the Israelites' return to God, thus saving them from destruction.

This is the basis of the Jewish people's belief in the reappearance of Elijah as the guide to redemption. In the course of subsequent centuries, this belief found manifold expression in the doctrines of redemption in Talmudic-Aggadic literature.

CHAPTER II

The Elijah-Figure in the Apocrypha

In the Apocrypha (between 200 BCE and 200 CE) which is close to
the biblical books in time and mostly also in content, the prophet
Elijah is repeatedly mentioned directly or by way of suggestion.

In the historical books of the Maccabees (*c.* 120 BCE), their
leader Mattathias, in his valedictory address enumerating the
Jewish heroes of past ages, describes also Elijah's zealous activity
for the Torah and his ascent into heaven (I Macc. 2: 58).[1] Later it
is reported that when the sanctuary which had been devastated by
the Syrians was restored, the stones of the desecrated altar were
stored in a special place on the Temple Mount, 'until a prophet
should come and decide [what should be done] concerning them'
(I Macc. 4: 46).[2] Similarly, when Mattathias' son Simon is nomi-
nated as his successor, it is said that he shall be prince and priest
'until some day the true prophet shall arise in Israel' (I Macc.
14: 41).[3] These seem to be references to Elijah's return, to be
expected before national redemption.

More space is accorded to Elijah's activity in the Book of Ben
Sira (150 BCE) within the framework of a poetic representation of
Israel's biblical history (48: 1–12):[4]

1 Until there arose a prophet like fire,
  Whose word was like a burning furnace.
2 And he broke for them the staff of bread,
  And by his zeal made them few in number.
3 By the word of God he shut up the heavens;
  Fire also descended thrice.

4 How terrible wast thou, Elijah!
  And he who is like thee shall be glorified.
5 Who didst raise up a dead man from death,
  And from Sheol, according to the good pleasure of [God];
6 Who broughtest down kings to the Pit,
  And them that were honoured from their beds [of sickness];
7 Who heardest rebukes in Sinai,
  And judgements of vengeance in Horeb.
8 Who anointedst kings for retribution,
  And a prophet as successor in thy place.
9 Who wast taken upwards in a whirlwind,
  And by fiery troops to the heavens.
10 Who art ready for the time, as it is written,
  To still the wrath before the fierce anger of God,
  To turn the heart of the fathers unto the children,
  And to restore the tribes of Israel.
11 Blessed is he that seeth thee, and dieth,[5]
  And blessed art thou thyself for thou livest.
12 Elijah was hidden in the [heavenly] chambers,
  Then was Elisha filled with his spirit.

It is noteworthy that the author adds to the Malachi quotation 'to turn the heart of the fathers unto the children' that he will restore the tribes of Israel. This reference to the national aspect of redemption may be explained historically, because the Book of Ben Sira was composed later than Malachi's prophecy. The words which follow in the text: 'blessed is he that seeth thee and dieth', are mostly seen by the commentators as referring to Elisha. But in view of the following verse 12, this is not justifiable. More probably it refers to the visions of Elijah by some devout people of that time.

In I (Ethiopic) Book of Enoch (c. 120 BCE), the original Hebrew text of which has been lost, in the history of the Israelites the relationship of the people to their God is represented allegorically as that of a flock of sheep to their master. It says there (89: 51-2):[6] 'And again I saw these sheep that they again erred, and went many ways and forsook their house, and the Lord of the sheep called some from amongst the sheep and sent them to the sheep, but the sheep began to slay them. And one of them was saved and was not slain, and it sped away and cried aloud over the sheep and brought it up to me, and caused it to dwell there.' This is a clear reference to Elijah, who is here represented as the only prophet of God in Ahab's time to be saved and, according to tradition, carried off to Enoch in heaven.

A later chapter describes first the 'seven world-weeks' which have already passed since the birth of Enoch, before his prophecy, at the beginning of the Book of Enoch. Of the sixth world-week it says that all who lived in it were blinded and their hearts godlessly forsook wisdom, 'and in it a man shall ascend; and at its close the house of dominion [the temple] shall be burnt with fire, and the whole race of the chosen root shall be dispersed' (93: 8).[7] The mention of a man's ascent doubtless refers to Elijah. The Messiah will reign from the eighth to the tenth world-week and then the Last Judgment will follow.

'The Martyrdom of Isaiah', also called 'The Ascent of Isaiah' (c. 100 BCE), states: 'And Elijah the prophet of Tebon of Gilead was reproving Ahaziah and Samaria, and prophesied regarding Ahaziah that he should die on his bed of sickness, and that Samaria should be delivered into the hand of Laba Nasr because he had slain the prophets of God' (2: 14).[8]

In II Book of Baruch (c. 100 BCE) Elijah's being fed by the ravens is given (77: 24–5) as one of the examples showing that God as well as the devout sent birds out as messengers.[9]

IV Book of Ezra (c. 100 BCE) mentions (7: 109) Elijah's prayers for rain and for the resuscitation of the child.[10] The same book prophesies that 'the men who have been taken up, who have not tasted death from their birth, shall appear' before the Messiah. 'Then shall the heart of the inhabitants [of the world] be changed and be converted to a different spirit' (6: 26).[11] This refers to Elijah, as is apparent from the clear echoing of the Malachi prophecy; apart from this it refers presumably also to Enoch.[12] The Bible (Gen. 5: 24) says of Enoch merely: 'And Enoch walked with God, and he was not; for God took him.' It was this unusual wording which probably gave rise to the belief in his miraculous transcendence. Thus in I (Ethiopic) Book of Enoch (70: 2), Enoch 'was raised aloft on the chariots of the spirit and his name vanished amongst them [from those who dwelt on the earth].'¹³ In II (Slavonic) Book of Enoch ('The Book of the Secrets of Enoch') two angels carry him up to the seventh heaven by degrees (1: 1–10; 3: 1–3).¹⁴

It is noteworthy that in the apocryphal literature Elijah's ascent to heaven—representing the hero's transformation—is transferred not only to Enoch but also to other biblical personages such as Moses, Isaiah and Ezra, although there are no clues to this to be found in the relevant biblical texts.¹⁵

II Book of the Sybillines, originally a Jewish work (c. 150 CE) which later partly underwent Christian revision, says in its description of the Last Judgment: 'And then the Tishbite descends from heaven to earth, driving the heavenly chariot, and gives the people who inhabit the earth three signs, the signs of life ending.' According to this source, at the Last Judgment held by the archangels Elijah also appears: he is a witness, together with Moses, the patriarchs, Joshua, Daniel, Jonah and Habakkuk.¹⁶

To sum up: in so far as the Jewish apocryphal literature of the last two pre-Christian and the first two Christian centuries does not have a pronounced apocalyptic character, only Ben Sira presents, as shown above, an elaboration of the Malachi prophecy. In apocalyptic descriptions contemporary with the Apocrypha (200–250), the Elijah-figure as such recedes, but for the first time there are references to the precursor of the Messiah, while Malachi and Ben Sira represent Elijah as the saviour himself, sent by God.

But from the writings of Philo Judaeus, the Gospels and Justin Martyr's *Dialogue with Trypho*, which were composed during the same period as the Apocrypha, it is apparent that at this time among both the scholars and the people the Jewish concept of redemption continued to develop, taking on more definite characteristics.

Philo records of Elijah himself that 'he did not die but was carried up with a whirlwind as it were into heaven and went up there to be among the angels'.¹⁷ In *De Praemiis et Poenis*, Philo expects the future to hold the religious-ethical revival of the Israelites, their eventual repentance, and the gathering in of the exiles: 'The returning exiles will be guided by some vision, more divine than is compatible with its being of the nature of man, invisible indeed to everyone else, but manifest only to those who were saved.'[18] Thus he talks of a redeemer who corresponds to the figure which Malachi and Ben Sira identify with Elijah.

According to Justin Martyr, Trypho the Jew says: 'As to [the] Christ, if indeed he is born and exists somewhere, he is unknown and does not yet know himself nor has he any power, until Elijah comes and anoints him and makes him manifest to all.'[19]

The Gospels and Justin Martyr's *Dialogue with Trypho* unequivocally show that until the beginning of the Christian era the ordinary Jewish people as well as the spiritual elite expected the return of Elijah as the precursor and attendant of the Messiah from the house of David (see chapter IX).

CHAPTER III

Elijah in Aggadic Literature (the Talmud and Midrashim)

The personality of Elijah, with its aura of mystery, made an increasing impression on the Jewish people. This finds relatively little expression, as has been shown, in the immediate post-biblical literature, the Apocrypha. It was different in the Talmudic-Aggadic world of legends and ideas which originated at about the same time, and which was decisive for the development of Jewish culture. Initially disseminated for several generations by oral tradition and evolved through research, it found its first written expression in the Mishnah (*c.* 200 CE). Then an intensive and fertile further development during the next three to four centuries culminated in the editions of the Babylonian and the Jerusalem Talmud (*c.* 500 CE), and later, until the ninth century, in the recording of numerous Aggadic Midrashim (collections of legends and homilies accompanying the biblical text). In all of them Elijah is mentioned innumerable times, frequently in short, sometimes only abrupt, utterances, sometimes in more or less detailed accounts or in sayings, advice, religious judgments attributed to him. Two extensive Aggadah collections are attributed to him, i.e. to his 'house of study'.[*][1]

Following the general character of Aggadic literature, these are

---

* The Aggadic passages in the two Talmuds as well as the Aggadic Midrashim are referred to in this chapter collectively as 'Aggadah', and 'Aggadist' denotes any of the rabbinic scholars quoted in the Talmud or a Midrash passage

mostly supplements and free interpretations, frequently also at first sight arbitrary, but always meaningful, re-interpretations of the biblical text. The Aggadists were, moreover, particularly concerned with Elijah's origin and his fate after his mysterious ascent. But beyond that—and this is what is surprising and significant—Elijah appears personally as a figure of this world in numerous episodes taking place in the Talmudic-Aggadic period itself. He intervenes, advising and acting, in the daily course of events. Finally, his later role at the time of the Messianic redemption is frequently and variously discussed by the Aggadists.

Among the Aggadic 'supplements' to the biblical record of Elijah, the repeated discussions of his probable origin may be mentioned first. The fact that neither his father's name nor the tribe to which he belonged is given initiated the debate as to whether he was a descendant of the sons of one of the two matriarchs Leah or Rachel. His belonging to the tribe of Gad, the son of Leah, is substantiated in the Aggadah historically and geographically by the fact that Gilead, the place where he originally lived, was situated in the district of the tribe of Gad. At the same time, the word *Gad* is interpreted as 'luck' in the world and also as 'destroyer' of the peoples oppressing the Israelites at the time of the redemption.[2] His descent from the tribe of Gad is also emphasised in a particularly interesting Aggadic interpretation of a verse of Jacob's blessing (Gen. 49: 16–19) which gives prophetically the characteristics of the future tribes of Israel. Between the blessing for Dan and the blessing for Gad, Jacob exclaims: 'I wait for Thy salvation, O Lord.' According to the Aggadah this means it is not the Samson descendent from Dan who will bring redemption to the Israelites but the one who comes from the later tribe of Gad; as it is referred to in Malachi's saying: 'Behold, I will send you Elijah the prophet'.[3]

Samson corresponds, even with respect to his name, to the mythological 'sun hero', but is finally not victorious and not transcending. Although he destroys the Phoenician princes who are fighting the Israelites, and who had captured and blinded him, he kills himself together with them: 'Let me die with the Philistines' (Judg. 16: 28–30). Even if Samson's prayer and his readiness to die may be explained as transformation and sacrifice of his ego, there is nowhere in Jewish thought any hint of his transcending or returning to earth, neither is he a key figure in Jewish tradition.

According to other opinions, Elijah was a descendant of Benjamin, that is from Rachel—based on a mention of the name Elijah in a list of the tribe of Benjamin (I Chr. 8: 27) and a free interpretation of the relevant texts.[4] According to R. Pedat, Elijah was a citizen of Jerusalem, part of which belonged to the tribe of Judah and part to the tribe of Benjamin, and was there a member of the Sanhedrin, the highest religious authority.[5] The ancient tradition that Edom, the arch-enemy of the Israelites, would one day be finally defeated by Rachel's sons[6] was presumably also used as an argument. Rachel, Jacob's wife who was his first love, was closer to the heart of the people than Leah; Jeremiah describes her as weeping over the fate of her children until God promises her that they shall return to their country. The Aggadah calls her the centre of Jacob's house.[7] Another Aggadah emphasises that he who one day redeems the Israelite people will be a descendant of Benjamin, the smallest and weakest tribe.[8]

A third opinion is that Elijah was a Levite. This assumption is based primarily on the parallels, repeatedly emphasised by the Aggadists, between Elijah and Moses, the first prophet and redeemer of the Israelites. 'Two prophets are descendants of the house of Levi: Moses and Elijah.'[9] The assumption that Elijah was a priest rests above all on his identification with the Aaronide Phinehas, the zealot at the time of the wandering in the wilderness.[10] In the Aggadic collection ascribed to Elijah's school (*Seder Eliyahu Rabbah*) he himself declares that he is a descendant of Rachel.[11] However, when he appears in other Aggadic accounts, he is repeatedly addressed as 'priest'.[12]

These various suppositions and arguments do show that the interest in Elijah's origin was in the first instance directed at his spiritual heritage: which of the matriarchs could be regarded as the ancestress of the future redeemer; which of the personages of the past as his ancestor.[13]

45

Elijah's deeds related in the Bible are repeatedly praised and glorified in Aggadic literature. 'May his memory be blessed', is added to his name in the Talmud and in many Aggadot, and attention is also drawn to the fact that he is one of the few who are called 'a man of God'.[14] Elijah is often numbered also amongst the *Zaddikim* (righteous, pious)[15] who can through their piety perform the same miracles as God[16] or, indeed, 'command God' inasmuch as they are able temporarily to suspend the God-given laws of nature or to influence his decisions.[17] Some Aggadists pronounce Elijah free of sin and compare him with Adam before the Fall.[18] It is also emphasised that in contrast to secular rulers, Elijah in his greatness never called himself divine.[19]

But for all their great veneration of Elijah, the majority of the Aggadists who concern themselves with him do not shrink from explicitly emphasising his weaknesses. Freely interpreting and elaborating the biblical account, they differ from it considerably at times in their representation of his character.

Thus the abruptness of Elijah's first appearance in the Bible prompts in the Aggadah a surprising interpretation of his threat of drought. God is said to have commanded Elijah to go and console Ahab's commander-in-chief, who is mentioned in the Bible in the previous verse in another connection. Elijah objects that he would on this visit certainly hear irreverent remarks about God which would enrage him. Therefore God promises that he will make every curse which he may utter on this occasion come true. Then when Ahab boasts that he is practising idolatry with impunity, Elijah prophesies: 'As ... the God of Israel, liveth, before whom I stand, there shall not be dew nor rain these years, but according to my word', and thus obliges God to bring about a drought and a severe famine in the country for several years.*[20]

God provides for Elijah on his flight at first in a miraculous way: the ravens who bring meat and bread to his hiding-place are said to have been chosen, as long ago as the Flood, to look after Elijah later, during a famine.[21] But God causes the brook from

* According to a different version (BT Sanhedrin 113a and M. Tehillim 78. 5), Ahab and Elijah pay the visit together, without being divinely commanded, and Elijah prophesies the drought without obtaining a promise from God

which Elijah drinks to dry up, so as to let him feel for himself the serious consequences of the famine which he has imposed. He then prompts him to flee further to the pagan widow in Zarephath, who feeds him. When Elijah later asks God to revive the widow's dead son, God commands him to return the 'key' to the dew, for only by means of dew can he revive the dead.* The lack of rain should therefore, according to the Aggadists, be regarded as having been imposed on purpose by the prophet.

In the Aggadic view, Elijah is much stricter and more punitive than the God for whom he fights. He even wilfully imposes a harsh test on the widow who is to feed him according to God's command.[23] Although later the Aggadah makes him ask mercy for her son in particularly moving words,†[24] it is emphasised that Elijah took pity only on individual human beings and had no compassion for his people. The Midrash formulates this: Elijah considered the dignity of the father (God) but not the dignity of the son (Israel).[25] When God wants to send Elijah to Ahab in order to inform him of the end of the drought, he objects that the king has not yet returned to God.[26] But God reminds him that after the creation of the world he watered the earth for the sake of the sole human being (Adam). Elijah has to carry out the divine command.[27]

The account of the divine judgment on Mount Carmel is also elaborated by the Aggadists. Carmel is said to have been chosen as the site of this revelation as compensation for the choice of Horeb for the great revelation to Moses and the Israelites.[28] The bullock which in the contest was intended for Baal is said to have refused to be sacrificed to the idol while his brother animal was being offered up to God, until Elijah explained to it that his being offered would also sanctify the name of God.[29] The trench Elijah

* BT Sanhedrin 113a says that the three keys—of rain, of giving life and of resurrecting the dead—God had reserved for himself, and even a divine messenger was allowed to use only one of them at a time, temporarily[22]

† After the death of her son, the widow says to Elijah: 'What have I to do with thee, O thou man of God? art thou come unto me to call my sin to remembrance, and to slay my son?' (I Kings 17: 18). On this verse, so difficult to understand, the Aggadist comments that the woman reproached Elijah because it would be said that they had had sexual relations, and the death of her son would be regarded as her punishment for it (*Pirke de-R. Eliezer*, ch. 33, p. 240)

made about the altar was the same size as the courtyard of the tabernacle made by Moses in the desert.[30]

But here, too, Elijah's excessive zeal is very much emphasised by the Aggadists. Not only does he wilfully provoke the divine judgment but he even commands the sun to stand still, so as to have more time for his purpose.[31] His words: 'Thou hast turned their heart back again', are interpreted as: 'You have turned the heart of the people away from you', that is, as a reproach to God who allowed the people to become apostate. He would proclaim this aloud, if God would not answer his prayer.[32] Here, as previously when Elijah controlled the rain, his fight for God becomes a struggle with God, a tendency to control him magically. However, elsewhere the Talmud comments that God admitted that he had done the people a wrong, as he had given mankind the instinct to do evil.[33]

According to another Aggadah, on Mount Carmel Elijah demands that his prayer be granted so that the Messianic redemption of the people which he is one day to bring about will not be in doubt,[34] but, in spite of his insistence, his prayer was answered only after he had mentioned in it the merits of the patriarchs.[35] Moreover, later, after the divine judgment, while waiting for the expected rain, Elijah points to the sign of the covenant on his body.[36] The Aggadists here want to emphasise that God's mercy and his revelation were invoked not by Elijah's excessive zeal but by the 'merit of the patriarchs'.

The events which now follow—Elijah's flight from Jezebel's revenge, his psychic breakdown in the desert and his sustenance by the angel—are hardly commented on in the Aggadah. His journey to Horeb is seen as if God had almost forcibly directed him to the mountain of the revelation, so that he might plead there for mercy for Israel. He ought to have said there: 'They [the children of Israel] are your sons, the sons of those who were proved faithful, the sons of Abraham, Isaac, Jacob.' But he had complained only of his own misery, the failure of his fight for God, and had accused his people of having broken the covenant with God.[37]

Another Midrash says: 'Elijah ought to have gone to the place in which his forefathers had stood [Horeb] and prayed for mercy for Israel; he did not do so.' God therefore says to him reproachfully: 'You have prayed for yourself, turn back'.[38] According to another Aggadah, God reprimands him: 'They have broken my covenant and not yours, destroyed my altars and not yours, killed my priests and not yours. Therefore how does it concern you?'[39] And 'God sought to calm Elijah, and after his revelation in the small voice of silence he waited for three hours [for Elijah's understanding]. When Elijah then repeats his complaint once more,* he is told: "Go, return on thy way to the wilderness of Damascus." "What you are asking I cannot grant." '[40] And in another passage: 'anoint Elisha in your stead', which means: 'I no longer want you as my prophet.'[41]

Thus, Elijah's fanatical harshness in his fight for God is not only criticised in Aggadic literature but especially underlined and, indeed, exaggerated. The ending of his prophetic mission is represented as a punishment, although in the biblical text there is no basis for this. Elijah was not open to God's mercy and love. Even the direct revelation he experienced did not change him.

Most Jewish interpreters of the Bible, especially R. J. E. Halevy, agree with the Aggadic view of Elijah's character, over-reaction and exaggerations.[42] The Midrash literature contains only one defence of Elijah's accusations: 'When Elijah saw that the Israelites were letting themselves be led astray by Ahab, he said: "better three years of famine than that they should descend into the abyss [hell]". Indeed, Elijah did it out of love.'[43]

About Elijah's revelation, one Aggadah says that he did not understand the meaning of the four phenomena—storm, earthquake, fire and the voice of silence—until God explained them to him as the four worlds which man has to traverse: the storm signifies life on earth, the earthquake death, the fire the punishment of hell. The voice of silence means the Last Judgment, when 'God alone is exalted'. This revelation, which in its biblical wording and context addresses Elijah in his 'here and now', is

---

* This also shows that the severe Aggadic condemnation of Elijah's excess of zeal is based on the verbal repetition of his accusation after he had experienced the theophany. The verse in question (I Kings 19: 14) is regarded by most exegetes as an inadvertent duplication of verse 19: 10

accordingly applied by the Aggadists allegorically to human fate generally.[44]

In the Aggadic view, Elijah's decisive transformation therefore does not take place at Horeb but on his last journey and at his ascent. On parting, Elijah and Elisha discuss, according to various Aggadic scholars, 'the reciting of the verse "Hear, O Israel"—or the creation of the world or the consolation of Jerusalem or the chariot of the divine throne.'*[45] These are the central religious themes: the unity of God, the cosmogony, the redemption and the theophany.

Their discussion is seen by other Aggadists as symbolised by the fiery chariot and horses: the one is compared to the Torah, the other to the oral tradition. And a messenger dispatched by God, the whirlwind, had to separate the two absorbed in the conversation on the Torah, so as to guide Elijah aloft.[46] Several Aggadists emphasise that Elijah 'ascended on the horse of the king [God]',[47] that is, was honoured by the grace of God.

In the Talmudic-Aggadic view, the pious generally die a physical death. 'Their body lies in peace on their bed, and their souls find safety beneath the throne of God and are joined to the eternal life' (BT Shabbat 152b). With regard to Elijah's ascent, however, it is generally accepted that his soul rose to heaven together with his living body. He is one of nine personages to whom this was granted,[48] among whom was Enoch, with whom he is often compared and of whom it says in Genesis (5: 24) 'and he was not; for God took him' (see also p. 40 n. 12). Only Rabbi Jose ben Ḥalafta says: 'Moses and Elijah never ascended, and the divine majesty never descended [at Horeb]'.[49] It seems that Rabbi Jose is trying to guard against an anthropomorphic concept of

* The Aggadist relates Elijah's chariot to the chariot of the divine throne of Ezekiel's vision (see p. 29).

The religious philosopher Joseph Albo (c. 1400) says of Elijah's theophany that 'he was informed of the division of existence into three worlds: the world of genesis and decay, the world of the spheres and the world of the angels. Also that there is one Being over them, who binds together all the parts of nature and controls them and watches over their effects in the lower world, realising His purpose and will. This is God, who is absolutely different from them. His quiddity [essence] is absolutely unknown and he can be described only in negative attributes, which are called "a still small voice of silence"' (Sefer ha-Ikkarim, vol. 2, ch. 31, pp. 217–19)

God and a deification of man, corresponding to the interpretation of the fiery chariot which has been mentioned; he therefore regards Elijah's physical ascent also as allegorical, as do some later traditional Bible commentators.[50]

In any case, Elijah's death is mentioned nowhere; at most it is his 'disappearance' or 'temporary concealment'. Thus in a historical work of the talmudic period, also ascribed to Rabbi Jose ben Ḥalafta: 'Elijah was concealed from the eyes of the world in the second year of the reign of King Ahaziah. He will reappear at the coming of the Messiah, will be concealed once more until the time of Gog and Magog, and now [in the meantime] he is writing the history of all times.'[51] Flavius Josephus (c. 100 CE) comments: 'He disappeared from the sight of men, and no one knows where he is.'[52] Thus there exists a general consensus that Elijah continues to live: for example: 'Seven men embrace the whole world: Methuselah [still] saw Adam, Shem saw Methuselah, Jacob saw Shem, Amram saw Jacob, Ahijah from Shilo saw Amram, Elijah saw Ahijah and is still alive.'[53] Another version adds: 'till the Messiah comes'.[54] This passage, however, expresses not only the eternal existence of Elijah, but emphasises that his spiritual tradition goes back to Adam.

In the heavens, Elijah belongs to God's immediate entourage: he is initiated into his resolutions and secrets,[55] the decisions of the 'heavenly house of study' are known to him.*[56] Elijah records the deeds of individual people[58] as well as the history of mankind.[59] He is also in charge of guarding the souls of the dead; he directs every pious man to his place in paradise; at the beginning of every Sabbath he brings the sinful souls to heaven and at the end of the Sabbath leads them back to their punishment; after they have atoned for their sins he escorts them to their final place in heaven.[60]

Much more is said in Aggadic literature about Elijah's activity

---

* Talmudic and Aggadic literature suggest that the souls of great scholars and pious men will dwell in the 'upper' (heavenly) house of study and discuss and decide religious views and commandments with the participation of the divine.[57] For instance, Elijah knows that particularly devout prayers for the resurrection of the dead can be effective, but he is punished for revealing the secret (BT Baba Meẓia 85b)

on earth than about his task in heaven. 'He can appear on earth with four wingbeats'[61] and 'can move across it'.[62] According to one view, 'he soars as an eagle* above the face of the earth and observes the hidden activities of men.'[63]

His activity on earth in the time of the Talmud is described in numerous stories with the most diverse variations. He appears as many figures, mostly not distinguishable from an ordinary Jewish man, especially frequently described as 'that old man',[65] but occasionally also as an Arab,[66] a horseman,[67] a royal— usually Roman—official[68]—once even as a harlot.[69] His disguise is thus whatever may best serve his helpful, successful intervention. Occasionally he may figure in a dream, in order to tell someone something of importance.[70] He appears so to help the Jewish people, especially in times of danger and persecution, but above all individuals in their private troubles.

As the Persian court official Harbonah, in the story of Esther, he contributes decisively, through his seemingly accidental arrival, to the rescue of Persian Jewry.[71] When he does not intervene directly in events where the Jewish people are in danger, he asks for divine help. He then refers to the merits of the patriarchs,[72] or himself hurries to them and to Moses, wakes them up and asks them to intervene so that God may avert the calamity.[73] He is constantly in touch with the patriarchs, and also serves them daily at their religious ablutions before prayer.[74] The enemies of the Israelites are well aware that their attacks are time and again frustrated 'by an old man'.[75]

Elijah's help to individuals is described as extraordinarily diverse. At the decisive moment, he rescues from extreme danger; he clears by his evidence or successfully defends those innocently accused;[76] he frees the unjustly condemned;[77] he heals the dangerously ill;[78] he saves those whose lives are threatened in various ways; indeed, he advises people whose fate has already

---

* The eagle, a mythological symbol of the sun and of spiritualisation, is also a biblical metaphor for the loving father who gives security to his young and at the same time guides them towards independence. Thus Exod. 19: 4: 'I bare you on eagles' wings, and brought you unto myself'; and Deut. 32: 11: 'As an eagle that stirreth up her nest, hovereth over her young, spreadeth abroad her wings, taketh them, beareth them on her pinions—the Lord alone did lead him [Israel]'[64]

been sealed by divine decree how, by means of righteous actions or good deeds, they may still avert it and live.[79] He brings a man and his wife together;[80] he makes peace between personal enemies;[81] he reassures of his innocence a pious man who is afraid of inadvertently having cohabited with a woman.[82] He takes a particular interest in the meek and humble: he ensures that the oppressed are given their rights. He has various ways of helping the poor—whether they are scholars or simple ordinary people, including Gentiles:[83] he gives them presents or coins which miraculously multiply;[84] indeed, he does not shrink on one occasion from selling himself as a slave for the benefit of a poor head of a family.[85] His ways and means of giving help sometimes may be natural or accidental, but always at the right time and in the right place, and sometimes obviously miraculous.

It is characteristic of Elijah that, while helping generously and magnanimously, when necessary he tries to improve the attitude of the one in need. Thus he can link his presents to a poor man with the admonition to use his future wealth to support the needy in his turn, and threatens to take away his possessions if he does not heed the precept,[86] or he withholds the profits from a merchant who has become successful through his blessing until he gratefully acknowledges divine help.[87]

Elijah has a very close relationship with many rabbis of the Talmudic-Aggadic period, especially with R. Eliezer,[88] R. Nahum-Ish-Gamzu,[89] R. Akiva,[90] R. Meir,[91] R. Jose,[92] R. Judah ha-Nasi,[93] R. Judah, the brother of R. Salla,[94] and R. Simeon bar Yoḥai.[95] He tends not to appear to them, as he does to the simple man, as an equal, or in appropriate disguise. The expression usually is: 'The rabbi . . . met Elijah and talked to him', or 'Elijah was with the rabbi': they were aware that they were meeting Elijah.* To them, also, he is always ready to give help when needed.[97] But beyond that he is also their teacher, counsellor and personal friend. On the

---

* The former expression, 'met Elijah', refers in each case to a single encounter with Elijah, while the latter indicates more of a constant relationship with him. In the view of R. Isaac Abrarvanel (exegete and philosopher, 1437–1508), the scholars' encounters with Elijah mentioned in the Talmud either signify visions in meditation or dreams, or the scholars called the surprising new experiences which came to them the 'Giluy Eliyahu' ('Elijah's Revelations') (*Yeshuot Meshiḥo*, p. 21)[96]

basis of his comprehensive knowledge, surpassing that of the human mind, he instructs for instance one rabbi on God's purpose in creating seemingly useless animals or even harmful insects and why He allows earthquakes and other natural catastrophes to happen.[98] To another scholar he explains the complementary qualities and abilities of men and women:[99] 'He who marries a suitable woman is kissed by Elijah'.[100]

He furthers the elucidation of difficult biblical texts. He mediates between the 'Divine' and the rabbinic 'house of study', through repeating 'below' what has been said 'above'.[101] Confronted with the frequently wide divergence of scholars' opinions, he repeatedly states that God values as true the view of every one of them, [102] thus indicating the relativity of rational human thought. The majority in the 'house of study' once decided against the opinion of one rabbi, although this had been confirmed by a divine voice. Elijah later reports that God had said smilingly about this: 'My children have defeated me.'[103] On another occasion Elijah relates that the opinions of R. Meir were not mentioned in the heavenly 'house of study' because he had been a pupil of the heretic Elisha ben Abuya. A sage commented on this: 'R. Meir found a pomegranate, took from it the fruit and threw the peel away.' Then Elijah announced: 'Now God, too, is beginning to value R. Meir as his friend and to quote his theses.'[104]

In many other additional respects, Elijah furthers the study of the Torah.[105] He transmits messages between the scholars,[106] reveals mistakes, resolves doubts, reminds them of what has been forgotten;[107] he brings them new pupils through inducing gifted young men to give up their occupation and to study; if need be, he provides them with material support, so that they may devote themselves to religious studies without worry.[108] At times he himself appears as a teacher and initiates those particularly thirsty for knowledge into the profundities of the Torah.

But Elijah is not only concerned about extending and deepening the scholars' knowledge of the Torah. He does not merely encourage them as a fatherly friend and fulfil their personal wishes. Above all, he tries through his instruction to further their individual spiritual development,[109] not shrinking, if necessary, from making stern admonitions. He makes demands on the scholars and leaders of the people which, in religious and ethic respects, far exceed those made on the average person: he punishes them, especially by withdrawing his friendship, when they do not meet his requirements.[110] On the other hand, he warns them not to demand too much of ordinary people.[111]

A particularly close friendship existed between Elijah and the famous talmudic sage R. Joshua ben Levi. Among other things, it is said of them that they studied the law together,[112] and once, when they were dealing with a religious decision made by R. Simeon bar Yoḥai who had since died, they visited him in Paradise in order to question him about it.[113] On another occasion, R. Joshua met the prophet Elijah at the entrance to R. Simeon's tomb and asked: 'Shall I one day reach the world to come?' Elijah answered him: 'If the master wishes.' R. Joshua then said: 'I have seen two people and heard the voice of a third.'*[114] Then he asked when the Messiah would come, and Elijah advises the rabbi to ask the Messiah himself—he would find him among the beggars and the sick in front of the gates of Rome. R. Joshua then receives the answer from the Messiah: 'Today.' Elijah later explains to the rabbi that this 'today' means 'on the day on which you will listen to the divine voice'.†[115]

A later Aggadah reports that Elijah once fulfilled R. Joshua's dearest wish—to be allowed to accompany him on one of his journeys through the world. Elijah then lets him experience some instances of apparently cruel human fate and demonic events. When the sage, in despair about what he has seen, breaks his original promise not to ask any questions, Elijah leaves him. But first he explains to his friend that, however unjust and cruel these events may appear to the human observer, each of them has a divine, providential meaning.[116]‡

* According to Rashi's comment to this passage, 'the voice of a third' refers to the *shekhinah*, the divine immanence. According to R. Livai of Prague, it was revealed to R. Joshua through Elijah's presence (*Nezaḥ Yisrael*, ch. 28)
† The Hebrew word '*ha-yom*' means both 'today' and 'on the day', in keeping with Psalm 95: 7
‡ The same story appears in Islamic literature about al-Khadir and Moses; see pp. 152–3

It is also related that Elijah let the rabbi, while alive, see *Gehinnom* (hell) in all its details,[117] and the Talmud mentions that, after R. Joshua's death, Elijah loudly announced his arrival in Paradise and let him meet R. Simeon bar Yoḥai there.[118]

Another scholar, Rabbi Beroka, met Elijah in the market-place of a large town and asked him who among the crowd of people would one day enter Paradise. Elijah showed him a prison warder who was just then passing, who secretly tried to lighten the lot of the convicts he was guarding; also two clowns, whose humour cheers people up and so brings them closer to each other.[119] Of the prophet himself, the Talmud says: 'When Elijah is present in a town, the dogs play. When the angel of death comes, they bark.'[120] Psychologically, the Elijah-personality as a symbol of the ability to relate positively, and of union, is placed here opposite death as the principle of aggression and separation.

The Talmud-Aggadah presents Elijah's activity as extensive; he is the omniscient helper, teacher, admonishing all circles of people; his influence on the scholars is far reaching because of his profound knowledge of the Torah and his nearness to God. But in respect of *halakhah* (religious law), his authority is limited. The Talmud expressly states that Elijah, as all prophets, is not entitled to repeal laws or to proclaim new ones,[121] such a right being reserved for him only in the Messianic age. Until then the majority of scholars at any given time have to decide on the practical extension or limitation of the laws of the Torah. In the interpretation of the text, however, as well as in the actual possibilities of putting legal decisions into practice, Elijah's superiority is recognised. For his knowledge of the Torah and of temporal facts surpasses that of human beings. He can thus help the rabbinic judges in the administration and the practical application of justice. It is frequently mentioned in the Talmud that an apparently insoluble legal problem or a legal claim which cannot be decided in practical jurisdiction should be suspended until Elijah appears. In talmudic literature this is frequently expressed by the word '*teku*', which can be understood grammatically as 'let it stand'; it is also explained as being the initials of 'Tishbi yetarez kushiot u-vayot'—[the Tishbite will solve difficulties and problems].[122]

Outstanding among the Midrash collections are the works known as *Seder Eliyahu Rabbah* and *Seder Eliyahu Zutta*, frequently cited in the Talmud and Midrashim as 'Tana debe Eliyahu'. The thorough literary and historical researches of M. Ish-Shalom reveal that they were first compiled shortly before the completion of the Mishnah at the time of the first Amoraim (*c.* 150 CE). It is apparent from the uniformity of the fundamental ideas and the linguistic style that it is a complete work in its own right and not, like the other Midrashim, a compilation of successive interpretations of the Scriptures or a collection of separate Aggadic sayings. The authors were presumably a group of scholars influenced by 'Elijah's inspiration' who had founded a 'house of study' in his name.[123] The Talmud records that the book was dictated to one of the early Amoraim, Rav Anan, by Elijah himself.[124] In spite of many digressions on the most diverse religious and ethical topics in which the editor of the work frequently loses himself, there is an unmistakable basic theme, a sort of religious philosophy of history which becomes apparent again and again. *Seder Eliyahu Rabbah* begins with the story of the expulsion of man from Paradise and describes the course of thrice 2,000 years—namely 2,000 years of chaos, 2,000 years of Torah and 2,000 years of the Messianic age—until the return of man to Paradise. The 'way back' planned by God and provided for in the act of creation itself is for mankind generally the 'way on earth' (*derekh erez*)—defined as the way of what is beautiful, appropriate, useful and just in the life of human society. But for the Jewish people the way back is said to be especially devised to lead to the 'tree of life' which symbolises the godhead and to which the Torah leads when it is observed in every respect, 'for the sake of the divine'. Before the final redemption of mankind, the Jewish people will be freed from the yoke of oppression and will return to their native soil. The tyrants and oppressors themselves will be punished, but in the relationship between man and man there must be no distinction between Gentile and Jew. The fate of the individual is determined by the standards by which he measures himself and others, and he may reach adhesion to God through love, reverence, humility and truthfulness.

These two works frequently mention Elijah's personal appearance; he is then repeatedly introduced as 'father Elijah'. He tells of men he met on his numerous journeys, relates the conversations he held with them, the questions he answered, how he advised and admonished them. The books moreover contain numerous religious and ethical demands addressed to the general public. They concern especially the study of the Torah, sincerity of prayer, family life, friendship and honesty in human relations.

Talmudic-Aggadic literature frequently emphasises Elijah's role as 'the angel of the covenant'. As has been mentioned, as early as the time of Moses, after the revelation at Horeb, at the beginning of the wanderings in the wilderness, an angel was appointed who was to lead the Israelites on behalf of God and as his representative. Later, in the time of Joshua and the Judges, he is explicitly called 'the angel of the covenant'. He has to supervise the keeping of the covenant made between God and his people. In the prophecy of Malachi, the angel of the covenant and the prophet Elijah will bring about the decision at the Last Judgment (see pp. 33–4). In Aggadic literature, Elijah is identified with the angel of the covenant, his appointment being regarded as God's answer to Elijah's accusation that the Israelites 'have broken your covenant'. The Aggadah relates that at the time of the Israelite kings, after the realm had been divided, the ritual of the covenant, the circumcision of the boys (Gen. 17: 9–13), was not performed, and that Elijah's accusation referred also to this, not only to the people's worship of Baal. That is why Elijah has since to watch personally over the performance of the boys' circumcision on the eighth day of their lives. A special chair, 'the chair of Elijah', should therefore always be provided for him at circumcisions.[125]

The biblical term for circumcision, *brit* (the making of the covenant), and the fact that it is undertaken as early as the eighth day after the boy's birth, show that in the Bible the act no longer appears as paternal castration—in contrast to pubertal initiation rites of primitive tribes. Nor can the biblical command to circumcise be regarded as the intervention of God seen only as the father who wants to bring the newly-born into his power. On the basis of his research into circumcision rites in New Guinea, the anthropologist and psychoanalyst Géza Róheim reached the conclusion: 'The penis in the foreskin is the child in the mother, and it is separated from her through the circumcision.' Compare the report of Richard Thurnwald that in some East African tribes the father tells his son, after he has circumcised him: 'My son, now you have left the wrapper of your mother.' Thurnwald sees this as the psycho-social transformation of the boy.[126]

The biblical circumcision would then be the child's symbolic release from the exclusive bond with its mother, which enables it to establish personal relationships with its fellow-men and with God. This also limits the father-aspect of the Divine and makes possible the covenant, as the *partnership* between man and God.

The biblical Elijah who, in the Books of Kings and especially as represented in the Aggadah, fights extremely zealously for the covenant with God, now becomes in the Aggadah also the angel of the covenant with the individual, the patron of the individual relationship between man and his fellow-men and between man and God. As such, he is alive in the people and intervenes in events not only in the Aggadists' time: his presence is felt in every family throughout future generations.

Above all, however, the Aggadists are concerned with Elijah's appearance at the time of the redemption and with his part in it. The oldest original talmudic writing, the Mishnah, deals with the prophecy of Malachi. Tractate Eduyot, in which the oral traditions of the earlier scholars are recorded, discusses the purpose, according to Malachi, of Elijah's future appearance: In the name of R. Johanan, who relies on an old tradition, R. Joshua says that Elijah comes to remove those who have arbitrarily approached and to bring close those who are arbitrarily remote. R. Judah says: 'Elijah comes only to bring close and not to remove.' R. Simeon says: '[he comes] so as to reconcile the controversies.' Later sages say: '[he comes] so as to make peace on earth as it says in Malachi: "Behold, I will send you Elijah".'[127]

These different interpretations of the Malachi prophecy must be understood in their historic context. In the time of R. Johanan and R. Judah ben Betera, the liberation of Erez-Yisrael from Roman rule was thought to be imminent. A precondition for national redemption would be, according to Malachi (2: 14 ff.), the abolition of marriages with pagan women; the restoration of the family purity of the people and especially of the Levites who were serving in the Temple. Therefore, since Elijah came before the redemption he had to solve these problems—referred to as the troubled relationship between 'fathers and sons'—either in the spirit of strict justice or with generosity. In the time of R. Simeon, about a hundred years later, the people were split into different sects. The Sadducees and the Boethusians denied that the oral tradition had binding authority, and even among the scholars who acknowledged its authority there existed far-reaching differences of opinion in Hillel's and Shammai's authoritative 'houses of study'. Therefore at this time—probably with reference to Malachi's admonition to remain faithful to the law of Moses—it was hoped above all that Elijah would reconcile the religious, sectarian and legal differences. The scholars of a still later period awaited Elijah as peacemaker: between sons and fathers, i.e. between them and God, and also finally as one who would bring peace to the world—probably because the expectation of a national revival had been disappointed and because the idea of universal redemption was gaining ground.

The Mishnah accordingly shows that every generation expected Elijah to solve whatever were its most burning religious and national problems and finally to bring universal peace, the Messianic age.

The Messianic idea, as outlined by the prophets, had—like the deliverance of the Israelites from Egypt—a national and a spiritual character: deliverance from foreign rule, return of the exiles from the dispersion, restoration of the kingdom, redevelopment of the country, rebuilding of the Temple in Jerusalem. It also stressed the religious and ethical regeneration of the people, and the realisation of the dependence of the Israelites and their fate on the fulfilment of the divine will. Ultimately the redemption of the Israelites would be linked with that of the world, the *one* God would be acknowledged by all mankind and his kingdom established on earth. But its coming may be preceded by the dreadful 'day of divine judgment' predicted by Malachi for the Jewish people only, and by Ezekiel and Daniel for all nations. This will be the time of apocalyptic events: apostasy, moral degeneration and threatened destruction of mankind by fire, sword, famine and natural catastrophes. Only a small remnant of the Jewish people and of mankind generally will experience the dawn of the new aeon, the resurrection of the dead. Then a new covenant will be made between God and man, the covenant of eternal peace.

Malachi lets Elijah appear before the Last Judgment so as to lead the Jewish people back to God and thus save them from complete destruction. Most prophets, however, expected a scion of the house of David to re-establish the Jewish kingdom and to bring about the kingdom of God on earth.

David once united the tribes of Israel and successfully consolidated the Jewish realm. He was also, according to biblical tradition, the Psalmist who saw in his fate the sign of God and accepted humbly even his personal suffering. His royal throne, too, he felt not merely to be a bestowal to him and his descendants by divine grace, but an expression of God's rule over the Israelites. Therefore the prophets envisaged a 'son of David' as the national and spiritual redeemer.

These predictions by the prophets expressed the Jewish people's faith in redemption and indicated its general outline, and initiated the ideas concerning the future national liberation and spiritual redemption. The Talmudic-Aggadic and later Midrash literature, which correspond to the respective historic conditions in which they were written and also to the individual attitudes of scholars and Aggadists, contain various conceptions and representations of the events of the redemption, their preconditions, details and sequence. A uniform doctrine of redemption was not dogmatically determined even in later generations.

Maimonides (R. Moses ben Maimon, 1135–1204), in his description of the stages of the redemption, says that the Messianic age will begin with outbreaks of war ('Gog and Magog') and the prophet Elijah will come before or after these, so as to lead the Jewish people on to the right path and to prepare them for redemption. He then adds: 'Concerning all these and other similar events, nobody knows how they will happen. The prophets apparently do not make them clear, and the scholars base their traditions only on the various biblical texts and therefore hold differing views.'[128]

A closer analysis of the various opinions and descriptions put forward by the Jewish commentators on the Talmud and Midrash and by medieval religious philosophers, however, reveals two fundamentally different conceptions of the process of redemption. They are apparently based upon a talmudic controversy on whether the return of the Jewish people to God is an indispensable prerequisite for the beginning of the redemption.[129]

Accordingly, there are two possibilities. If the entire Jewish people or the majority return to God, their national liberation and the universal redemption of mankind will consequently come about, together with spiritual redemption through Elijah and the Messiah ben David. Should they not return, national liberation will begin at a time determined by God either as a natural, historic event, similar to the return of the Israelites from the Babylonian exile, or through apocalyptic upheavals as a result of which only a small remnant of the Jewish people will remain. After this 'beginning of the redemption' (also called 'signs' or 'heels' of the Messiah or 'Messianic Days'), the return to the Holy Land, its rebuilding and national independence, Elijah, who is to lead the Jewish people back to God, will appear, and with him the Messiah who will establish the kingdom of God, the world of universal peace. A new aeon will then begin.

Both conceptions appear in numerous variations, but agree that the accomplishment of final redemption lies in the hands of Elijah and the Messiah ben David. The preparatory, and especially the spiritual, tasks are mostly assigned to Elijah, the actual liberation and redemption to the Messiah, in which he is supported by Elijah.[130]

While some Aggadists ascribe to the Messiah not only a real pre-existence before the time of redemption,[131] but also an ideal pre-existence since the creation of the world,*[132] they stress that Elijah's return at some future time was predetermined even before Malachi's prophecy. It was promised to the patriarch Jacob, and in five passages in the Bible a letter (*vav*) missing in Elijah's name has been added to the name of Jacob—'as a pledge that Jacob's sons would one day be redeemed through Elijah'.[133] When God summoned Moses from the burning bush, he too was told that Elijah would come as redeemer.[134]

Elijah and the Messiah have, however, met on earth even before the latter's appearance at the time of the redemption. It is said that, on the day on which the Temple was destroyed, it was announced to Elijah that the saviour of Israel had already been born. He finds the new-born, stained with blood, in Bethlehem, and makes him a present. When he returns to the child five years later, he is deaf, dumb and lame and is blown out to sea in his presence. Then Elijah rends his clothes and complains to God. But a divine voice comforts him, saying that the Messiah shall return 'at the end of days'.[135]

Another Aggadah relates how Elijah comforted the Messiah in one of the halls of Paradise. He held the Messiah's head against his chest and said: 'Bear with the suffering which God has imposed upon you until the end of days because of the sins of the Jewish people; be calm, the end is near.'[136]

Within the framework of a detailed talmudic discussion about the time of the Messianic redemption, Elijah says to R. Judah that the world will exist for at least eighty-five jubilees (4,250 years) and the scion of David will appear in the last jubilee. But Elijah cannot answer his question whether the Messiah will come at the beginning or at the end of the last jubilee and whether this will then come to an end. R. Ashi, the editor of the Babylonian Talmud, thinks that Elijah intimated here that the Messiah could not be expected earlier but could be from then on.[137]

Regarding the moment of Elijah's return at the time of the redemption, one Aggadah mentions that Elijah will one day

---

* The spirit of God hovering over the face of the waters (Gen. 1: 2) is said to refer to the spirit of the Messiah (see p. 64)

appear together with the Messiah 'on the night of the redemption', the Passover night, during which the Israelites were once liberated from Egypt.[138] But generally no definite day was predicted for Elijah's final coming; he could be expected at any time, just before the Messiah, except on the day before the Sabbath and the holy days, so as not to interfere with the preparations for these.[139] According to some opinions he would also not appear on the Sabbath and on the holy days themselves.[140] But Elijah's actual final return is above all connected with the Jewish people's return to God. In the Torah (Deut. 30: 2–5) redemption is made dependent upon it; the prophets and many Aggadists draw attention to this again and again. The Midrash Rabbah interprets Genesis 1: 2: 'And the spirit of God moved upon the face of the waters', as referring to the spirit of the Messiah.[141] 'And what', it goes on to ask, 'makes him gradually draw closer? The *teshuvah* (return). For it resembles the water, for it says: "Let your heart flow like water towards God." '[142] This intimates the close connection between redemption, return, and the spirit of God by which the biblical Elijah is moved.

Elijah's coming can therefore be hastened through observance of the Torah.[143] A thesis of R. Phinehas ben Yair recorded in the Mishnah, which is later frequently quoted and commented on in the *mussar* literature (ethics), names the various stages of the return which lead to the redemption: 'The Torah leads to attention, attention to zeal, zeal to purity, purity to abstinence, abstinence to holiness, holiness to humility, humility to fear of sin, fear of sin to piety, piety to the holy spirit and this to the resurrection of the dead through Elijah.'[144] One Aggadist thinks especially important the observance of the commandment to let the mother bird fly away before taking the eggs or the nestlings.[145]

An exhaustive commentary in an Aggadic chapter on *teshuvah* (repentance, return to God) concludes: 'Rabbi Judah said: If the people of Israel will not repent, they shall not be redeemed. Israel will repent only because of suffering, oppression and exile, and because they have no sustenance. Israel will never repent with full sincerity until Elijah comes, as it is said: "Behold, I will send you Elijah the prophet before the coming of the great and terrible day of the Lord." '[146]

A sensitive interpretation of the verse 'I lay me down and I sleep' refers to the spiritual awakening of the Jewish people by Elijah; 'the Jewish community says "I lay"—i.e. without prophecy, and "I sleep"—i.e. without the holy spirit; and I am awakened through Elijah, and God raises me up through the king, the Messiah.'[147] Likewise in the Psalms (43: 3): 'O send out Thy light and Thy truth; let them lead me' is interpreted to mean that the light is Elijah, the son of Aaron, and the truth is the Messiah, son of David.[148] Similarly, the words in the Song of Songs (7: 14): 'at our doors are all manner of precious fruits', are also said to refer to Elijah.[149]

The external events at Elijah's appearance are described differently in accordance with the different views of the process of the redemption held at various times. Before the arrival of the Messiah, Elijah brings back the vessels lost at the destruction of the Temple, with the manna, the water of ablution and consecrated oil, [150] the last to anoint the Messiah king.

Regarding the details of Elijah's appearance itself, a free interpretation of a prophecy (Mic. 2: 13) says, for instance: Elijah will come three days before the Messiah and proclaim his arrival from the mountain tops of the Holy Land. On the first day he laments its desolation, and his voice is heard all over the world. He prophesies the coming of peace, and 'the sinners rejoice at this'. On the second day he proclaims 'the good has come'; on the third, 'the salvation of the world has come.' But at the same time he tells the sinners that it is not coming for them. Then God appears in his royal majesty before all the inhabitants of the world, redeems the Jewish people and reveals himself to them. Hence the passage: 'The breaker is gone up before them; they have broken forth and passed on, by the gate, and are gone out thereat; and their king is passed on before them, and the Lord at the head of them.' In his commentary to the Hebrew Bible, R. David Kimḥi remarks about Micah 2: 13 that an unnamed Aggadic source identifies 'the breaker through' with Elijah and 'their king' with the Messiah. Moreover, this identification is apparently obvious from the context of the whole passage itself.*¹⁵¹

Another (apocalyptic) Midrash describes Elijah's appearance at the time of the struggle with Gog and Magog, the enemies threatening the Jewish people and their country, who are also regarded as the demonic anti-Messianic powers and forces generally. In the midst of the struggle, at a time of general terror, God opens a subterranean way for Elijah, who leaves the scholars in Jerusalem and sets out across the desert for Midian, where, after many miraculous events, he meets the Messiah who is waiting there, and who then begins his triumphant procession across the world. Elijah remains there and issues the book 'Ha-Yashar' ('The Righteous'), of which 'the Torah is only one single line'¹⁵²—this seems to imply that the complete Torah will be revealed only at the time of the redemption, through Elijah, as its contents correspond to the new aeon which is dawning.†

Several pseudo-epigraphic books (300–800 CE) deal more fully with the apocalyptic events 'at the end of days'. First, with manifold variations, comes the description of the appearance of the fighting Messiah ben Joseph who precedes the Messiah ben David. Thousands fall in fierce wars with the hostile powers. Fire, destruction and famine prevail; the Messiah ben Joseph himself is slain in Jerusalem; the Jews spared by the war hide in caves or are sheltered by heavenly clouds. At the moment of the most extreme danger and distress, the final redemption is brought about through Elijah and the Messiah ben David. In some descriptions there are renewed struggles led by the Messiah ben Joseph who has been revived by Elijah. In other versions the anti-Messianic powers are conquered by God himself. Then his realm becomes visible to all mankind.¹⁵⁴

The concept of the Messiah ben Joseph, seen historically, means that the redeemer of the Kingdom of Judah is matched

---

* The reference to Elijah as 'the breaker through' corresponds to his frequently sudden, unexpected appearances in the Bible, and implies here the possibility of the sudden breakthrough of the coming kingdom of God (see p. 189)

† The receiving of a new Torah in the heavenly house of study by the Messiah through Elijah's mediation is described in detail in the Midrash **Torat ha-Mashiah**¹⁵³ (*Midreshe Geulah*, pp. 349–50)

with a redeemer of the realm of the ten tribes. This tradition is based on the words of God mentioned in Zechariah (12: 9–10): 'And it shall come to pass in that day, that I will seek to destroy all the nations that come against Jerusalem. And I will pour upon the house of David, and upon the inhabitants of Jerusalem, the spirit of grace and of supplication: and they shall look unto Me because they have thrust him through; and they shall mourn for him'.

The Jerusalem and the Babylonian Talmuds see in this a reference to the Messiah ben Joseph, to his victorious appearance in the wars at the end of days and to his death.[155] These references are then variously elaborated in the apocalyptic descriptions mentioned above. The duplication of the Messiah-figure seems, psychologically, to be based on the separation of the spiritual and universal aspect of redemption from the political and historical one of national liberation.[156]

The Acts of Daniel says: 'and the Messiah ben David, Elijah and Zerubbabel[157] climb the Mount of Olives. The Messiah lets Elijah blow the ram's horn. The primeval light of the creation shines again, the light of the moon becomes like the light of the sun, and the sick are healed. Through Elijah's second blast on the trumpet the dead are resurrected; they come to the Messiah from all directions through the sky on eagles' wings. A pillar of fire rises from the restored sanctuary and becomes visible to the whole world. At the third blast of the trumpet the *shekhinah* (the divine immanence) reveals itself'.[158]

The 'primeval light' of the creation was, according to the Aggadah (BT Ḥagigah 12a), generally withdrawn and preserved only for the *zaddikim* but would reappear for mankind in the redeemed world. The meaning of this is essentially the same as that of the harmonisation of sun and moon also mentioned in the Talmud. It refers to the Aggadah that God reduced the size of the moon but would restore it again in the distant future (BT Ḥullin 60b). Psychologically it means that the harmonisation between the 'masculine' consciousness and the 'feminine' unconscious is the basis of the redemption. This harmony, frequently mentioned in Aggadic and Kabbalist literature, appears temporarily in periods

67

of peace and spiritual enlightenment, and its final lasting appearance means universal redemption.

In the so-called Book of Elijah, the angel Michael lets Elijah foresee on Mount Carmel the end of days in an overwhelming dream vision which takes him through apocalyptic events across the whole world. The vision ends with the victory of the Messiah and the descent to earth of the heavenly Jerusalem with God's Temple.[159]

A detailed interpretation of the Jewish Apocalypse cannot be attempted here. On the historic plane, it seems to give expression to the people's hopes and fears concerning national and territorial restoration, and to the surmise that the fate of the Jews may be finally changed only after the spiritual transformation of mankind and within the setting of universal peace. These specifically Jewish expectations accord with the view long held by many peoples and religions that apocalyptic events will have to be experienced before the redemption of mankind. Psychologically, this is probably based on the ambiguity of human aggression and the possibility of its integration by man's dissolving the projections of his 'shadow' and by the 'union of opposites' (see pp. 191, 195).

At the time of redemption, Elijah's activity does not affect only the community; he also gives comfort and help to individuals.[160] At the Last Judgment, with his plea before God, he supports the request of innocent children who died young to forgive the sins of their parents.[161]

The resurrection of the dead is also in his hands; through this, at the end of days, he indeed proves himself to be Elijah.[162] For his resuscitation of the Phoenician widow's son he had received from God the key to the gift of dew and rain. The rain which quickens the earth and makes it fruitful, as a symbol of spiritual purification and resurrection, is mentioned in the Talmud with the words: 'The day of rain is like the day of resurrection of the dead.'[163]

Elijah's mission is not over with the final redemption and the establishment of the Messianic realm. As one of the 'eight princes' mentioned by the prophet Micah (5: 4), in the Aggadic view he supports the Messiah with advice,[164] and in particular makes the legal decisions. He is also regarded as one of the four craftsmen mentioned by the prophet Zechariah (2: 3), who, according to the biblical text, are to destroy the enemies of the Jewish people. The Aggadah identifies these men as Elijah, the two Messianic personages and the Kohen-Zedek (the priest of righteousness)[165]—or, according to another version, the priest-king mentioned in Genesis (14: 18), Melchizedek,* who are to undertake the rebuilding of the Holy Land and of the Temple.[167] The redeemer-figure here appears in four aspects: the prophetic, the spiritual, the political and the priestly.

Many Aggadists, however, as well as the authors of the Aramaic translation of the Bible, assign to Elijah himself the function of the high priest at the time of the redemption.[168] This is based on the view that he belonged to the tribe of Levi, that he offered the sacrifice on Mount Carmel, and that in Talmudic-Aggadic writings he is repeatedly mentioned as a priest, or is identified with the Aaronide Phinehas.

In general, as has been shown, the two figures of the redemption, Elijah and the Messiah ben David, are assigned different tasks: Elijah the spiritual preparation for, and the Messiah the actual accomplishment of, redemption. In several Aggadic descriptions, however, the Messiah carries out some of Elijah's tasks or, conversely, Elijah those of the Messiah. Sometimes they even merge completely into a single redeemer-figure. It is mentioned, for instance, that 'Elijah' is one of the epithets of the Messiah,[169] or he appears without the Messiah to proclaim the redemption, which is accomplished directly by God: 'In the future [at the time of the redemption] I guide you and send

---

* Melchizedek is regarded by some Aggadists as a believing Caananite, by others as Noah's son Shem. The Babylonian Talmud (Nedarim 32b) records that a transgression against God's majesty lost him his priesthood, which passed to Abraham. According to Psalm 110, Melchizedek is the judge of the nations, enthroned at the right hand of God. In a fragment of the Dead Sea scrolls, the central motif is the coming of Melchizedek as the Heavenly Judge in the Last Judgment, and when Jesus was asked whether he was the Messiah, he answered: 'Hereafter shall ye see the Son of man sitting *on the right hand* of power' (Matt. 26: 64 *et al.*; Flusser, op. cit.). Similarly in Daniel (7: 9, 10, 13, 22): 'The Ancient of days' [God] and '*one like unto* a son of man' [Melchizedek] gave the Last Judgment[166]

Elijah before you.'[170] Moreover, it is said in a Midrash: 'The prophet Isaiah does not say: "those redeemed by Elijah" or "those redeemed by the Messiah" but "the ransomed of the Lord"' (35. 10).[171] And in Midrash Ekhah Rabbah it says: what is the name of the Messiah? R. Abba b. Kahana says: 'His name is the Lord, for it says in Jeremiah (23: 6): "In his [the son of David's] days, Judah shall be saved, and Israel shall dwell safely; and this is his name whereby he shall be called, the Lord is our righteousness." '[172] Elijah and the Messiah here appear as redeeming aspects of God himself.

The question arises whether and to what extent the Talmudic-Aggadic writings present Elijah also as bringing about personal salvation. In the Bible, repeated hints of individual redemption may be found: e.g. when the Psalmist (69: 19) says: 'Draw nigh unto my soul, and redeem it'; and Job (19: 25) :'I know that my redeemer liveth.' However, nowhere is a personage mentioned as the mediator of the salvation. But it is to be noted that in his revelations to chosen scholars and also to men 'of the people', Elijah not only offered instruction on religious and ethical duties but also sought to direct their individual development. He was their spiritual adviser. We may also note the Aggadic saying: 'The door [to redemption] is not opened altogether, but Elijah appears in one town and is invisible in another; he talks to one man and not to another.'[173] The individual is also referred to in the remark in *Pirke de-Rabbi Eliezer*: 'The good way has two byways, one of righteousness and the other of love, and Elijah is placed exactly between the two ways. When a man comes to enter [one of these], Elijah cries aloud concerning him, saying: "Open ye the gates".'[174] The thesis of R. Phinehas ben Yair mentioned above (p. 64) may also refer rather to individual than to universal redemption.

The Aggadah makes an especially interesting comparison of Elijah with other biblical personages. Thus as the last, final redeemer, he is compared with Moses, the first deliverer of the Israelites. Both are sent directly by God. It is said that Moses hinted at Elijah with the words: 'send, I pray Thee, by the hand of him whom Thou wilt send' (Exod. 4: 13), with which he tried to escape his summons at the burning bush. And God answers: 'Him whom you mean I shall send in the distant future.'[175] Hosea's saying (12:13): 'And by a prophet the Lord brought Israel out of Egypt, and by a prophet was he preserved', is seen as referring to Moses and Elijah: 'Two prophets are descended from the house of Levi, Moses the first and Elijah the last, and both deliver the Israelites as messengers. Moses delivered them from Egypt . . . and Elijah delivers them in the future from the power of Edom [Rome] . . . and this deliverance will be for ever.' Attention is then drawn to numerous parallels in the life and fate of Moses and Elijah, among many others the wandering in the desert lasting forty years and forty days respectively; the personal revelation which both experienced in the rock-cave on Horeb; Elijah disappeared from the earth, just as the grave of Moses remained hidden to posterity. But it is also emphasised that God said to Moses at Horeb: 'Stand here with me', but to Elijah (I Kings 19: 13): 'What doest thou here?'[176] Moses asked there for forgiveness for the Israelites, Elijah complained about them. In another Aggadah, God says to Moses: 'Just as you have all your life given your soul for them [the Israelites] in this world, so Elijah and you shall appear together in the future.'[177] It is mentioned elsewhere that Elijah had been the pupil of Moses.*[178]

The Aggadic comparison of Elisha with Elijah is obvious, and indeed contained in the biblical text: the prophetic power of the teacher is passed on to the pupil; he too, divides the Jordan, does not let the oil in the widow's jug run out, revives the child of his benefactress. Furthermore, he performs many miracles—twice the number of Elijah's, according to his wish for 'a double portion of Elijah's spirit'.[179] Elisha's miracles are attributed to his prayers and his submission to the divine will and he is called, as Elijah, 'the man of God'. But like his master, in his zeal he is occasionally described as going beyond the instructions which he has received.[180]

The Aggadah sees a special relationship between Elijah and the

* Rashi comments on this passage that this refers to a spiritual discipleship. But the *Sefer Yuḥasin ha-Shalom* (p. 8) mentions a chain of tradition in which the Torah was passed on by Moses through Joshua, Phinehas, Samuel, David and Ahijah to Elijah, and by him through Elisha to the later prophets up to Ezra

prophet Jonah. The Bible represents Jonah as struggling with God. He insists on God's strict justice and does not want to acknowledge his merciful understanding and forgiveness until he is transformed in the belly of the whale, and finally recognises God's love through the fate of the gourd.[181] It is his task to warn men to repent. Obviously it is the parallel religious development and transformation undergone by Elijah and Jonah which prompts the Aggadic saying that the boy resuscitated by Elijah's breath later became the prophet Jonah.[182] Others say that Jonah was one of Elijah's four pupils, besides Micah, Obadiah and Elisha.[183] The passage in the Psalms (8: 8): 'the fowl of the air, and the fish of the sea' is taken to refer to Elijah's and Jonah's transformations which happened respectively in heaven and in the sea.*[184] According to yet another Aggadist, the boy resuscitated by Elijah would later appear as the Messiah ben Joseph.[185] This corresponds to the view represented above that under certain conditions the appearance of the Messiah ben David must be preceded by a Messiah descendent from Joseph, who has been killed and, according to some Midrashim, is revived by Elijah.

While Moses, Elisha and Jonah are mentioned in more or less far-fetched comparisons with Elijah, Aggadic literature actually identifies Elijah with the priest Phinehas ben Eleazar, one of Aaron's grandsons.

IV Book of Moses records that in their wandering through the wilderness many Israelites took Midianite wives and through this came to participate in pagan rites of worship. When Zimri, a prince of one of the tribes, openly took a Midianite woman to his tent, Phinehas killed both in his zeal for God and for the purity of Israelite family life, thus appeasing God's anger and saving the Israelites from the plague imposed on them. God rewarded him for his intervention: 'Behold, I give unto him My covenant of peace' (Num. 25: 1–15). In the Book of Joshua (22: 13 ff., 31 ff.), as well as later, at the time of the Judges (20: 28), Phinehas appears in various situations as a zealous fighter for God.

---

* The hero's voyage in the body of the whale corresponds mythologically to the battle with the dragon, the negative aspect of the 'Great Mother'. They are both symbols of transformation (see p. 19)

Phinehas ben Eleazar is also mentioned as one of the princes in the time of King David (I Chr. 9: 20), and some interpreters equate him with the Aaronide of the same name. Phinehas' intermittent activity recorded in the Bible accordingly extended over a period of more than 300 years, so that he resembles the Elijah-figure which later appears again and again in Jewish history.

Beyond this, the Aggadists regard as the priest Phinehas some of the unnamed messengers, angels and prophets who appear in the Books of Joshua and Judges. Thus they see Phinehas-Elijah also as one of the two spies Joshua sent to Jericho, who hid in the house of the harlot Rahab (Josh. 2).[186] They mention, too, that in the time of Jephthah the Judge he refused to see him and release him from his vow to sacrifice his daughter (Judg. 11: 30 ff.).[187]

This identification of Elijah with Phinehas is categorically repeated in Aggadic writings in the words 'Elijah is Phinehas'.[188] This is most clearly emphasised by an Aggadist who lets God say reproachfully to Elijah: 'You are always zealous! In Shittim [at the time of the wanderings in the desert] you were zealous because of the illicit intercourse... here [at Horeb] you are zealous because Israel has broken my covenant.'*[189] Rabbi Simeon ben Lakish says: 'Phinehas is Elijah, for God said to Phinehas: "You have made peace between Me and Israel in this world, thus you shall also make peace between Me and My children in the world to come." '[190] In the *Pirke de-Rabbi Eliezer* we find: 'God changed Phinehas' name to "Elijah of Toshave Gilead", for in Gilead [Elijah's place of origin] the Israelites turned back to God through him [Phinehas], and it says (Mal. 2: 5): "My covenant was with him of life and peace"—that means life here on earth and in the world to come.'†[191] Some Aggadists transfer Elijah's future tasks to Phinehas, even without emphasising the change of name. Thus Phinehas, too, is assigned eternal life by

* The Babylonian Talmud (Sanhedrin 82b) and the Jerusalem Talmud (Sanhedrin 9. 7) also question the *a priori* justification of Phinehas' action, even though he was rewarded for it by God

† R. Joseph Albo comments on this: The permanent existence of the soul and the body of Phinehas-Elijah will result if the harmony between the opposite elements continue . . . then the cause of dissolution disappears (*Sefer ha-Ikkarim*, vol. 4, pt 2, pp. 494-5)

some of them: 'He will always stand and absolve the Jewish people until the time of the resurrection of the dead.'[192] Accordingly, the absolution of the Israelites by Phinehas is also transferred to Elijah: 'Phinehas is Elijah, and if he [Elijah] were not, we would not be able to live in the sinful Edom [the Diaspora]; and our teachers say of him: since the destruction of the Temple, he daily offers up two sacrifices so as to absolve the Jewish people, and on their skins he records daily events.'*[193] The Aramaic translation of the Bible adds to the biblical phrase, 'I give unto him [Phinehas] My covenant of peace', 'I make him a constant angel, who lives for ever and will proclaim the redemption at the end of days.'[195] Equally, the angel of the covenant mentioned by Malachi is identified both with Phinehas and with Elijah (see p. 34), and this also explains why Elijah, as has been said, is repeatedly called a priest in Aggadic literature and is to assume the function of the high priest at the time of the redemption (see p. 69).

The repeated identification of Elijah with both the figure of the Messiah himself and the priest Phinehas is traced by Aptowitzer and other historians to the aspirations of the Hasmonean princes who were themselves sons of a high priest and wished to replace the traditional claim of the house of David to rule Israel with their own claim to it as descendants of Phinehas-Elijah.[196] This does not, of course, reduce the significance of the fact that the Aggadists—who by the way were not at all sympathetic to Hasmonean rule—saw Phinehas and Elijah not merely as extremely similar in character but as identical personalities who appeared again and again in Jewish history; hence they regarded Elijah not merely as the biblical and historical prophetic heroic figure. Neither did they represent him, glorified through legends, as an ideal worthy of imitation. Confronted with the 'living' Elijah, they saw him as a living person first for their own generation; beyond this they saw in him a timeless

---

* In the Aggadic view, the sacrifice takes place in the 'upper [heavenly] Temple' which existed even before the creation of the world and will remain after the destruction of the Jerusalem Temple; it will descend to earth at the time of the redemption. According to most of the Aggadot on the subject, the daily sacrifice there is offered by the angel Michael or by Metatron[194]

personality belonging to the biblical past who would have a decisive influence on the future course of Jewish history.

How did this actualisation of Elijah come about? The Israelite prophets had opposed the Jewish kings' ardent striving for national power by referring to the covenant between God and the patriarchs, and the resultant demands on the Jews, collectively and individually. They also increasingly emphasised the universal aspect of God, which was visible even in the biblical representation of the creation and of the early history of the nations.

The same emphasis existed among the successors of the prophets, the 'Men of the Great Synod', and was developed further later by the Aggadists. Because of the constantly increasing restrictions on the religious and political freedom of the Jewish people, this tendency found expression in a tradition at first oral and later written. Then there occurred the long foreseen catastrophe: the downfall of the state and the destruction of the central sanctuary, jeopardising the continuing existence of the Jews as the people of God. Besides the task of preserving and elaborating the biblical laws as the constitutional element for the people as a whole, the problem of individual religiousness became even more acute than before. It was apparently this critical situation which led the spiritual leaders to an intensive confrontation with Elijah's personality since it was he who, according to the tradition going back to Malachi, was to bring about the return of the individual and the people to God and the coming of the redemption (see pp. 33–5).

They recognised more and more the eternal essence of Elijah's personality, his striving to make the divine will manifest in the world, his struggling with his people and with his own ego. With this Elijah the Aggadists lived; they met him, were taught and guided by him. It seems that in their confrontation with him they became aware of their own, and also the general human spiritual ambivalence in meeting earthly and divine demands, and that they realised that a transcendence of the painful human limitations would be possible only through divine grace.

Thus the Aggadic presentation of the biblical Elijah, which was

75

at first predominantly negative, is quite understandable: the over-emphasis on his blind zeal, his autocratic behaviour, his suppression of any love for the people, his one-sided image of God, his inflexibility; also the Aggadic 'overlooking', as it were, of his transformation, which is not explicitly mentioned in the biblical text but can be clearly perceived in Elijah's going to the mountain of God, his being seized by the theophany and his last journey on earth. It seems that the Aggadists regarded his ascent to heaven as an act of grace—the divine judgment that Elijah's excessive zeal for God's cause and his harshness towards his people masked the ardour of his love of God. God now lets Elijah experience for himself his aspect of goodness and grace which Elijah tended to ignore.*

While in the Book of Kings Elijah matures towards his transcendence by beginning to change on earth, and nothing is said about his 'fate' after his ascent, the Aggadists regard his ascent itself as the beginning of his transformation. They present him as being changed, immortal, consulted by God in heaven and being his angelic messenger on earth, a friend of men, who not only extends sympathetic help but strives to bring out the positive, the good inherent in everyone. They see him as an angel of the covenant, watching over the circumcision which symbolises the possibility of a direct relationship between man and God as well as between one human being and another (see p. 59).

Elijah's positive attitude to his surroundings, which can scarcely be seen in the biblical record because it is mostly repressed, becomes fully apparent in the Aggadic Elijah returning to earth. His image of God and of man is transformed.

Neither are the negative aspects of the biblical Elijah fully repressed in the returning Aggadic Elijah. His zeal is no longer a blind zeal for a one-sided image of God but becomes, in the service of the Divine, devotion to mankind and the world.† He therefore may admonish and even severely punish a man when

---

* The philosopher Baḥya Ibn Pakuda mentions that Elijah as worshipper of God and his true obedient servant was rewarded by him for his sufferings for his cause[197]

† The Hebrew word *kin'ah* means not only jealousy or zeal but also eagerness for a cause in a positive sense (see p. 163)

he considers it necessary for his psychic development. Elijah's character as a human being has now been perfected and made harmonious. The Aggadists, as it were, transferred to heaven the transformation which Elijah's own insight and strength were insufficient to accomplish on earth.

Thus transformed, redeemed, he can now become he who transforms and redeems. As Malachi prophesied and as the Aggadah emphasises, Elijah's essential task in the process of the redemption is *teshuvah*—the answer, return, coming to one's Self. It means answering in response to the divine as well as to the human voice; becoming aware of and actualising for oneself the existential unity of mankind and becoming conscious of the Divine which embraces man and reveals itself to him. One's own self-realisation, one's being redeemed and accessible, released from the shell of the ego, can also bring about the release of one's fellow-man. It also makes the way to God accessible to him and may become the decisive step to his redemption.

In the encounter between the spiritual leaders and Elijah, they transformed his figure and were themselves transformed by it; their own image of God and man was extended. The Divine and the human within them drew closer together.

This shows the effectiveness of the constellation of the Elijah-archetype. The Aggadists experience within themselves Elijah's struggle, his transformation and his return to the world. This was their own redemption.

The manifold and lively Aggadic representations of Elijah's personality and of his activity made a deep and lasting impression on their contemporaries and on posterity and maintained the firm belief of the Jewish people that, at times of spiritual need or external danger in exile, God sends a helper who will finally be the immediate precursor of the future redemption of the Jewish people and of mankind.

77

CHAPTER IV

Elijah in Jewish Mysticism

It is in the nature of mysticism that its phenomena can be separated neither historically nor in their literary representation, and perhaps least of all psychologically, from the traditionally recognised phenomena of the religion within which they originated. Thus, for instance, the individual and to some extent also the collective revelations of God which occur within the framework of the more highly developed religions, and the prophecies to which they gave rise, in principle cannot be differentiated from mystical experiences.

Mystics, in the sense of personages who sought direct contact with the Divine through introspection and meditation, and who derived from their experiences more or less clearly defined esoteric doctrines, are first mentioned in Jewish literature in the early Talmudic-Aggadic writings. In the circle of R. Johanan ben Zakkai's disciples living in the second century, an esoteric cosmogony (*Ma'aseh Bereshit*) developed out of the biblical record of the creation, and a theosophy of the divine realm (*Ma'aseh Merkavah*) out of Ezekiel's vision of the chariot of the divine throne.*[1] Hints concerning their content as well as warnings and precautionary measures regarding passing them on to pupils imply that the next generations of his scholars formed mystic circles. The Talmud also contains numerous Aggadic sayings of a

---

* Theosophy, here and throughout this study, means the elaboration and conception of the mystics' direct experiences of the Divine and of their spontaneous reflections of them

78

mystic character and almost pantheistic conceptions of the god-head. They might be regarded as the result of the Aggadists' experiences and as the starting-points for further mystic percep-tions and speculations. For instance the Aggadic saying: 'God is the site of the world and not the world the site of God', indicates that man can actively partake in God, and the saying: 'every-thing that God created above, he [also] created below', a macrocosmic-microcosmic parallelism.[2]

Of the esoteric writings already mentioned in the Talmud, the oldest text (third to fifth century), apparently completely pre-served, is the *Sefer Yeẓirah* (*Book of Creation*), a cosmogony ascribed to the patriarch Abraham. Some profound commen-taries on it were written during the following centuries.[3]

The later pseudo-epigraphic and apocalyptic literature, in so far as it is contemporary with talmudic writings, is also permeated with numerous mystical elements (see pp. 51–2). Coming after them and influenced by them are III Book of Enoch and the Hekhalot and Merkavah literature—most of the Hekhalot writings survive only fragmentarily. Their central theme is the mystical ascent of the soul through the heavenly palaces to the divine throne. Then follows the *Sefer ha-Bahir* ('The Luminous Book') *me-ha-Tanna Rabbi Neḥunya ben ha-Kanah*, compiled in the twelfth century from considerably earlier Aggadic-mystical sources.[4] Further writings emerged from the increasingly wide-spread mystic movements among the Jews of Germany (Ḥaside Ashkenaz),[5] southern France, Spain and eastern countries, and these, influenced to varying degrees by early Jewish religious philosophy, the mystical, especially the gnostic doctrines of the surroundings, and by the spirit of their times, enriched and developed each other.

Then in Spain, in the thirteenth century, there was discovered the *Zohar* (*Book of Splendour*) 'by R. Simeon bar Yoḥai'. According to Gershom Scholem's comprehensive research,[6] this book, composed by Moses de Leon (*c.* 1280), soon became the standard work of Jewish mysticism, hardly less respected and influential in the religious life of the Jewish people than the Bible and Talmud. Almost all later mystics based their own speculations on the Zohar and regarded them as no more than further interpretations and obvious inferences from its world of ideas. The Kabbalist movement reached its climax in the sixteenth century with the Kabbalist circle in Safed (Palestine), the principal representatives of which, though obviously strongly influenced by the Zohar, were creative and formed new conceptions in their own right.

All these more or less converging mystical trends, fed by the mythic elements in the Bible and the Aggadah and their symbols, may first be considered in their totality as a mythical revival of Judaism, but they go far beyond this, as will subsequently become apparent. The extraordinary range of the Kabbalist world of ideas and its far-reaching influence on Jewish religious life seem to result from the miseries of the dispersion and persecution of the Jewish people and from the inability of the rational doctrines of Jewish philosophy to satisfy the religious longing of individuals and wider circles among Jews.

It is hardly surprising that Elijah, who was to the Aggadic spiritual leaders of the people a mediator between them and divine wisdom, also plays an extremely significant part in the personal experiences of Jewish mystics and in their recorded mystical speculations.

R. Simeon bar Yoḥai, with whom the title and content of the classical Kabbalist Zohar are inseparably linked, was one of the most important teachers of the Mishnah in the second century. The Talmud records that he and his son R. Eleazar had to flee from Roman persecution and hid for twelve years in a cave, buried in the sand, until the prophet Elijah appeared to them and told them of the emperor's death and of their deliverance. When they left the cave and began to travel across the country, 'everything they looked at burned', and a divine voice sent them back into the cave.[7] After a further twelve months this voice permitted them to go out into the world again and, from then on, 'what Eleazar destroyed, R. Simeon restored' (see p. 53 n. 95). The story of their stay in the cave (symbolising, like the womb, absolute immersion in the subconscious; see p. 18) clearly indicates the introspective attitude of R. Simeon and R. Eleazar and their mystical experiences which made them at first deny the life on earth: their gaze burns the world created by God. By renewed introspection their outlook changes, so that they can understand and accept destruction and renewal. The Talmud thus rejects the ascetic, life-denying mystic in favour of the positive mystic who through and after his mystical experience accepts God's world and realises the Jewish tradition in a new, profounder meaning.

The Zohar records the first part of this talmudic Aggadah, the flight of the two scholars and their stay in the cave, but with the supplement: 'and Elijah appeared to them [during their twelve years' stay there] twice daily and instructed them.'[8]

The talmudic story and the additions of the Zohar clearly indicate the origin and development of the tradition which sees R. Simeon as the creator of Jewish mysticism on the basis of the Elijah-revelation ('Giluy Eliyahu') which was granted to him. Accordingly, he frequently meets Elijah in his wanderings through the Holy Land with his son and their pupils, which provide the setting in the Zohar. At these meetings Elijah is usually immediately recognised by R. Simeon or his scholars.[9] Only occasionally they see him as an old man or wayfarer, and during the ensuing conversation they realise that they are talking to Elijah. Sometimes the mystics receive Elijah's prophecies in dreams.[10] It is often reported that R. Simeon himself summons Elijah and tells him to ask God's permission to come to R. Simeon to instruct him,[11] or he invites him to a meeting of the mystics.[12]

Elijah's appearance never remains purely visionary; a dialogue always ensues. Elijah prophesies, instructs, answers the questions put to him or at times himself asks R. Simeon to interpret a biblical verse or to solve a religious problem. In these conversations, Elijah transmits to R. Simeon—and through him to the circle of mystics—'the secrets of the divine "house of study"'. In the Zohar, this means the hidden mystic meaning of the Torah.

Reports of the 'Giluy Eliyahu' which was accorded to Jewish mystics are not confined to the Zohar. The comparatively sparse references to unequivocal mystic experiences of teachers of the Mishnah and the Talmud usually do not explicitly mention inspiration by Elijah, but it has to be taken into consideration that, as has been shown (p. 53 n. 96), Elijah's spirit was alive in their time and in their circle and had a direct influence on them. After the completion of the Talmud at the beginning of the ninth century, R. Joseph ben Abba, head of the famous rabbinic house of study in Pumbedita, is mentioned as a mystic who was under the influence of the 'Giluy Eliyahu'.[13] It is also reported that on the annual procession round the Mount of Olives on the festival of Sukkot, R. Hai Gaon, the head of this school in the eleventh century, was accompanied by Elijah and talked with him.[14]

The *Sefer Yezirah*, the *Sefer ha-Bahir* and the Hekhalot and Merkavah literature make no mention of the 'Giluy Eliyahu'. However, the Hekhalot as well as the Responsa of the Geonim[15] contain instructions to the adept how to prepare for the ascent to the 'heavenly palaces': he should put his head between his knees, as Elijah did on Mount Carmel when he prayed meditatively for rain. This position corresponds almost exactly to that typical of the embryo in the womb and means, psychologically, complete immersion in the unconscious.

From the twelfth century onwards there exist from a number of well-known mystics in Provence explicit reports on the 'Giluy Eliyahu': R. Abraham ben Isaac (Narbonne, c. 1150), the important Talmudist R. Abraham ben David (Posquières, 1150–98), his son R. Isaac the Blind (c. 1200) and R. Jacob ha-Nazir (c. 1250), and also from the outstanding mystics living in Germany who formed the Haside Ashkenaz (German Hasidim) circle: R. Judah he-Hasid (the Pious) of Worms (c. 1200) and his famous pupil R. Eleazar of Worms, presumably the authors of the *Sefer Hasidim*, and from R. Isaac of Acco (Palestine) and R. Menahem of Recanati (c. 1300, in Italy). The reports originate sometimes from the mystics themselves, sometimes from their pupils.[16]

According to the author, the *Sefer ha-Peliah* and *Sefer ha-Kanah*, too, were written under the direct influence of Elijah; the first book is a mystical interpretation of the biblical account of the creation, the second a comprehensive symbolism of the Torah commandments. In a preface the author reports that Elijah appeared to him, initiated him into the secrets of the divine 'house of study' and finally led him, from the tomb of the patriarch, up to 'the divine house of study' itself. There, however, he lost consciousness, whereupon Elijah brought him back to earth and instructed him in the mysteries of the creation.[17]

Elijah's revelations greatly influenced R. Luria Ashkenazi (1534–72), by far the most outstanding personage of the circle of Kabbalists living in Safed, whose doctrines were decisive for the following generations. His most important disciple, R. Ḥayyim Vital, to whom we owe the first written account of R. Luria's doctrine, was also inspired by Elijah. There is a legend that Elijah told the fathers of both of them, even before their births, that their sons would be great; he told R. Luria's father that he would be present in person at the circumcision of the child, and that they should therefore wait for him; and thus it happened.[18] R. Vital writes about his teacher: 'He was occupied only with the study of the Talmud . . . then Elijah appeared to him and advised him to withdraw to solitude . . . and so he sat in a house on the bank of the Nile, was seized by the holy spirit and Elijah constantly appeared to him and taught him the secrets of the Torah.' About two years before Vital died, Elijah told him to go to the Holy Land and settle there—he would also reveal himself to him there from time to time.[19] He did as he was told and settled in Safed. He sometimes walked with his pupils to the neighbouring village of Meron; there they sat down where, according to tradition, R. Simeon bar Yoḥai and his pupils once sat, and the souls of the dead teachers appeared to them. 'And this is', concludes the narrator, 'the secret meaning of the Aggadic doctrine that Elijah resurrects the dead.'*[20] Vital himself, according to his own statement, experienced the 'Giluy Eliyahu' after suitable preparation in accordance with his teacher's instructions,[21] and also participated in the revelations at Meron.

In his work *Sha'are ha-Kedushah* on esoteric ethics, R. Vital deals at length with the nature of prophecy, amongst other

---

* Apart from this psychological interpretation, the author in later chapters of his book deals in detail with the literal meaning of the resurrection of the dead through Elijah (pp. 42a, b, 51b)

themes, and also with divine revelations accessible to the individual in post-prophetic times. After the necessary preparation through conscientious observance of the religious commandments, through asceticism, immersion in the teaching of the Torah, devout prayer and meditation, spiritual illumination can be attained in five different ways: through the *ruaḥ ha-kodesh* ('holy spirit' *sensu strictiori*), a *maggid*,* the prophet Elijah, a deceased pious man or dreams. The latter are considered the lowest stage of revelation. The highest, the holy spirit, consists of 'illumination coming from the root of one's own soul'. The *maggid* is an angel created by the mystic himself through a particularly devout observance of a religious commandment, who then speaks to him. The 'Giluy Eliyahu' (*sensu strictiori*) is achieved through piety of the heart. The soul of a deceased pious man can appear to one whose soul is rooted as deeply as his.[23]

Summing up his detailed discussion, R. Vital emphasises that 'every one of these different stages of illumination can be attained with Elijah's help through consecrating oneself and studying the Torah, without other special efforts.'[24] By these 'efforts' R. Vital means the use of magical proceedings, conjurations and special invocations and *yiḥudim* (meditations upon God's name). He acknowledges the effectiveness of this magic, but warns against its use as, besides what is good and true, what is untrue and evil may also find expression in the revelation it provokes,† and he particularly emphasises that 'the best course is to attain Elijah's revelation through piety; and the greater the piety, the greater the revelation.'[26] Altogether, R. Vital considers only someone who can claim Elijah's inspiration to be a genuine mystic[27] whose writings are to be regarded as authoritative by the Kabbalists.

---

* The term '*maggid*' (literally, 'one who relates') has two separate connotations. It means a popular, usually itinerant, preacher,[22] and it can also mean an angel or a celestial messenger who conveys secrets to the Kabbalists in various mysterious ways

† An example of this is the fate of R. Joseph della Reina who, by means of magic formulae, summoned Elijah to reveal himself. He asked Elijah for instructions on how to conquer the angel of death and bring about the redemption. After an initial warning against this undertaking, Elijah gave him detailed instructions. Della Reina, however, made a mistake in carrying them out, failed miserably and finally committed suicide[25]

Interesting details of the 'Giluy Eliyahu' are described in the *Maggid Mesharim* of R. Joseph Karo (*c.* 1600), the famous author of the *Shulḥan Arukh* (the codification of Jewish law), who also belonged to the circle of mystics in Safed. The *maggid*, by whom he is regularly inspired verbally in the waking state, repeatedly promises him that after further spiritual purification Elijah will appear to him: 'You will see Elijah, dressed in white; he will sit opposite you and talk to you like a friend; others present will not see him; his voice will sound to them like yours.'[28] On another occasion the *maggid* makes a similar promise, and adds: 'He will be your teacher and master and teach you all the secrets of the Torah.'[29] The *maggid* also explains to him the three stages of the Elijah-vision: in a dream; in a waking state in which one can speak to Elijah but without being answered; in the waking state in which a dialogue with him is established.[30]

R. Moses Cordovero, also belonging to the circle of Safed Kabbalists and himself favoured with 'Giluy Eliyahu', describes in his 'Investigation Concerning Angels' how angels may appear as *maggidim*. He says: 'The angel enters the soul and the body [of a man], influences him and compels him to speak words of wisdom. After the disappearance of the angel he knows these things and [also knows] that someone has told them to him . . . and he understands them.' But Elijah is different:[31]

> he becomes part of the intellect of a man and reveals what was hidden to him. To the man it seems as if he had thought of it himself, as if something new had suddenly entered his consciousness. It may concern religious matters or future events in his life. And it comes stealthily, with a heaviness in the head, but without buzzing in the ears and without the feeling of something new [coming from outside] as with the *maggid*, but rather as if the man had told it to himself.

R. Judah ben Bezalel Livai (Maharal, the exalted Rabbi Löw of Prague, 1520–1609), talmudist, philosopher and mystic, to whom the creation of the Golem is ascribed, expressed himself similarly: 'It makes no difference whether Elijah reveals himself in a vision or not, for frequently he communicates his words to someone who does not know where they come from; it seems to him as if they came from himself, but they come from Elijah.'*³²

In the subsequent two centuries, most of the important mystics refer to the 'Giluy Eliyahu', in particular R. Israel Baal Shem Tov, the founder of the Ḥasidic movement of the eighteenth century, and the spiritual leaders of Ḥasidism who followed him (see p. 120). R. Elijah Gaon of Vilna, the famous rabbinic authority of that time (1720–97) and author of extensive commentaries on the Zohar, also felt inspired by Elijah. His most important pupil, R. Ḥayyim of Volozhin, records that his teacher spoke of 'the messages of the divine house of study' which were told to him awake and in dreams, and also of visits of the prophet Elijah, who revealed to him holy mysteries. This was granted to him, R. Elijah said, not because he wished it or prepared himself by meditation, but purely 'by the grace of God' when his own hard efforts to understand had failed.³³

Worthy of special mention is R. Moses Ḥayyim Luzzatto, who lived in Padua at about the same time (1707–47)—an extraordinary personality with multiple talents, thoroughly familiar with the Bible, the Talmud and the Kabbalah as well as with classical languages and contemporary secular culture. Apart from a textbook on religious and ethical self-education (*Mesilat Yesharim*), still widely used, and also lyrical poems and plays, he wrote a number of mystical books in the spirit of the Lurian Kabbalah. It is evident from Luzzatto's correspondence with his teacher, and of that with his friends with whom he formed a secret Messianic circle, that he was a genuine mystic. First a *maggid* appeared to him, who taught him how to prepare himself for Elijah's revelations. Elijah himself then frequently came to him—not at his call but at God's command. 'Elijah never appears only for the spiritual satisfaction of the individual, but so as to prepare for the Messianic redemption of the Jewish people those who had already attained their enlightenment. Only to these does he appear face to face; to others he is invisible.' Later

---

* He draws this conclusion mainly from a passage in the Talmud. It mentions that two scholars in different places suddenly found the same solution to a very difficult problem on the same day, and this is followed by a discussion of whether this was 'Giluy Eliyahu' (BT Eruvin 43a)

'Elijah's master, the angel Metatron' also appeared to Luzzatto.[34] Inspired by Elijah, Luzzatto wrote his most important work, 'The Second Zohar'. In it, Luzzatto is compared by Elijah with R. Simeon bar Yoḥai, the author of the Zohar. Of this work, only fragments survived, as Luzzatto later destroyed his Kabbalist books under pressure from rabbis who suspected him of Sabbatianism.[35]

The mystics who refer to the 'Giluy Eliyahu' almost always mention only the fact that the source of their mystical revelations was the 'Giluy Eliyahu', but rarely literally record the verbal content of the inspirations. Verbal records of Elijah's teachings and of his dialogues, especially with R. Simeon, with his son Eleazar or one of their pupils, are to be found almost exclusively in the Zohar. The principle themes are: the relationship between God and the Jewish people, the redemption and its prerequisites.

While he was still hiding in the cave, R. Simeon asked Elijah, in the name of the rabbinic house of study which was secretly in touch with him by means of carrier-pigeons: 'Why does the exhortation in Deuteronomy [ch. 28], which according to tradition refers to the second exile, contain only severe threats and punishments, but no consolations and hopes for future redemption, as does the exhortation in Leviticus [ch. 26] referring to the first exile?' Elijah answered: 'These threats, too, express the love of the angry father', and he then interpreted some of those threatening words and sentences, contrary to their literal meaning, as consolations and promises for the future. He concluded with the words: 'But all this depends on Israel's *teshuvah* (return to God) and he who has a heart understands this and knows how to return to his Lord.'[36]

On another occasion R. Simeon asked: 'It says: "In thy distress, when all these things are come upon thee" (Deut. 4: 30); all this has already befallen the Jewish people, but redemption has not yet come.' To this Elijah answered: 'God has considered this matter today, has listened to the angel Michael as advocate and Samael as plaintiff and then pronounced the verdict: the Jewish people shall be redeemed only when they have returned; but if they return even only by a hair's breadth I shall open wide the gates to them.'[37]

Once R. Ḥiyya was told by Elijah in a dream that the destruction of Jerusalem had been decided in heaven, but that the scholars could avert the catastrophe through their study of the Torah, the tree of life.[38] As Jerusalem had already been destroyed in the rabbi's time (*c.* 100 CE), this presumably referred to the spiritual Jerusalem, the *shekhinah*, which could remain united with the transcendent godhead through the study of the Torah.

Three questions were once put to R. Eleazar by a Gentile, but he was unable to answer and passed them on to Elijah: 'You Jews expect the Temple to be rebuilt, but does not the prophet Zechariah call the second Temple [meanwhile destroyed] the "final Temple"?' Elijah's answer was: 'The first two Temples were built by the hand of man and were destroyed because of the sins of the Jewish people. The third Temple will be built [as he explained from some verses in the Torah] by God himself, namely a lower Temple on earth and an upper one in heaven, and this is what we are expecting.'* The two other questions were: Why is it God's chosen people which are afflicted with so much suffering? Why are the Jews less healthy and weaker than other peoples in spite of observing the regulations concerning food which have been imposed upon them? Elijah answered: 'Israel is the heart of the world organism; the other nations are its various limbs. Just as the heart is closest to the [guiding] brain and the first to be affected by it and therefore the most sensitive, the Jewish people are especially susceptible to all suffering and require special food in order to survive at all.'[39]

Other conversations between R. Simeon and Elijah make apparent God's love of the Jewish people in general and of the the mystic in particular. Thus it is said that Elijah asked the rabbi to elucidate a problem discussed at the time in 'the heavenly house of study': What is the explanation of the fact that in the biblical Song of Songs—which the rabbinic Aggadah had interpreted as a love song between God and the Jewish people—the shepherd, that is God, says of himself: 'I ate . . . and drank'

---

* In the Kabbalah, the upper and lower sanctuary also mean the upper *shekhinah* (Binah) and the lower *shekhinah* (Malkhut); the lower Temple is regarded as the site of the divine immanence (see the diagram on p. 104)

[at the wedding feast]? R. Simeon answered: 'God shares the meal with the Jewish people just as a groom eats together with his bride, for her sake, even if he himself is not hungry and does not feel like it; and even that only in the house of the bride herself.' Elijah replied: 'Indeed, this is just what God Himself was about to answer, but He wanted to give you precedence.'[40] And in another passage the Zohar says that the mystery of the Song of Songs was revealed by Elijah.[41]

The possibility that a human being may succeed in accomplishing the *coniunctio mystica* between the transcendent divine emanation and his immanence, and the subsequent intimacy of the Great Individual with God, is formulated by Elijah: 'Through your endeavour to accomplish with each religious observance God's union with the *shekhinah*, they unite your spirit in the upper regions [as well] as in the lower ones; [you are] like a prince whom his parents love and whom they kiss and tend in love and peace.'[42]

The close reciprocal relationship between Elijah and the mystic in their common endeavour is clearly apparent also in the following: 'You speak,' Elijah says to R. Simeon, 'and then I shall speak; for, through both of us, it [the secret of the Torah] becomes lucid. We have God's permission to reveal the secrets above and below—you the lower and I the higher ones. But you are of greater significance: your words are recorded above, and mine—through you—on earth.'[43] Seen psychologically, this seems to imply that R. Simeon is the earthly prototype of the heavenly Elijah-archetype. About the mystic work which R. Simeon would one day publish, Elijah told him: 'Rabbi, how many people will delight in your book when it is published on earth at the end of days, and freedom on earth will be proclaimed by it!'[44] In the *Tikkune ha-Zohar*, Elijah himself solemnly presents to God the outline of the Kabbalist doctrine of divine emanation, and concludes by requesting R. Simeon to continue to reveal the secrets, as he was the first to receive permission to do so.[45]

Besides the description of these and many similar encounters of R. Simeon, his sons and his pupils with Elijah and the conversations held with him, the Zohar, as well as later Kabbalist writings

—especially those of the Lurianic school—contain numerous comments on the biblical Elijah. These are based on biblical passages or on their Aggadic interpretation, but are varied and deepened and mystical speculations are derived from them. The Kabbalists are especially concerned with the meaning of the name 'Elijah', with Elijah's transformation, his ascent to heaven, his survival, his return to earth as an angel; furthermore, they trace the blending of his soul with that of other biblical figures who lived before him.

Just as the Kabbalist mysticism of letters and words identifies God's name not with his essence but with his activity which can be experienced by man, it regards the names of human beings and also of angels as an expression of their individuality—i.e. as the character of their mission. The usual interpretation of the name 'Eliyahu' is 'Eli ("my God") is YHV', i.e. the first three letters of God's four-letter name YHVH. In the Kabbalah, the three letters YHV together signify the nine upper, transcendental *sefirot* of the emanation. The fourth letter, H, signifying the tenth immanent *sefirah*, corresponds to the initial letter 'h' of the word *ha-navi* (*the* prophet) by which Elijah is always called. Thus even the name 'Eliyahu' implies the *coniunctio* between the divine transcendence and immanence which is brought about by the prophet at the time of most extreme distress as 'unification of the divine name', as redemption.[46]

A similar interpretation, presumably an elaboration of this passage in the Zohar, is given by R. Joseph Karo in the *Maggid Mesharim*:[47] the 'h' of *ha-navi* R. Karo interprets as the physical appearance of Elijah, corresponding to the hypostasis of the nine upper *sefirot* in the immanent tenth *sefirah*. Furthermore, according to R. Karo,[48] the identification of Elijah-Phinehas becomes apparent through an exchange of letters, a method frequently used in the Kabbalah, which results in the identity of their names.

Like the Aggadah, the Zohar concerns itself extensively with Elijah's excessive zeal for God; thus it especially criticises his accusation that the Israelites had broken the covenant with God through refraining from circumcision; but it praises at the same time the positive significance of his zeal. Even during the flight into the desert his male-active soul became evident; 'that is why he did not die like other people, because it [his soul] sprang from the tree of life and not from the dust . . . and that is why his body separated from his spirit; and he disappeared . . . he remains a holy angel amongst other holy figures, is God's messenger in the world, and God lets miracles happen through him.' When Elijah was previously temporarily 'defeated by the female component of his soul' and wished for death, God commanded him to stand by the mountain and revealed himself to him in the 'small voice of silence'—'that is the innermost recess, from which all light shines forth'.[49] When Elijah then repeated once more: 'I have been very zealous for thee', God answered him: 'How much longer will you be zealous for me? You have shut the door [on death] so that death has no power over you as over everyone else, but the world cannot bear you and my sons [at the same time]. But wherever my sons carry out the covenant [circumcision], you shall be present.' The Zohar passage concludes: 'Behold, no one who is zealous for God is taken away by death like other people. Peace descends upon him, as it says of Phinehas: "Behold, I give unto him my covenant of peace." '[50]

According to Jewish tradition, also accepted by the Zohar, the soul consists of three parts. The lowest, 'nefesh', is the vegetative soul closely related to the body, animating it and directing the human instinct towards good or evil. The middle part of the soul, 'ruaḥ', represents man's spiritual striving and connects the 'nefesh' with the highest part of the soul, 'neshamah', which is in itself divine. However, 'nefesh' and 'neshamah' often occur in kabbalist texts as referring to the soul as a whole. 'Ruaḥ', the middle and mediating part, is frequently equated with Elijah.[51]

Lurianic Kabbalah regards what the Zohar calls Elijah's masculine soul as his higher soul (ruaḥ), corresponding to the angel Sandalphon sought by Elijah in the solitude of the desert. Elijah's soul called feminine in the Zohar is regarded as his earthly soul (nefesh), from which he wants to be released.[52] This conception corresponds to the transformation experienced by Elijah in the desert and at Horeb.

The revelation of the 'small voice of silence' is regarded in this passage of the Zohar as the *coniunctio mystica*, and 'the innermost recess, from which all light shines forth', is the bridal chamber; 'to this [to the queen] the king comes'—as the *Tikkune ha-Zohar* describes—'not in a storm, a fire or an earthquake, but as the voice, which comes after them as the fourth thing.'[53] In the Kabbalah, 'king' means the six lower transcendental formative *sefirot* collectively, and the king's medium of expression is the voice. 'Queen' means the lowest, the immanent *sefirah*; the queen's potential medium of expression is language, which will, however, become articulate only through union with the voice of the king. The union itself is accomplished in silence.[54] Storm, fire, earthquake are the *kelipot* (shells), the negative aspects, the sediments, of the emanation, in which the *shekhinah* is caught and from which it is freed by the *coniunctio*. Elijah is summoned: 'Clothe the king in the four white garments, the queen in the four golden ones, because it is written of her: "all her dignity is within, and her garments are woven of gold".'[55] In the colour symbolism of the Kabbalah, white is the colour of love [the transcendental Divine], gold the colour of stern judgment, one aspect of the immanence.

The Zohar, like the Bible and the Aggadah, represents Elijah as the hero zealous for the father-God who is temporarily defeated in his struggle but is raised up by the divine call. The revelation of the small voice of silence which is granted to Elijah is explicitly called here the *coniunctio mystica*. The transcendental-male Divine unites with the immanent-female, and reveals itself to it.

While the biblical Elijah conceals his face from the numinous, the mystical Elijah clothes the royal couple. The garments veil the essence of the Divine, but precisely through this may bring God closer to human comprehension. That there are four of each of the garments signifies the completeness of each of the two aspects of God. In their completeness they enter into the *coniunctio*.

It is noteworthy that Elijah does not directly participate in the *coniunctio*; his soul is not united with the Divine. He does not enter into the *coniunctio*, but it is revealed to him, and thus he matures towards his transformation into the divine messenger. He can no longer remain on earth as a human being; he has overcome death. He is raised up to heaven, into the divine realm, but he becomes at the same time God's messenger and guardian of the covenant between him and men.

In another passage of the Zohar Elijah experiences a transformation in his wanderings in the desert. 'God found in Elijah's time no man more pious than he, but when he accused the Israelites . . . he angered Him. He let him fall asleep [in the desert] and let him see Moses beseeching God for forty days to forgive the sin of the golden calf. . . . And God said to him [Elijah]: "You should do likewise and remember that the Israelites received the Torah at Horeb." ' That God said this to him 'was "the strength of that meal" (I Kings 19: 8), with which he went to Horeb; and Elijah did not leave his place before taking an oath that henceforth he would always stand up for the Israelites. Of everyone who does a good deed, Elijah now proclaims: "he has done this and that", and he does not rest until this merit has been recorded [in heaven].'[56] Elijah's attitude, now positive, to the individual within the collective, enables him to become a divine messenger in the world of man.

The actual event of Elijah's ascent is generally expressed, as in the above-mentioned passage of the Zohar (see p. 91), as the separation of the spirit [the soul] from the body. It is described in detail in other contexts and different versions. The Zohar applies the biblical question: 'Who hath ascended up into heaven, and descended?' (Prov. 30: 4)[57] not only to God himself and to Moses, but particularly and in great detail to Elijah. R. Simeon asks: 'How could Elijah ascend to heaven, as none of the firmaments tolerates even a grain of matter?', and answers: 'Elijah entered the whirlwind, wrapped it around him and ascended. And I have found the explanation of this mystery in the Book of Adam:[58] Among the beings in the world there is a spirit [a soul] who descends to earth and clothes himself in a body; his name is Elijah. In this body he ascends, the spirit separates from it and it remains in the whirlwind. He requires another body of light, in which he can be amongst the angels [in heaven]. When he descends to earth, he again clothes himself in the body which has remained in the world [in the whirlwind], and in it he appears below [on earth]. In the other body [of light] he appears above [in heaven]. That is the secret of the verse "who hath ascended up into heaven, and descended?" No man whose spirit ascends descends again, except Elijah.' The interpretation of the verse finishes: 'And what is his name? "Eliyahu". And what is the name of his son? "Eliyahu". Before he ascends he is Eliyahu, and when he descends as messenger and miracle worker he is Eliyahu.'[59]

Similarly, in another passage of the Zohar: 'When the human soul leaves the body so as to go to the other [heavenly] world, it cannot enter there until it has received another body made of light. This we know from Elijah; he had two bodies—in one he appeared before men, in another before the holy angels.'[60]

The general doctrine of the Zohar concerning the embodiment of souls and angels (see p. 91) maintains that the human soul [its middle *ruaḥ* part] is clothed in something like a sheath of the heavenly air of Paradise, which it takes off in 'the lower Paradise, before its entry into the world'. The souls which are allowed to ascend to heaven after death leave their earthly body in the grave, receive their ethereal sheath back in the lower Paradise and ascend in it.[61] The angels who descend from above put on similar sheaths in Paradise when they have to act as messengers on earth. To people, however, they appear mostly as human beings.[62]

According to the Zohar passage cited above, Elijah thus receives for his appearance in heaven a body of light [astral body] similar to that of pious men who are allowed to ascend after their death. His earthly body, however, in contrast to theirs, remains not in a grave but in the whirlwind, and he becomes incarnate in it whenever he descends. Like the other angels, he thus can appear in the world as a human being.

The identification of the name of the ascending Elijah with that of the descending Elijah called 'son'—emphasised at the end of the passage—means psychologically that the 'heavenly' Elijah as archetype is, as it were, the father of the earthly Elijah-figures appearing in the world from time to time. It agrees in this connection with the Zohar passage: 'Who ascended? Elijah. Who descended? Jonah, who came by virtue of Elijah', i.e. who is—according to the Midrash—the boy resuscitated by Elijah and who—according to the biblical description—is, in psychological terms, also a prototype of the hero-archetype (see p. 19, p. 72 and footnote).

In the passages cited here, the Zohar emphasises that Elijah is unique and cannot be compared with any other human being, as we find in the *Zohar Ḥadash* in the following rather different description of his transformation:

> When God wanted to send Elijah alive to heaven, the angel
> of death complained to God: 'Now everybody will protest
> [against his death]!' Then God answered him: 'I have created the
> world on the assumption that Elijah will ascend to heaven. He is
> not like other human beings and he can remove you from
> the world.' When the angel of death then descended, Elijah
> wanted to destroy him. God forbade him to do that. Then Elijah
> seized the angel of death and ascended [on him] to heaven. Thus
> it says in the Bible: 'Elijah went up by a whirlwind into heaven.'

Immediately before this, the *Zohar Ḥadash* remarks: 'The whirlwind is the angel of death, which makes the body of man "stormy".'[63] And elsewhere it says: 'And on it, the evil impulse, Elijah went up to heaven, as is written: "he went up by a whirlwind into heaven." '[64] Hence, Elijah's mediation between heaven and earth is one of the indispensable preconditions for the creation of the world and essential to its existence. The Zohar thus assigns to Elijah a potential existence, as the Aggadic writings do to the Messiah.

The angel of death, in Jewish tradition identical with Satan and man's evil impulses, is represented in the Bible as God's messenger and not as his opponent.[65] Elijah and the angel of death both have to submit to the divine will. The remark that the appearance of the angel of death as well as evil impulses arouse stormy emotions in men may refer to the psychological connection between man's unsatisfied desires and his fear of death.

The overcoming of evil impulses and of the angel of death are certainly decisive factors in Elijah's transformation. The integration of evil impulses, according to the talmudic saying 'serve God also with the evil instinct', also results in the integration of the fear of death.[66]

In another connection, the Zohar mentions that Elijah ascended with the help of God's twelve-letter name, which was revealed to him in 'the small voice of silence'.[67] According to the *Sefer ha-Bahir*, he was told this name of God by an angel on Mount Carmel.[68]

All these descriptions of the ascent—though differing in important details—unequivocally assume that the originally human Elijah was transformed into an angel, into a messenger of God.

A different view, quoted by the mystic R. Moses Cordovero as the opinion of Moses de Leon, holds that Elijah was one of God's angels at the time of the creation of the world. In contrast to other angels, he did not protest against the creation of man but welcomed it and offered to descend to the world to help him. Only then was he given the name of 'Elijah' and in the time of King Ahab was sent to earth for the first time. He strengthened the Israelites' belief in God, was again raised up to heaven and appointed the constant intercessor for the Israelites.[69]

This assumption that Elijah always existed as an angel means psychologically that he represents an aspect of the godhead who accords special care to man created in his image, who therefore longs to transcend his earthly existence.

Cordovero critically analyses and rejects this view that Elijah was initially an angel. He points out that talmudic scholars repeatedly discussed to which tribe Elijah belonged and never questioned that he belonged to mankind, and emphasises above all that the Zohar repeatedly described Elijah as a human being transformed into an angel.[70]

Nevertheless, the view that Elijah was always an angel who was sent to earth from time to time implicitly appears in some Kabbalist writings; e.g. where Elijah drew Abraham's attention to the ram which he sacrificed instead of Isaac.[71]

Cordovero differentiates between Elijah's and Enoch's rank as men transformed into angels and the rank of the *zaddikim*, as well as that of the patriarchs, especially that of Jacob and of Moses. Elijah and Enoch surpass the other *zaddikim* in their strong adherence to God, so that not only their *neshamah*, the divine part of their soul, ascended to heaven, as with that of the other *ẓaddikim*, but their *ruah* (spirit) was transformed into angels.[72]

To explain the difference between Elijah on the one hand and Jacob and Moses on the other, Cordovero cites a passage from the Zohar, where it is asked why Jacob and Moses when fleeing came to a well at which they met Rebecca—or Zipporah—and Elijah did not. The answer is that Jacob and Moses support the throne of the upper formative–male emanation of God. The waters of the 'well' represent the receptive female lowest emanation (*shekhinah*) and 'therefore gladly rise to meet Jacob and Moses, as the woman does the man', while Elijah 'is below the well'—he supports the *shekhinah* and therefore, as an angel, becomes its messenger,[73] without uniting with it.

The distinction between Elijah's rank and that of those who have always been angels the Zohar derives from the biblical verse 'let fowl fly above the earth' (Gen. 1: 20): The 'fowl' is the angel Michael, 'fly' refers to Gabriel, and 'above the earth' refers to Elijah, who 'is always on earth, as well as above it'. And while the angels are descendent from the second and third highest *sefirah* (divine wisdom and differentiating insight), Elijah's soul originated in the lower *sefirot*. This accords with his human origin and also enables him to be more effective on earth.[74]

In his discussion about the human nature of Elijah and his transformation into an angel, Cordovero deals with the view mentioned in earlier Kabbalist literature that Enoch was transformed by fire into the angel Metatron and Elijah into Sandalphon. Cordovero emphasises that Enoch's body was entirely burnt by the flames, but Elijah's became transformed into another body so that his spirit could appear on earth, when God sent him there as his messenger.*[75] This transformation of Enoch and Elijah is also repeatedly mentioned by the Lurianic Kabbalists: e.g. 'The

* Cordovero mentions that others identify Elijah with Methuselah. This identification can presumably be explained by the fact that Methuselah the son of Enoch lived, according to an Aggadic comment, like his father in a way pleasing to God and, before the Flood, called upon corrupt mankind to repent (*Midrash ha-Gadol* to Gen. 6: 13, vol. 1, p. 125). Methuselah thus resembles the Elijah-figure

bodies of Elijah and Enoch assumed [spiritual] features: Enoch became Metatron, Elijah's body became Sandalphon. . . . And if there were no longer any other *zaddikim* in the world, the world would continue to exist for their sake.'[76] 'Elijah is Sandalphon and this is his "other body of light" mentioned in the Zohar.'[77] What is the basis of the likeness between these two *zaddikim* and these angels?

The Talmud and the rabbinic Aggadah regard Metatron as the angel whom God appointed as his representative during the Israelites' wanderings in the desert and of whom it is said: 'My [God's] name is in him' (Exod. 23: 20–1).[78] He is the highest angel, to whom the guardian angels of all peoples are subject.[79] He reigns in heaven where he sits recording Israel's merits and receiving the people's prayers; he also initiates children who died very young into the Torah.[80] During the exile, according to the Midrash Rabbah, Metatron offers the souls of the pious in the heavenly Temple as an expiatory offering for the Jewish people,[81] and as early as the Jerusalem Targum he is referred to as the transformed Enoch.[82] III Book of Enoch, which in time and also in its essential content belongs to Hekhalot and Merkavah mysticism, describes his ascent from the sinful world, together with the *shekhinah*. While his body is consumed by the flames, his soul is transformed into the angel Metatron.[83] His function as 'the angel of the [divine] countenance' and 'prince of the world' is also variously described in other Hekhalot writings. He is the teacher and guide of the mystics, and the souls of the pious are entrusted to him.[84]

According to the Zohar and later Kabbalist literature, Enoch–Metatron received 'the highest splendour', namely the noblest part of Adam's soul, which he had forfeited by his sin.[85] Metatron represents the *shekhinah*—he is her body, i.e. her son[86]—as well as the 'middle line', the synthesis of the opposite stages of divine emanation.[87] He rules in the world *yezirah*, the world of formation (see p. 105) which is also the world of the angels.[88] He is the firstling of creation, the human being created in God's likeness who revealed himself to Moses and Ezekiel.[89] ' "In the beginning God created", i.e. Metatron, as the *kadmon* [the very first] of the heavenly hosts.'[90] He is incarnate in the great pious men of all times.[91]

The angel Sandalphon is described in the Talmud as 'a pillar standing on the earth and reaching up to the *ḥayyot* (living creatures), the supporters of the chariot of the divine throne'. 'He stands behind the chariot of the divine throne and braids crowns for God.'[92] As the transformed Elijah he is apparently first mentioned in the *Sefer Temunah*.[93] According to the Zohar, he receives the prayers of the Jewish people and twists them into wreaths [crowns] for God; the *Zohar Ḥadash* says that he is the guardian of the mysteries which he keeps in his 'sandal', as 'the weight of the whole body is kept in the shoe.'[94] According to the Lurianic Kabbalah, he continues to offer daily sacrifice in the heavenly Temple after the destruction of the earthly one.[95] He is also the guardian of the birds—i.e. the souls which are called 'birds'.[96] In one of the later Midrashim, Sandalphon is called the mediator between the Jewish people and their heavenly father.[97] He reigns in the world of making, which means also on earth.[98] He directs everything there, and connects matter and spirit.[99]

It is especially noteworthy that in early as well as in later mystical literature, the attributes and tasks ascribed to Metatron are often ascribed to Sandalphon, and vice versa. Thus in the Zohar, Metatron also is called 'messenger', and Sandalphon, there and in a manuscript about R. Judah he-Ḥasid's interpretation of the Torah, 'prince of the countenance'.[100] Another manuscript, also originating from the Ḥaside Ashkenaz circle, gives 'Yehuel' as the first of Metatron's seventy names; attention is then drawn to the coincidence of these letters with those of Eliyahu's name, 'for the "Giluy Eliyahu" is derived from Yehuel'.[101] According to Rabbi Karo, Elijah as well as Enoch is transformed into Metatron.[102]

Generally, a clear distinction is made between Enoch-Metatron and Elijah-Sandalphon, but they are frequently seen as one united figure. The connection between Metatron and Sandalphon is especially emphasised in the following: 'All the angels of the chariot of the divine throne are contained in Metatron and Sandalphon through the mystery of Enoch and Elijah.'[103] 'The angels

Metatron and Sandalphon cling to each other like brothers and cannot be separated even by the Jewish people's involvement in sin.'[104] 'Enoch and Elijah correspond to the two heavenly cherubim Metatron and Sandalphon, who were portrayed embracing each other on the cover of the Ark of the Covenant.'[105]

The relationship of Metatron to Sandalphon as well as between them and Elijah and Enoch is understandable. Elijah and Enoch had been created as human beings in God's likeness. In their life on earth they realised their inherent potential. They succeeded in bridging the gulf between God and man; they transcended their human limitations and were transformed into angels.

Within the mystic figure of the godhead, Metatron and Sandalphon represent the unity of the differently evolving divine emanation. Together they represent the virtual 'middle line' uniting the opposites, which as it were descends vertically from the highest *sefirah* (Keter) to the lowest: 'The middle line are the *sefirot* Da'at, Tiferet, Yesod; it is the light of love which descends from above to the *shekhinah*.'[106] In Lurianic writings, the middle line is usually equated in its entirety, including Keter, with *adam kadmon* (see the diagram).

Metatron represents the actual unity reigning in the upper worlds of the emanation and is, according to R. Meir ibn Gabbai (c. 1500), identical with *adam kadmon*, the human figure on the chariot of the divine throne in Ezekiel's vision.[107] Sandalphon represents the potential unification of the lowest emanation, the *shekhinah* (immanence), with the transcendental godhead. He can appear to people and through his revelation, 'Giluy Eliyahu', show them the way to bring about the potential unification with the divine.

Elijah's activity does not consist exclusively of transmitting mysteries to the chosen. As has been mentioned before (pp. 93, 58–9), he is in the Kabbalah, as in the Aggadah, the angel—the guarantor—of the covenant. The Zohar demands that every father of a new-born boy summon Elijah to the circumcision, and prepare a special chair for him. Elijah will then appear and testify before God to the fulfilment of the covenant.[108]

The identification of Elijah with the Aaronide Phinehas is also

evident to the mystic. A Zoharic passage says that 'Elijah'—
according to the historical context he ought here to be called
'Phinehas'—had in his time received the 'covenant of peace' from
Moses because of his justified ardour (see pp. 72–4.). Since, in his
excessive zeal, Elijah was accusing the Israelites of breaking the
covenant, he has to give back to Moses his covenant of peace. That
is why he goes to Horeb, but there Moses says to him: 'Go to the
children of Israel as angel of the covenant, and they will give back
to you the covenant of peace.'[109] This sentence means that through
Elijah's presence at the circumcision, which symbolises mans'
direct relationship to God and to his fellow-men, Elijah himself
will restore his own harmony. Rabbi N. Z. J. Volozhin explains
that by giving to Phinehas the 'covenant of peace', God compen-
sated for his excessive zeal and made his soul harmonious.[110]

The Zohar, however, bases its identification of Phinehas with
Elijah not only on their zeal for God and the 'covenant of peace.'
The expectation often mentioned in the Talmud that, in the time
of the Messiah, Elijah shall solve all religious legal problems is
substantiated in the Zohar with the promise once made to Moses
that Aaron shall be his prophet. Accordingly, 'Aaron's son', i.e.
his grandson Phinehas = Elijah will solve these problems at the
Messianic redemption.[111]

Here and in other passages,[112] the identity of the two personages is derived, as in the Talmud, from biblical verses, and
explained through the similarity of their characters; the Zohar
however also implies Phinehas' incarnation in Elijah, and later
Kabbalist writings are explicit about it.

According to the Zohar, the reincarnation of souls in other
bodies (metempsychosis) occurs mainly among the childless and
those who transgress sexual prohibitions. Amends have to be
made in a second life for non-observance of the covenant, or for
violating it—'covenant' referring in Jewish mysticism to the
relationship of the Jewish people with God, as well as to the erotic-
sexual relationship of man and woman (see 3 Zohar 57b). Interestingly enough, Phinehas himself is mentioned as an example of
such amends (*tikkun*, restitution) being made. He reincarnated the
souls of Aaron's sons Nadab and Abihu, who died, according to

the Zohar, not only because they were over-zealous in offering 'alien fire' [a sacrifice not commanded by God], but also because they failed to observe the divine commandment to procreate (Lev. 10: 2; Num. 3: 4). But 'only their body died, their soul passed on to Phinehas', when 'in his zeal to punish the sinners [Zimri and the Midianite woman], his own soul left him for a moment'.[113] Furthermore it says in connection with this *gilgul* (transmigration) of Nadab-Abihu-Phinehas: the offence they had committed in offering 'alien fire' was atoned for by Phinehas when he punished the cohabitation of the Israelite prince with the 'alien woman'.[114] Although the metempsychosis occurs because of Nadab's and Abihu's childlessness, it does so in a man who at the same time atones for their other sin.

The later Kabbalists—especially those of the Lurianic school—maintain that the transmigration of souls occurs with everyone so as to bring about man's *tikkun*. Since all souls were from the beginning inherent in Adam, because of his fall they were all bound to sin. Moreover, every soul has to be given the opportunity through its migration to practise the observance of all Torah commandments.*[115] Thus a complicated transmigration has to be accomplished in the history of mankind to reach the original condition, the purity of the souls of all Adam's descendants, which constitutes their redemption. This process involves not only the actual *gilgul*—the incarnation of an 'old' soul in a new body; far more frequent is the *ibbur* (transition, fertilising) of a soul within a body by 'sparks' which pass into it from another soul to unite with it temporarily or permanently.[116] Migration of souls occurs in accordance with their affinity to each other and their individual need for *tikkun*.[117]

This process of transmigration and restitution of souls, embracing the whole of mankind, is exemplified in Lurianic writings by a few outstanding personalities of Jewish history. Among them is a detailed account of the development of Elijah's soul by R. Ḥayyim Vital. Two parts of the *ruaḥ* (spirit) of Adam's soul,

---

* This claim arises out of the Aggadic doctrine that man's physical and spiritual members correspond to the 613 commandments of the Torah. Therefore, according to the Kabbalist view, without the observance of every one of them, human perfection cannot be attained

arising out of the world of the highest emanation (*aẓilut*), passed, after his original sin, through Cain, Gad and Benjamin into Elijah's body[118] and formed his original, his own soul. It then merged with the soul of Phinehas on the occasion of his action in the desert, after he had previously absorbed the soul of Aaron's sons Nadab and Abihu. The original soul of Phinehas as well as the soul shared by Nadab and Abihu issued from a rather lower stage of Adam [the *nefesh* of the *aẓilut*].

The complete Elijah-soul therefore consisted of four parts. Two are 'spiritual'; the one, transcendent, originating in Gad, the other, immanent, originating in Benjamin, corresponding to the biblical Elijah 'borne up by the spirit'[119] and his descent from Leah [Gad] or Rachel [Benjamin] presumed by the Aggadists (see pp. 44–5). These two spiritual parts would enable him to live for ever,[120] the transcendent part always remaining in heaven, the immanent part also descending to earth. The two other, lower parts of the soul (*nefesh*), also one transcendent and one immanent, would unite with the corresponding higher spiritual parts.[121] 'The four parts of Elijah's soul are matched by the four wing-beats with which he hovers above the world'[122] and the union of the four parts is sealed by the Torah verse: 'I give to him my covenant, peace.'[123]

The quaternity of the parts of Elijah's soul and his four wing-beats may be interpreted psychologically as the four basic functions of the soul.[124] By their unification, through being made conscious, the soul achieves its completeness. The Hebrew word '*shalom*' means not only 'peace' but also 'completeness' or 'harmony'. *Brit shalom* accordingly also means 'covenant of completeness'. R. Vital emphasises in conclusion that through precisely the lower components of Elijah's soul, he was enabled to be effective in the world of man. 'That is why, in the time of the Messiah, he will make the souls [of men] complete and will with divine help lead back the fathers together with the children.'[125]

Elijah's significance and his special functions in the process of redemption differ in accordance with the various Kabbalist theosophic doctrines and corresponding conceptions of the redemption. In the Zohar, the *en-soph* (the infinite), the hidden divine Being, manifests itself in ten *sefirot* (stages or aspects of the emanation). The lowest stage [Malkhut] embraces earth and mankind; it is the immanent female aspect of God (*shekhinah*) and also represents the collective soul of the Jewish people.

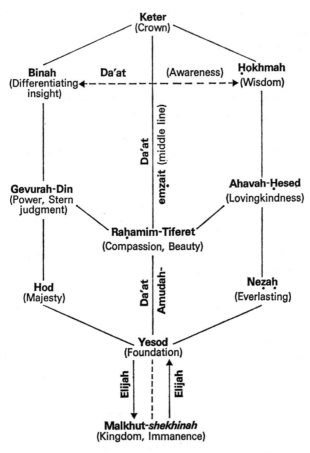

The ten *sefirot* of *adam kadmon* (primordial spiritual man) representing the mystical configuration of the divine manifestation (the site of Elijah is marked)

According to a doctrine in the *Tikkune ha-Zohar*, elaborated by Cordovero and Vital, from the *en-soph* four worlds emanated. They evolve from each other, each of them containing the ten *sefirot*, or the Lurianic *parzufim* (countenances). The first is *azilut* (emanation *sensu strictiori*), corresponding to Ḥokhmah; the second is the world of creation, corresponding to Binah; the third is the world of formation, corresponding to the six middle *sefirot*, and the last is the world of making, corresponding to Malkhut-*shekhinah*, the divine immanence.[126]

Adam's sin, either the plucking of the fruit from the tree of knowledge or the separation of the tree of knowledge from the tree of life, is seen in the Kabbalah as signifying the separation of the *shekhinah* from the nine upper transcendent *sefirot*. Their reunification, the *unio mystica*, is the redemption: the return of man to the original direct relationship with the living godhead.

According to the Zohar, man is summoned to this return by Elijah, the prototype of the dynamic union of heaven and earth. He shows that the difficult way of return through devotion to prayer, the Torah and good deeds is indispensable to redemption, but can be alleviated through God's love of mankind and with his help.[127]

The Lurianic Kabbalah, developed after the expulsion of the Jews from Spain and the disillusionment over the non-appearance of the Messiah who had been expected immediately afterwards, changed and amplified Zoharic theosophy: the *en-soph* 'withdraws at first into itself', so that the emanation worlds have 'space' to be formed, but it leaves a small residue in this space. Then a new 'ray of light' is emitted by the *en-soph*, alternately flooding back and forth, thus dynamically unfolding its creative potential. But at the highest stage of the emanation, *adam kadmon*, the powerful flood of divine light results in 'the breaking of the vessels' which had also been emanated. The light withdraws almost completely. What was about to come into existence could not take shape and the *kelipot* of the broken vessels with the divine sparks which adhere to them plunge down to form 'the abyss of evil'. The harmony of the emanation has been disturbed.

R. Luria's doctrine of 'the withdrawing of the *en-soph*', 'the residue of light', 'the breaking of the vessels' and the origin of evil seems to be a mythical expression of the ambivalence of the Creation—emanating from the infinite, absolute Being, but by its very manifestation impairing, as it were, the divine unity.

Through a renewed emission of light, the world of *tikkun* then emerges. In it develop *parzufim* in which the *sefirot* remain differentiated but harmoniously attuned to each other. The *parzufim* represent at the same time the personal aspects of the godhead (see p. 180), and thus appear in all emanated worlds. At the lowest stage of the emanation, the world of making, however, the sin of the human Adam brings about the fall of mankind and its world. Through this, the *shekhinah* was separated from the higher *sefirot*. The *tikkun* was not achieved. Divine sparks remain dispersed, bound to evil. The *shekhinah* is in exile, just as are the Jewish people.

It is now encumbent on man, primarily the Jewish people, 'to gather the dispersed sparks', i.e. to separate them from the evil and unite them with the Divine. Thus evil will be made powerless and lose the possibility of existing, and the original harmony of God, world and mankind will be restored. This task can be carried out through *kavvanot* (intentions): i.e. mystical contemplation of the words of prayer, as well as observance of the Torah commandments in the knowledge and awareness of their significance within the cosmic process of restitution. Every individual soul has in the course of its wanderings (metempsychosis) to gather the sparks which belong to itself, that is, to accomplish its own *tikkun* as its own individual contribution to the *tikkun* of the universe. The attainment of the cosmic redemption is thus at the same time the redemption of the Jewish people, the coming of the Messiah.

Within the framework of this comprehensive conception, which had a profound influence on the world of Jewish thought, the angels Enoch-Metatron and Elijah-Sandalphon represent the possibility of attaining this goal and show the way to it. Metatron guards the souls which have already been redeemed. Sandalphon takes care of those still wandering about in exile, and through his inspiration, the 'Giluy Eliyahu', the great mystics of any period can attain their own *tikkun* and show their followers the way to theirs. This finally leads to the collective *tikkun*. Then, when human endeavour has freed almost all the divine sparks, Elijah will evoke the divine act of grace which completes the redemption of the universe.

A particularly impressive metaphorical description of the last phase of the redemption is given by R. Naphtali Bacharach, a mystic of the Lurianic school: Elijah-Sandalphon calls for God's compassion for the Jewish people: 'Behold the mother-bird which has strayed from its nest, the *shekhinah* who weeps for the Jewish people.' Then heaven and earth tremble, God sheds two tears into the ocean, and commands Elijah-Sandalphon to resurrect the dead with dew and Metatron to wake the Messiah. Then peace descends on the world and 'God and his name will be one'.[128]

The metaphor of God shedding two tears into the ocean when the Jewish people are in distress occurs in the Talmud.[129] Here in mysticism it means that the divine compassion, the aspect of the *sefirah* Tiferet, turns towards the 'ocean', one of the names of the *sefirah* Malkhut-*shekhinah*, through the mediation of the *sefirah* Yesod, i.e. through Elijah, who represents the lower part of the 'middle line'. Thus 'He', the transcendent Divine, and 'his name', the immanent one, become united in man's consciousness.

The central position occupied by the Elijah-figure in the development of Jewish mysticism is understandable in the religious and the psychological context. That Elijah, surrounded by mystery in the Bible, came to earth from heaven and in human shape met the Aggadists of talmudic times as their teacher and friend, was to them a profound religious experience. Becoming aware of the possibility of bridging the gulf between creator and creature—the yearning of the religious man—they intensified their own search for the way to unity with the Divine. The closer the personal relationship of the seeker with the transformed Elijah returned to earth, the more illuminating their shared path into the depth. As in the biblical description of Elijah's transformation, sparks of the master's soul passed on to his pupil Elisha—according to the Kabbalists, symbolised by the cloak passed on to Elisha[130]—Elijah's spirit enfolds the Torah scholars, quickens for them the Bible's mythical world of symbolism, and activates their creative potential as expressed in the

profundities of the Aggadah. Thus Elijah shows them the way to
immersion into the depths of cosmogeny and the divine realm.
The Aggadists become mystics.

Inspired and guided by Elijah's spirit and the specific Judaic
symbolism connected with him, the mystics penetrate into it, and
with it deeper and deeper into the Divine. The extended experience of God thus newly gained then allows them to understand
more profoundly and more meaningfully the biblical commandments and the traditional symbols, which become transformed
like themselves.

From the early Kabbalists' brief references to Elijah-revelations
and from their detailed descriptions in the Zohar and the explana-
tions of R. Ḥayyim Vital, it appears that these were visual and
auditory phenomena which occurred sometimes spontaneously,
sometimes after meditative preparation, and which often culminated in a relationship of dialogue with Elijah (see pp. 80 ff.).

According to some later Kabbalists—e.g. R. Livai of Prague
and R. Moses Cordovero—the 'Giluy Eliyahu' is experienced not
sensually but as a mystical soliloquy. R. Cordovero distinguished
it clearly from the *maggid*-revelation which compels the mystic to
speak [automatic speech]. His words: 'it seems to the mystic as if
he has said something to himself', and R. Livai's remark that
'inspiration by Elijah is often experienced by the recipient as his
own thought' point to a dialogue between the conscious ego and
the subconscious layers of the mystic's soul (see pp. 84–5 and 86).

Nearly all mystical experiences are generally called 'Elijah's
revelations', which is in accord with R. Vital's conclusions
that all the different stages of illumination can be attained with
Elijah's help. R. Joseph Karo's references to *maggid*- and Elijah-
revelations are equivocal. When he was reciting the Mishnah, he
was regularly visited by a *maggid* as a voice issuing from his own
mouth [automatic speech]—this he felt to be the *shekhinah*. The
maggid repeatedly promised him that he would reach the highest
degree of Elijah-revelation. It has also been said that R. Ḥayyim
Luzzatto's mystical writings—the so-called 'Second Zohar'—
were dictated by Elijah [automatic writing].

From a psychological point of view, R. Karo's mystical

experiences as well as those of the Gaon of Vilna and probably those of most of the great talmudic scholars are compensatory. They complete their preponderant male-rational religious attitude by making conscious their previously partly repressed, more feminine, intuitive and irrational attitude.[131]

R. Abraham Abulafia, one of the most important Jewish mystics of the thirteenth century and apparently the only one who wrote down a detailed personal record of his immediate mystical experiences, emphasises that a spiritual teacher appeared during his meditation on God's name—'a mover within opened the gates of the holy mysteries of the soul'. In supreme ecstasy he experiences him as the angel Metatron, and identifies himself with him.[132] Metatron, who bears 'the name of his master' (God), is, as mentioned above, connected and sometimes identified with Sandalphon-Elijah in the Kabbalah. The mystic, ascending through meditation on God's name, unites with the angelic bearer of God's name who, however, remains between him and the godhead. It seems that a complete *unio mystica* is not attained.

This also corresponds to the view that the revelation which was granted to Elijah before his transformation was an experience of the *unio mystica*: the union Tiferet-*shekhinah*, the transcendent-male aspect of God with the immanent-female one. He feels himself participating in the accomplishment of the *coniunctio* through clothing the king and queen in their wedding garments (see p. 92). But he himself does not enter the *unio mystica*.

The identification of the mystic with Elijah (Sandalphon or Metatron) seems to be the limit of what Jewish mystics generally can attain. Elijah-Sandalphon, 'standing on earth and reaching into heaven', is the prototype of the Jewish mystic himself who, transformed, remains bound to the earth, in contrast to the 'uroboric'* mystic who retreats from the world and remains a recluse (see p. 81).

The 'Giluy Eliyahu' means for the mystic the influx of new experiences of God which flow into those which are already integrated, transform them further and may culminate in the

* From *uroboros*, a hoop-like snake that bites its own tail, which symbolises the unconscious

experience of a union with the Divine. But the humility of both the ecstatic and the contemplative mystic makes him distinguish between the Divine and himself even in their union. To him revelation is a grace, the revealed remains a token of grace.

The changing frequency and intensity of the 'Giluy Eliyahu', the difficulties and spiritual dangers on the mystic's way to God, make him reflect on the biblical-Aggadic Elijah-figure, and these reflections may then precipitate new disclosures. The mystic, according to prevalent tradition, sees in Elijah a man who had surpassed his human limitations. He is therefore particularly fascinated by the details of Elijah's transformation, feeling this process of transformation taking place within himself. The mystic gets to know from his own experience the solitary walk in the desert, the search for his lost soul, the longing for the 'mountain of the revelation' and the dark night of its cave. But Elijah accompanies him, he is for him the divine guide who keeps him alive in the wilderness, enables him to reach the mountain, calls him forth from the darkness of the cave and finally lets him hear 'the small voice of silence' (I Kings 19: 3–15; see also pp. 14 and 31). Thus the ecstatic and the meditative mystic feels himself led and protected by Elijah on his way into the depth. Through him he is confronted with himself and brought to his individual experience of God. To the more theosophic mystic, the words of the Torah become transparent through the intuition accorded to him by Elijah, and manifest themselves as a revelation of the creative living God. Every Jewish mystic goes Elijah's way.

Jewish mysticism essentially arose out of meditations about the first biblical words, that 'in the beginning' God created the world and the first man (see p. 78), and about the vision of Ezekiel, who saw on the divine chariot 'a likeness as the appearance of a man' (Ezek. 1: 26). From these a straight line seems to lead to the conception of the later Kabbalists who saw in the highest, first divine emanation the mystic figure of the godhead, *adam kadmon*, the prototype of primordial spiritual man. Correspondingly, on the earthly plane, the biblical Adam was created in God's likeness, and his fall meant the loss of his unity with God. In Enoch-Metatron and Elijah-Sandalphon the living soul of Adam in its original purity was restored, because they made their way on earth with God. This obviously made the mystics conscious of the relation between the entirely integrated man of this world and the divine *adam kadmon*. It seems that Enoch-Metatron, 'who works from above to below', indicates God's love and his care for man, while Elijah-Sandalphon, 'who works from below to above', indicates man's longing for God and his striving to transcend his human limitations.

CHAPTER V

Elijah in the Pseudo-Messianic Sabbatian Movement

The Elijah-figure which is inseparably linked with the appearance of the Messiah played a decisive part in the pseudo-Messianic movement which arose in the seventeenth century around Shabbetai Zevi. Certainly, after the Inquisition and the expulsion of the Jews from Spain, growing despair over the interminable sufferings of centuries of exile found a religious-positive compensation in the creative elaboration of the Kabbalah. The Lurianic conception that not only the Jewish people were in exile but also the Divine; that the redemption of the Jewish people and the 'redemption of God' were identical; that every individual could contribute to its approach—spread from the small circle of genuine mystics to the rabbinic world in general and out to the spiritual elite of the people. Amongst the Jewish masses in their daily suffering, however, the demands of their individual *tikkun* could not suppress the passionate longing for an immediate Messianic-national redemption. Then, in the middle of the seventeenth century, the Cossacks under Bogdan Chmielnicki rebelled against Polish rule, subjecting the Polish and Russian Jewry to unspeakable misery. The catastrophes of these times were interpreted as *ikve ha-Mashiaḥ* ('heels of the Messiah'), the demonic-apocalyptic prelude to redemption. The arrival of the Messiah was expected daily.

It is not surprising that in this extremely tense atmosphere, here and there a religious-emotional ecstatic mind would play with the thought of being the Messiah so passionately awaited by the people. Shabbetai Ẓevi (1626–76), born in Smyrna, became within a short time the centre of a comprehensive pseudo-Messianic movement.

Contemporary accounts mention that he had a particularly impressive appearance with strong personal magnetism, strove even as a youth for his *tikkun* by means of strict asceticism and studies of the Kabbalah, but was regarded as only a little above average intellectually and rather unstable emotionally. According to the clear testimony of his personal friends, he vacillated almost constantly between manic and depressive moods. He was seized early by the belief in his vocation to be the Messiah, but was also frequently beset by doubts about himself and his destiny. In his public behaviour he repeatedly came into sharp conflict with Jewish tradition, was banished from Smyrna because of this and eventually settled in Jerusalem. Even here he would hardly have been able to overcome his doubts about himself or been acknowledged beyond his circle of personal friends, if in Nathan of Gaza he had not found his herald and prophet.

Nathan (1644–80)—extraordinarily talented, psychologically stable, a diligent student of the Talmud and Kabbalah—was regarded even as a young man as familiar with the secrets of the individual *tikkun*. In a phase of depression Shabbetai Ẓevi sought help and advice from him and this meeting so much confirmed Shabbetai's belief in his vocation as the Messiah that shortly afterwards he proclaimed himself as such in public.

Nathan himself wrote about the reason for, and the start of his relationship with Shabbetai Ẓevi in a detailed open letter composed after the subsequent apostasy of Shabbetai:[1] in an overwhelming divine revelation in the twentieth year of his life, he had been called to be a prophet, and the appearance of the Messiah in the figure of Shabbetai Ẓevi had been foretold to him. Later, after Shabbetai had proclaimed himself to be the Messiah, Nathan had, in a new vision of 'the angel of the covenant', received permission to speak of his previous revelation. At the same time further details had been revealed to him of 'the days of the

Messiah' which had now come, although the whole of the Jewish people had not yet returned to God.

After this appearance of the angel of the covenant, who is, according to Jewish tradition, identified with Elijah (see pp. 36, 58, 101), Nathan, as herald and prophet of the 'Messiah' Shabbetai, himself became the personification of the Elijah-figure, without expressly calling himself by this name. He became the mainstay of a rapidly expanding Messianic movement, previously unparalleled in Jewish history, which spread from Palestine to the Diaspora and in the course of which Elijah is said to have repeatedly appeared in synagogues and streets of different towns. But Nathan created above all the ideology of the Sabbatian movement. He introduced into the Lurianic doctrine of redemption a theme of gnostic origin: the soul of the redeemer had initially to fight a hard and lengthy battle with the 'dragon of evil', with alternate victories and defeats. This explained the noticeable variations of Shabbetai's moods, his often absurd behaviour and above all also his anti-nomistic attitude to Jewish tradition.

But before long the Messianic ecstasy came to an abrupt end. Shabbetai was arrested by the Sultan of Turkey, and became a Muslim in 1666. The overwhelming majority of his followers left him, bitterly disappointed, but in many countries there were groups, some larger, some smaller, which continued for decades after his death to believe in Shabbetai's Messianic vocation.

Nathan, in the open letter mentioned above, endeavoured to explain Shabbetai's apostasy by means of mystic speculation. His conversion to Islam was a necessary stage in his Messianic mission, and he would certainly return to complete his work of redemption. The letter concludes: 'May God in his great compassion have mercy on us and let the hearts of the whole of Israel acknowledge the truth. And may he send Elijah to make peace in Israel. It seems to me that our sages referred by this[2] to the grave reproaches which exist in Israel regarding this faith [in Shabbetai Zevi] ... The verse[3] ends "lest I come and smite the land with utter destruction" ... A punishment as grave as this can refer only to the holy faith in our noble lord Shabbetai Zevi. For everyone who is rooted in it has, as it were, fulfilled the whole

Torah . . . These are some of the ways of the holy faith, the fundamentals of which were proclaimed to me by the angel of the covenant.'[4]

This letter by Nathan, though serving to justify Shabbetai's apostasy and unintentionally Nathan himself too, bears the stamp of subjective truth. It shows the unshakeable faith of a mystic, rooted in the Jewish tradition, in the revelation of Elijah. Seized by it, he is himself unconsciously forced into the role of an Elijah-figure, as herald and helper of a supposed Messiah. And even after the quite obvious psychotic breakdown of the Messiah-personality proclaimed by him, he believes that Shabbetai will return by a new revelation of Elijah to the whole Jewish people.[5]

CHAPTER VI

Elijah in Ḥasidism: his Psychological Integration

Almost immediately after the tragic collapse of the pseudo-Messianic movement around Shabbetai Ẓevi and influenced by it in the first phase of its development, Ḥasidism originated in Russia at the beginning of the eighteenth century.

Instead of 'the days of the Messiah', of the expected deliverance from exile and of spiritual renewal, there had come bitter disappointment and with it confusion and social misery for the Jewish people. The nihilist atmosphere of Sabbatianism—and shortly afterwards that of the circle of followers of Jacob Frank, who fiercely proclaimed 'redemption by holy sin' and was later converted to Christianity—had seriously threatened the continuing existence of religious tradition; especially as this atmosphere remained alive in numerous, mostly disguised, Sabbatian conventicles. But the depth of the tragic events also harboured buds of regeneration through the dynamics of Jewish mysticism. A small spiritual elite had succeeded in 'redeeming the divine sparks from the abyss' and kindling through them a genuine, new religious movement within the Jewish tradition.

The founders of Ḥasidism were not so much the official leaders of the Jewish communities, the rabbis who mainly concentrated on talmudic learning, but the *maggidim*, the circle of itinerant preachers. They were mystics, or at least familiar with the theosophical doctrines of the Lurianic Kabbalah, and through their vocation were in direct contact with the Jewish masses and were well aware of their spiritual and social distress. As founders of the Ḥasidic movement stand the personalities of R. Israel ben Eliezer Baal Shem Tov ('Master of the Good Name'—1700–60) and his closest pupils, R. Jacob Joseph of Pulnoye and R. Dov Baer of Meseritz, 'the Great *Maggid*' (1710–72). Around them gathered an esoteric circle of *maggidim* and Torah scholars, who later became the leading spirits of the various Ḥasidic groups which arose rapidly in Lithuania, White Russia, Poland, Hungary and as far as Palestine.

As the Lurianic Kabbalah had transformed the original ideology of the Zohar without affecting the core of its essence, it was now transformed, more through a shifting of the emphasis than through fundamental changes. The theosophical doctrines of the Lurianic Kabbalah, its speculative ideas and concepts were transformed—first within the contemplative personalities of the Ḥasidic leaders themselves—to direct, individual, mystic experiences. Under their spell, they became creative and vital fields of energy, by which numerous individuals amongst the people who flocked to them were lastingly influenced.

Thus Jewish mysticism adapted itself to the new situation of the people. The expectation of a personal Messiah-figure who would bring national redemption receded into the background once more, as previously in the Lurianic Kabbalah. Supreme emphasis was placed on the inescapable task of the individual to 'redeem the divine sparks' corresponding to his individual soul. But this task was now no longer seen as the seemingly endless wandering and transforming of individual souls by metempsychosis, but almost exclusively as concerning the immediate preoccupations of the people's daily life.

In connection with the phrase in the Psalms: 'Draw nigh unto my soul, and redeem it', Rabbi Moses Ḥayyim Ephraim of Sudlikov cites his grandfather, the Baal Shem Tov: 'Every individual is under the obligation to redeem his soul',[1] and also: 'The redemption is the awakening from sleep; i.e. from being unaware of the divine presence.'[2] R. Jacob Joseph of Pulnoye also refers to the doctrine of personal redemption which had been handed down to him by his master: 'That man recognises that God is hidden even in all his psychic and physical miseries . . . (as happened to the Israelites in Egypt) that is the essence of the redemption of all men and at all times. As it is written: "Out of my straits I called upon the Lord" and "Thou who didst set me free when I was in distress". That is true redemption';[3] and 'My teacher told me: before praying for general redemption, one should pray for the redemption of one's own soul'.[4] Personal redemption through becoming aware of the divine immanence in one's own soul is repeatedly demanded in different ways— sometimes explicitly, sometimes by implication—by the various Ḥasidic trends, according to the individual personalities of their leaders, the *zaddikim*.

Ḥasidic teaching, thoroughly rooted in traditional Judaism, does not on the whole accord primary importance to belief in a national and universal Messiah-personality. It does believe in 'the coming of the Messiah', but regards it mainly as the pinnacle of the 'Messiah structure', to which each individual has to contribute. The coming of the Messiah is considered to be, so to speak, the final stone of the edifice, the confirmation that all men have attained their personal salvation. Then God himself will improve the external conditions of the world at the coming of the redeemer.[5]

In a letter to his brother-in-law R. Gershon of Kutov, the Baal Shem Tov wrote, according to the authentic text (Koretz, 1791), that in his spiritual ascent he met the Messiah and asked him: 'when are you coming?'. And he answered: 'By this shalt thou know it: when your teaching will become renowned and revealed throughout the world, and when thy springs [will] be dispersed abroad, [imparting to others] what I taught you and you apprehended [so that] they too will be able to perform contemplative unifications and ascents [of the soul] *like you*. Then shall all the "shells" perish and it will be a time of acceptability and salvation.' Apparently these experiences of the Baal Shem Tov were the basis of the great emphasis on individual redemption in early Ḥasidism.

A particularly extreme view is presented by R. Mordecai

Joseph Leiner: not only individual redemption but also future universal redemption consists merely of a change in man's psychological attitude: he has to become aware that everything that occurs, including so-called evil, is the will of God.[6]

Rabbi Ze'ev Wolf of Zhitomir dwells with particular emphasis on the prescription that everyone would have to earn his own redemption, 'for only the knowledge of the mature man leads him beyond his own limitations.' Through the coming of an outstanding spiritual leader who would be able to show everyone the way to his redemption, the individual would be deprived of his free will and with it of the essence of his personal redemption.[7]

In Ḥasidism, the way to personal redemption is above all through meditative prayer. Immersion in *kavvanot* (intentions)—to direct the words of the prayer to their corresponding spiritual site within the higher worlds, as demanded by the Lurianic Kabbalah (see p. 106)—has to be replaced by the *kavvanat ha-lev* (intention of the heart)—striving for *devekut* (cleaving to God) through meditation on the structure of the words of the prayer or through the immersion of the heart in the contents of the prayer, not for the benefit of the individual himself but for the *shekhinah* of which he is a part.[8] Sometimes Ḥasidic prayer is called 'praying with a broken heart'.[9] Beyond this, contemplation, the abstention of the soul from all activity, enables the individual to become aware of the Divine within himself.[10] Furthermore, when studying the Torah, everyone would have to fan into flame the individual sparks corresponding to his own soul which are hidden in the text. Similarly, when observing religious commandments, one should strive to penetrate to the vital inner meaning which directly appeals to oneself.[11]

Besides the demand that through intensification of the religious-traditional life one should strive for *devekut*, the biblical instruction: 'in all thy ways acknowledge Him' (Prov. 3: 6) should apply in its Ḥasidic interpretation: divine providence lets man encounter at every step in his life—at any time and in any place—people, events, things, which appeal to him and which demand that he redeem the divine sparks in them congenial to his soul.[12] This means that man should endeavour to enter into vital, meaningful relationship with everything he encounters, no matter how 'accidental' it may appear.

Like the great mystics of earlier generations, the leading spirits of the Ḥasidic movement, the *zaddikim*, also experienced the 'Giluy Eliyahu'. R. Jacob Joseph of Pulnoye wrote: 'Aḥiyah ha-Shiloni, who received [the Torah tradition] from our teacher Moses ... and later belonged to the Davidian court of justice, was the teacher of Elijah and the teacher of the Baal Shem Tov'.[13] R. Solomon of Lutzk mentions in the name of R. Dov Baer of Meseritz, whose teachings he published: 'and he [the Baal Shem Tov] had the "Giluy Eliyahu" and other sublime revelations, and he began to explain the different sublime degrees of the "Giluy Eliyahu".'[14]

Numerous encounters between the Baal Shem Tov and Elijah, some with legendary elaborations, are described in detail in his biography, *Shivḥe ha-Besht* (*Praises of the Baal Shem Tov*). It says there that Elijah appeared to his father as a beggar, desecrating the Sabbath, but was received hospitably without reproach; Elijah foretold to him the birth of his son Israel and his future outstanding significance; later, Elijah appeared to the Baal Shem Tov himself, when he was a youth and in distress, had comforted him, had several times rescued him from danger and had revealed himself to him also in the hour of his death.[15]

R. Dov Baer, the majority of his pupils, and some later *zaddikim* were also inspired by Elijah, as is evident either from their own hints or from reports of their closest pupils or friends.[16] The extremely rich Ḥasidic folklore provides detailed accounts of numerous, frequently miraculous, encounters of the *zaddikim* and their most outstanding followers with Elijah.[17]

In Ḥasidic literature there are relatively few commentaries on the biblical record of Elijah, and they generally do not go far beyond the Aggadah and Kabbalah. Some interpretations, however, may be mentioned, in which the specifically Ḥasidic attitude is evident. The biblical comment concerning Phinehas, always also identified with Elijah in Ḥasidic literature, 'when he was zealous for me [God] in their [the Israelites'] midst', means that even when acting zealously, Phinehas-Elijah was closely connected with his people.[18] Elijah wore a belt of '*or*' (according to the Hebrew spelling, 'skin'), but his body consisted of '*or*' (spelled differently, meaning 'light').[19] Elijah's sacrifice on Mount Carmel was contrary to the biblical commandment to offer sacrifices only in the Temple, on the altar with a special ramp leading up to it, but he was entitled to disregard this commandment, since he himself personified the ramp, the ascent to God's altar, and succeeded in leading the Israelites back to God.[20] R. Zadok ha-Kohen, who developed the above-mentioned deterministic doctrine of R. Leiner (see pp. 118–19), calls Elijah's sacrifice on Mount Carmel a sin, but one necessary for the Israelites' return. In connection with this, R. Zadok shows that Elijah's personality represents the union of opposites—according to the Zohar, he had absorbed the soul of Phinehas, who had sinned out of fear of God, and also the souls of Nadab and Abihu, whose sin arose out of love for God.[21] R. Barukh of Medziboz said that the greatness of Elijah's deed [on Mount Carmel] was not that he performed a miracle, but that when the fire fell down from heaven all those present did not mention the miracle, but exclaimed: 'The Lord, he is the God.'[22] Elijah was allowed to ascend to heaven because of his devotion to God, which arose out of supreme love.[23] Elisha's wish for a double portion of Elijah's spirit, and Elijah's answer, 'if thou see me when I am taken from thee' (II Kings 2. 9–10), R. Naḥman of Bratzlav explains with a reference to the doctrine of the Zohar 'that every *zaddik* had two spiritual souls, one on earth and one in heaven'.[24] As the pupil's soul shares a root with his master's, Elisha would, at the sight of Elijah's ascent,—at the moment when Elijah's heavenly soul comes down to lift up the earthly one—receive also the heavenly portion of his master's spirit.[25] Although Elijah (like all human beings) was formed out of the transitory four basic elements, in him they had become a unity which endured to become eternal, and therefore he was able to live for ever.[26]

The Ḥasidic conception of Elijah's part in the process of redemption is unique, his activity being entirely appropriate to the personal redemption to which Ḥasidism gives prominence.

R. Menahem Nahum of Tchernobil expresses this particularly clearly and in detail:[27]

'Behold, I . . . send you Elijah the prophet before the coming of the [great and terrible] day of the Lord . . . And he shall turn the heart of the fathers' (Mal. 3: 23-4). It is true, as before the coming of the Messiah there will be Elijah's proclamation and through it an increase of Da'at (awareness, realisation)—as it is written: 'For the earth shall be full of the knowledge of the Lord' (Isa. 11: 9)—so, in the same way, this happens within every man of Israel and at any time . . . The predominance of the materialistic and evil, the lower part of man, over his higher [spiritual] part, makes the heretic believe that there are two separate forces in man. But in reality man is an absolute unity and can accomplish this . . . And behold, when man has a positive intimation [inspiration]—thus [for instance] when studying the Torah, when he endeavours to understand a difficult passage—then, before his knowledge is extended, he has a sort of intimation, he feels a [new] idea appearing in his brain. This is the Elijah-factor. Then his knowledge is extended and filled with vitality, and he is also easily able to unite his several parts, including the base and the good. One who [in this way] announces something good [adequate], becomes invested with a spark of Elijah, as he [Elijah] has always been the herald of everything good, and later, as is well known, became incarnate in Phinehas; and then, when he announces [to someone] something good, that one quickly says that he has become aware of Elijah within himself, even if others are not aware of him [Elijah]. . . .[28] And when he has this knowledge he can begin to serve God by means of the Elijah-function which has become incarnate within him, and he can ascend gradually . . . and, through extending his awareness, cleave to God . . . Therefore it is written: 'Behold, I send you Elijah the prophet'; I 'send', that means: now, at the present time; every hour the Elijah-factor is sent to every man before 'the day of the Lord' . . . and the union of the good and the bad is [then] accomplished. As it is written: 'In all thy ways acknowledge him' (Prov. 3: 6), and he turns 'the heart of the children to their fathers'.

And in another passage, with reference to the biblical verse concerning Phinehas: 'Behold, I give unto him My covenant of peace' (Num. 25: 12), it is again emphasised that Elijah is ever-present in everyone. And[29]

It is true that all the passionate striving of those who serve God is caused by the Elijah-factor. He proclaims all that is whole . . . the union of thought and speech . . . and after this there comes the Messiah aspect . . . as the Baal Shem Tov said: 'Every individual has to prepare his share of the Messianic structure and to carry it out, until the whole structure has been erected.' And the result is: wherever there is unity this means *shalom* [peace, wholeness] . . . and that is possible only through Elijah and . . . he is always present before this union is achieved, and the unity is called the 'coming of the day of the Lord'.

The 'unity' is formulated by R. Menahem Nahum in the same chapter: 'The heart of any individual may become God's site, so that none of its parts is separated from its origins; thus man can make himself and all creation [the world] one with the infinite [God].'[30] The same author says in another passage: 'Every awakening of the soul, the female spring of water, is in everyone as the Elijah-factor . . . that is why one says: "Elijah has revealed himself to someone", for this factor is hidden within every human being.'[31]

This author's son, R. Mordecai of Tchernobil, makes a free interpretation of the words of the Psalmist: 'Who makest the clouds Thy chariot' (104: 3) about one of the aspects of the Elijah-function:[32]

The cloudy densities of this world which obscure the infinite divine light—when these barriers and partitions are broken through, the chariot of the divine throne appears. But how can one tear this cloudiness apart? This [can happen] through the passionate longing for God which every Jew has by nature and from birth, and this is called 'Elijah'; this is the secret of the female [spring of] water which man awakens in himself; his longing for the creator.

R. Elimelekh of Lizhensk is said to have taught his pupils that through divine revelation and the return to God of the Israelites which Elijah brought about on Mount Carmel, he is connected with all the souls of Israel. And as Elijah is the angel of the covenant, a part of his soul is transmitted to every newborn child, a smaller or a larger part according to the psychical potential of the child. Therefore, it may happen that a small soul becomes whole

through pleasing God with its life, and that Elijah reveals himself
to it, while the soul of a great man—as is well known from the
example of the famous eleventh-century Spanish Hebrew
philologist and exegete, R. Ibn Ezra—in spite of all its striving
does not succeed in realising his correspondingly great Elijah-
potential.[33]

A more general statement is: 'Wherever a sanctification of God
occurs [through human action], it represents a stage of the Elijah-
function.'[34] The internalising of Elijah is taken even further in a
saying by R. Yiẓḥak of Berditchev: 'Nowadays the Messiah can
come even without the previous appearance of Elijah, if we
prepare our hearts without troubling him. We can make our-
selves capable of receiving the Messiah every day if we obey the
divine voice.'[35]

Elijah therefore becomes, in the view of Ḥasidism, above all an
internal psychic factor which exists potentially in every human
being. It is the awakening of the longing (dormant in all people)
for a spiritual experience of God; the opening up of man's soul;
his striving to overcome the internal and external resistance of
his human nature and of life on earth. But at the same time
'Elijah' is also the divine call granted to those who long and strive
for God: he is the 'messenger', the sudden illumination; consciousness becomes extended; part of the transcendental divine
becomes immanent; through the Elijah-factor man attains Da'at.

In traditional Jewish writings, Da'at means not only knowledge
as the result of the experience of the senses and rational thought,
but to some extent in the Bible[36] and the Aggadah, nearly always
in mysticism and especially in Ḥasidism,[37] perfect knowledge,
existential awareness, arising out of direct relationship. This
meaning of Da'at is derived from the verse (Gen. 4: 1): 'And the
man knew Eve his wife'; from knowledge in the erotic relationship.

Of Da'at in this sense, also called extended or perfect Da'at,[38]
Ḥasidic literature—apart from the above-mentioned passages by
R. Menahem Nahum and R. Ze'ev Wolf—says, for instance: 'It
fills the soul with vitality.'[39] 'It is a complete knowledge and fills

all chambers [organs] of man, which are part of the divine immanation, while it [plain knowledge] is as a rule restricted to the brain.'[40] 'It fills all the chambers of the heart and unites body and soul, unites speaking and doing with the thought.'[41] 'It unites love with fear.'[42] 'It decides between two [opposites] and unites them.'[43] 'It unites everything in the root [God].'[44] 'It is the knowledge—going beyond rational knowledge—of the unity of everything ... Therefore the *tikkun* actually consists of the revelation of Da'at; it unifies his [man's] qualities.'[45] 'Da'at leads out of the confines of the *galut* (Diaspora).'[46] 'Forgetting is the cause of the *galut*, and redemption comes through Da'at [the recovery of consciousness].'[47] And frequently one encounters in Ḥasidic writings the short saying: 'Through Da'at comes redemption.'*[48]

Da'at in the Ḥasidic sense is therefore the knowledge which stretches beyond the intellect of man, seizes him emotionally and urges him towards making the known real. Further progress in psychic transformation can lead to the suspension of the boundary between subject and object.[50] The experience of God-images— the sight of different divine aspects—is transformed in Ḥasidism through the Elijah-factor to the existential realisation of God, to the direct experience of the unity of all that exists.

R. Menahem Mendel of Lubavitch (called 'Zemaḥ-Zedek'), one of the spiritual leaders of the theosophically profound and psychologically systematising Ḥabad Ḥasidism, symbolically applies the prophecy that Elijah will turn 'the heart of the children to their fathers' in his mystical commentary on the Song of Songs to the divine emanation itself: the seven lower, differentiated, stages of the emanation—also called 'children'—will be united with each other as well as with the always united higher, intrinsically divine *sefirot* called 'father and mother'. This will happen because of Da'at, 'which is due to Elijah'.[51]

* Ḥasidic literature frequently refers to the fact that the first redemption of Israel, the liberation from Egypt through Moses, was also a liberation 'from the straits' through Da'at. This refers to a play on words: *yeẓiat miẓrayim* (exodus from Egypt) = *yeẓiat mi-ẓre-yam* (escape from the straits of the sea). Therefore not only Elijah, the final redeemer, but frequently also Moses, the first redeemer, is seen as a representative of Da'at. Occasionally it is also said of him: 'he is hidden in every Jew' [49]

In the Kabbalist description of the divine emanation as the 'tree of life' or 'figure of God', Da'at is generally not an actual stage of the emanation but is regarded as the coupling of the second and third highest *sefirot*: Ḥokhmah (the universal wisdom of God, also called father) and Binah (his differentiating insight, also called mother). Because of the union of these 'primordial parents', Da'at also unites 'the children' on the 'middle line', the lower stages of the emanation, which are already differentiated and separated as right and left pairs of opposites.*[52] The lowest tenth *sefirah*, which contains the human world, is as a result of the original sin of mankind not permanently connected with the trunk of the *sefirot*-tree, the 'middle line', but is 'in exile', dominated by opposites as long as human knowledge still segregates and separates; i.e. has not yet reached the higher stage of true perfect knowledge (Da'at).

Da'at has thus to be understood, in the sense of the above quotation from Zemaḥ-Zedek, as the centripetal-synthetic factor in the world of emanation evolving centrifugally-differentially. Thus the striking term 'Elijah' for *divine* Da'at is understandable: it is the unifying and as it were 'redeeming' tendency within the differentiating *sefirot* emanations.

In Aggadic writings as well as in the Kabbalah, the redemption of God through man is intimated.[53] In the Lurianic Kabbalah and in Ḥasidism, this thought is based to a marked extent on the conception that the godhead, in accordance with the limited possibilities of human wisdom, limits himself (*zimzum*) and reveals himself merely in seemingly opposing manifestations. Only when humanity has attained Da'at—the full realisation of the unity of man, world and God—and thus its own redemption, the godhead, too, will be as it were released from its own limitations.

The Elijah-dynamic on the macrocosmic plane of the divine emanation as seen by Ḥabad-Ḥasidism corresponds to the Elijah-

---

* See n. 52. According to Ḥabad-Ḥasidism, the highest *sefirah* (Keter) is concealed in the *en-soph*. Ḥokhmah and Binah are the first and second *sefirot*. Da'at is the third, which connects these two together and with the six lower *sefirot*. This middle line is, as mentioned above (p. 100), called Metatron-Sandalphon (-Elijah) in Kabbalist literature

Da'at factor on the microcosmic human plane, as extensively described by R. Menahem Nahum of Tchernobil (see p. 122).* The doctrine of macro-microcosmic correspondence,[55] clearly expressed in the Aggadic saying: 'All that God created above, He also created below', was also applied in the Kabbalah in the sense that every stage of the divine emanation is reflected in a corresponding aspect of the human soul. In Ḥasidism this correspondence does not remain metaphorical-theosophical but is applied psychologically and thus gives Jewish mysticism a new momentum. In the process of introspective psychic development man might attain, ascending in meditation as it were retrogradely through the stages of the divine emanation, the experience of the unity of himself, the Divine and the world.

The Kabbalah repeatedly uses for the dynamic of the divine emanation a play on words based on the fact that the words 'AIN' ('nothingness') and 'ANI' ('I') consist of the same letters. The world develops out of the 'AIN' (the divine nothingness) to the 'ANI' (the divine, personal I of the lowest *sefirah*) and can return from the 'I' back to the 'nothingness'.[56] Thus Ḥasidic mystics demand that man aim towards this retransformation within himself. 'The purpose of the creation of man consists of raising the worlds to their root—to their original "nothingness" —i.e. to make them cleave to God [to achieve *devekut*] through the Torah, prayer and good deeds, and above all through man considering himself to be nothing.'[57] R. Dov Baer of Meseritz's pupils regarded this instruction as an overcoming of human egocentricity by contemplation and also as a religious-moral demand for extreme humility.[58]

It is this Ḥasidic-mystic ascent of the 'I' to 'nothingness' for which the Elijah-Da'at-function in man strives and to which it guides him. When the Ḥasidic mystic approaches the divine 'nothingness' with this attitude and realises his human nothingness, the divine 'Being' lights up and he realises that he is part of it. The world becomes numinous and, as a manifestation of the

---

* Ḥabad-Ḥasidism accordingly, in the psychic-human sphere, regards Ḥokhmah-Binah as the spiritual, and the six lower *sefirot* as the emotional forces of man, which lead to actual realisation[54]

godhead, becomes real again. In the words of Ḥasidism: 'When man wishes to be created anew, he must attain nothingness through fear of God and humility, then he becomes created anew, becomes like a spring brimming with strength, an inexhaustible stream.'[59] 'He who becomes nothing partakes of the divine nothingness, and nothingness brings about being.'[60] 'In everything he sees, he always sees God.'[61] 'His thoughts reveal the thinking of God.'[62] 'God speaks out of his mouth.'[63] Thus the Ḥasidic mystic attains *devekut*, his redemption in the sense of conscious participation in divine unity.

In spite of the central position which *devekut* occupies in Ḥasidic doctrine, it is repeatedly emphasised that a constant complete *devekut* seems neither possible nor desirable. This is usually expressed in a free interpretation of the words of the prophet, 'and the living creatures ran and returned' (Ezek. 1: 14)[64] and in the saying of the Baal Shem Tov, 'constant bliss is no bliss.'[65] The Jewish mystic, therefore, is one who becomes transformed, and remains in the world, as is evident from the talmudic Aggadah of R. Simeon bar Yoḥai (see pp. 80–1), and as is expressed in the talmudic reference to 'the angel Sandalphon', the transformed Elijah, who 'stands on earth and reaches into heaven',[66] and also by Elijah's ascent and descent (see pp. 52, 93–4).

The way shown by Ḥasidism to man's individual redemption attainable through Da'at, activated and guided by the intrinsic psychical Elijah-factor with its tremendous demands, could of course be followed by only a few. Doubtless it was followed by many Ḥasidic leaders, especially of the first generation after the Baal Shem Tov and the Great *Maggid*. They became aware of the divine presence within themselves, in their fellow-men and in whatever exists, alive or inanimate; they were illuminated and filled by it; their personality was opened equally to what is in heaven and on earth. Through this they had an attraction for their surroundings which seemed almost magical. A profound spiritual and emotional relationship tended to develop between the Ḥasidic rabbi called *ẓaddik* and those who flocked around him.

The term '*ẓaddik*' for the Ḥasidic rabbi requires explanation.

The *ẓaddik* of the Bible is the man who observes the commandments of the Torah regarding God and the world. The Talmud
and the Aggadah furthermore call '*ẓaddik*' the Great Individual
who transcends his human limitations; once he is, interestingly
enough, compared with the sun.[67] There is, for example, an
Aggadic saying that all miracles which God performs could also
be performed by *ẓaddikim*,[68] and that what God will do [to all
men] in the world to come he [in some cases] allows *ẓaddikim* to
carry out in the present world;[69] in both of these passages, Elijah
is mentioned as one of these *ẓaddikim*. The Talmud says:[70] 'The
world is based on one pillar and this is called *ẓaddik*, because it is
written: "the righteous [*ẓaddik*] is an everlasting foundation" '
(Prov. 10: 25). The *Sefer ha-Bahir* cites this talmudic passage,
adding: 'He rises up from earth, to heaven.'[71]

In the Kabbalah, '*ẓaddik*' is the special name for Yesod, the
ninth *sefirah* of the divine emanation which also represents the
phallus in the mystical figure of the godhead. The flow of
the emanation arising out of the infinite concentrates in Yesod,
the last of the six middle *sefirot*, and can fructify the tenth, female,
sefirah, the *shekhinah*.

This *sefirah*, Yesod, is also called, apart from '*ẓaddik*', 'the
living God', 'the life of the worlds', 'symbol of the covenant',
'redeeming angel', 'everything in heaven and on earth', and
'peace' (in the sense of harmony).[72]

There are Ḥasidic descriptions of the '*ẓaddik* of the human
world', corresponding to the '*ẓaddik* of the higher worlds', of the
divine emanation: 'As the *sefirah* Yesod lets the divine abundance
stream down from above, so the lower [earthly] *ẓaddik* is able to
do this. He is like a ladder on which angels ascend and descend;
he is like a channel which directs the [divine] flow down to mankind',[73] and 'The earth conceives from heaven, as the woman
conceives from a man, develops and gives birth . . . but there has
to be a mediating link between the opposites: that is the *ẓaddik*;
he is the mediator, for his soul comes from above and his body
from below.'[74]

R. Elimelekh of Lizhensk says: 'The essential stimulus to returning and acknowledging God is received by mankind from the

ẓaddik, who has in love and awe reached adhesion to God and makes him one. The Divine in the *ẓaddik* makes him holy, and through this the heart of man is awakened and made ready to return', and 'The *ẓaddik* has to be the prototype for the redemption; whatever will one day be within everybody at the time of the redemption, has already to be within him'.[75]

Similar Ḥasidic sayings are: 'The *ẓaddik* can awaken fear of God and the wish to return in the heart of the whole Jewish people, for he is connected with them all.'[76] 'The *ẓaddik* has succeeded in returning, and as "master of the return" he can bring the Jewish people to righteousness and make them return.'[77] 'Not everyone can make himself one with God, but if he follows the *ẓaddik*, he can ascend through him.'[78]

R. Naḥman of Bratzlav says:[79]

> It is essential that there is peace [harmony] among man's qualities, i.e. that he is not divided in his qualities and his experiences. And the *ẓaddikim* are called 'covenant of peace'. . . . For when God appointed Phinehas as priest, He said: 'Behold, I give unto him my covenant of peace' [Num. 25: 12] . . . And the individual points, in which one may differ from another, are also branches of the *ẓaddik*, who has within him the general [view] point of the Jewish people.

The characteristics of the *ẓaddik* in the Aggadah and Kabbalah thus correspond to the characteristic traits of the Elijah-Sandalphon-figure. And as the biblical Elijah, transformed and redeemed in his ascent to heaven, became the spiritual guide of the Aggadists and mystics, so the Ḥasidic rabbi who had achieved adhesion, his individual redemption, became the *ẓaddik* to his still unredeemed fellow-men. He had realised and activated his own inner Elijah-function, and through this became to his followers the personification of the Elijah-potential still dormant within themselves.

The Great *Maggid* himself says: 'Every individual sees in the *ẓaddik* his own share, or his image.'[80] He thus describes a phenomenon that in psychology is called 'projection'. The Ḥasid projects his 'Elijah-factor', his unconscious striving for transcendence on to the personality of his rabbi, the *ẓaddik*.

Many thousands of Ḥasidim were fascinated by the numinosity of their rabbi, and saw in him the mediator between themselves and God. In spiritual or material difficulty, with unshakeable confidence they always turned to him for advice. A considerable number of followers came to live for months or even years in his immediate vicinity, and his spiritual guidance activated their own individual Elijah-function and enabled them to develop it further. Many men may have been brought by psychic maturation in the Ḥasidic sense to the stage of at least temporary 'adhesion'.

The profound psychological understanding of the Ḥasidic rabbis is evident in many of their recorded sayings. As a characteristic example may be mentioned R. Jacob Joseph of Pulnoye's interpretation of the seemingly incomprehensible talmudic saying: 'The best doctor has to descend into hell.' 'The best doctor'—and by this R. Jacob Joseph undoubtedly means the *zaddik*—'is he who can heal the human soul, but for this he has to descend into the hell of the sinners.'[81] To R. Jacob Joseph, according to his further statements, sins tend to be committed because of an inner compulsion or lack of insight.[82]

Thus the *zaddik* became to his followers as it were Elijah returned to earth, who brought them closer to their personal salvation. The image of Elijah did not remain only in the eschatological sphere of future national and universal redemption, but entered the human soul. The longing for the numinous unity of God, world and man grew gradually more conscious. Thus Ḥasidism became a spiritual movement which pointed a new way to harmony between profound individual piety and Jewish tradition.

CHAPTER VII

Elijah in Liturgy and Ritual

The timeless significance of Elijah naturally finds manifold expression in Jewish liturgy and ritual.

As the prayer of the biblical Elijah: 'Hear me, O Lord, hear me, that this people may know that Thou, Lord, art God' (I Kings 18: 37) brought about the decisive revelation to the multitude on Mount Carmel,[1] so the Aggadic Elijah instructs one of the talmudic scholars on prayer and its efficacy. Certainly, the individual may in case of emergency say his prayers while walking along, but it pleases God especially when his sons praise 'his great name' in the synagogues and houses of study—he then regrets that he banished them 'from his table'—the altar of his temple.[2] A Ḥasidic interpretation of the details of this talmudic passage emphasises the close connection between prayer and redemption,[3] and the Kabbalists, as has been mentioned, represent Elijah transformed into an angel twining Israel's prayers into wreaths and crowns for God (see p. 99). It could be said that Elijah connecting heaven and earth, and hastening the coming of the redemption, corresponds to prayer as the relation of dialogue between man and God.[4]

Elijah is daily mentioned when grace is said after meals: 'May God in his mercy send us the prophet Elijah, may his memory be blessed, and may he bring us good tidings, help and comfort.' And in the benedictions after the weekly public Sabbath reading of a chapter from the Books of the Prophets, it says: 'Let us rejoice, O Lord, through your servant, the prophet Elijah, and through the kingdom of David, your Messiah, may he come soon and rejoice our heart.'

The passage which is read from the Books of the Prophets on the Sabbath always has a certain connection with the Torah passage which is read before it. Three times a year the passage from the prophets concerns Elijah. The description of the worship by the Israelites of the golden calf, and Moses' endeavours to lead the people back to God (Exod. 30: 11–33) is followed by a reading of the account of the contest with the worshippers of Baal arranged by Elijah on Mount Carmel (I Kings 18: 1–39). The account of Phinehas' zealous deed and his appointment to the office of priest which is his reward (Num. 25: 10 ff.) is followed by the description of Elijah's flight into the desert, his journey to Horeb and the revelation which is granted to him there (I Kings 18: 46; 19: 21). Finally, the reading on the so-called 'Great Sabbath', the Sabbath before the Passover feast commemorating the exodus from Egypt, is Malachi's final chapter (3: 4–24) which prophesies Elijah's return at the time of the redemption.

There are numerous mentions of Elijah in the *piyyutim* (poetic elaborations) of the prayers said on festivals, especially of the prayers for dew and rain. Similarly, the *seliḥot* (prayers of repentance) on fast days and in the weeks preceding the Day of Atonement include repeated supplications for a favourable hearing with reference to Elijah's prayer being answered on Mount Carmel.[5] And when the Day of Atonement is ending, Jewish communities stay, after twenty-four hours of fasting, dressed in shrouds to say the closing prayers which begin with the words: 'Open the gate unto us at the time when it is closing', and conclude with the exclamation, repeated collectively seven times, of the people at the revelation on Mount Carmel: 'The Lord, he is God.'

In particular, the ending of the Sabbath bears the mark of Elijah. Following the official liturgy, before and after the *havdalah* (the ceremony at the end of the Sabbath), 'Elijah songs' are sung in many Jewish homes. The best known, included in all traditional prayer-books, devotes several verses to Elijah's biblical miracles. It also mentions that his appearance in a dream promises good luck, and expresses the hope that he will soon proclaim the redemption. The refrain of this song is: 'The prophet Elijah, the Tishbite from Gilead, may he come to us soon with the son of David, the Messiah.' This is frequently followed by some other traditional songs, based mostly on folk legends about Elijah's good deeds performed for pious men and especially for those who keep the Sabbath strictly.

The particular 'Elijah-mood' at the close of the Sabbath arises from the view expressed in the Talmud that Elijah is to be expected at any time, but not on a Friday or on the Sabbath itself (see p. 64). Therefore his coming is most likely to be at the end of the Sabbath observance. Aggadic literature also relates that at the close of every Sabbath, Elijah records men's good deeds (see p. 51). Moreover, during the week, external pressure and inner distress is more noticeable to men, so that at the close of the day of rest Elijah's coming is particularly ardently desired.[6]

The celebrating of the end of the Sabbath as an evening dedicated largely to Elijah—joining as it were under his auspices the secular to the holy—is in itself in the nature of a ritual. Two further important and impressive rites have been observed by the Jewish people for over 2,000 years: the placing of 'Elijah's chair' at the beginning of the circumcision ceremony (see pp. 58, 100), and the references to Elijah-Phinehas and the 'covenant of life and peace' made with him in the grace after the festive meal which concludes the ceremony. Furthermore, in the Sephardic and Italian ritual, all those present sing an 'Elijah hymn' before the circumcision.

Particularly popular is a custom within the framework of the *Seder* evening, the first evening of the Passover festival celebrated annually by Jewish families on the night of 15 Nissan in memory of the exodus of the Israelites from Egypt. At a festive table set with *mazzot* (unleavened bread), bitter herbs and wine, through a recitation of the biblical account and its manifold Aggadic interpretations, the slavery of the Israelites in Egypt, the miracles which took place before the liberation and the night of the redemption are relived as in *illo tempore*. This brings to life the expectation repeatedly mentioned in traditional literature that during this very night, on which the first redemption of the Israelites took place through Moses, there will come the final redemption through Elijah and the Messiah who will follow him. Right at the beginning of the celebration, a special cup of wine, called 'Elijah's cup', is placed on the table. When grace has been said after the meal, the door of the house is opened by a child in expectation of Elijah's appearance, and biblical passages are recited which express the hope of the Jewish people to be delivered from oppression.[7] This custom has in the course of time given rise to many legends. They tell of Elijah's appearance, mostly in the guise of a venerable old man who sits down with the family at table, offers wise counsel or raises hopes for a happy future.

Elijah in Jewish Folklore

Elijah's personality plays an important part not only in the biblical record of historic events, in the Aggadah, in mysticism and in Ḥasidism, but also in Jewish folklore, and in fact to a particularly large extent. Traditional stories, anecdotes, poems and songs about Elijah exist in almost illimitable abundance, of any period and in various languages, originating in Jewish communities all over the world. Special localities, mostly synagogues and caves, predominantly in the land of Israel and the whole of the Near East, have been dedicated to Elijah. Illustrations of his biblical activities are included in prayer-books and especially in the Passover night liturgy (see pp. 134–5).

It is apparent that none of the biblical or post-biblical personalities, not even the patriarchs, Moses or David, occupy as prominent a place in folk literature as Elijah. He is not only the psychopomp of the Aggadists and the Kabbalists and the symbol of the psychic maturation factor in Ḥasidism, but also the explicit darling of the people.

The encounter with Elijah means to the leading Jewish personalities religious guidance, a spiritual confrontation, a drawing close to the Divine, the possibility of the salvation of the individual and the expectation of the redemption of the collective. To the collective itself Elijah became, through the influence of motifs in Talmudic-Aggadic literature and in the Midrashim, above all the heaven-sent helper, in the immediate psychic and material troubles of the individual, and also the guardian and rescuer of Jewish communities in the Diaspora.

Countless folk stories describe Elijah's sudden unexpected help. He cures serious illnesses, saves lives in danger, defends people in courts of law, frees those unjustly convicted, makes peace between adversaries, brings about happy marriages, blesses the barren, supports and comforts the poor, rewards good deeds, advises and instructs.

He appears mostly as a kind, wise old man, but also often in disguise, for instance as a beggar or a simple peasant, according to the occasion. Frequently he performs miracles. Time and space are at his command, so that his help is always available and never too late.* He helps especially the simple, the pious and the humble, those who suffer and those who are oppressed. He procures justice for them and punishes the unjust and presumptuous, even if these are learned or distinguished personalities. It is characteristic of Elijah's activity that both the help which he provides, and also the type and severity of the punishment imposed by him, are intended to bring home to the one concerned his error or his failing in order to help him attain religious and moral improvement and to educate himself.

Out of the extreme abundance of the Elijah stories a few may be taken to serve as characteristic examples.

R. Judah ha-Nasi betrothed his daughter to a pious youth, eager to learn and highly gifted, who stipulated that he should spend a few years before his marriage studying at a famous, far distant *yeshivah* (talmudic high school). As he did not return at the agreed time, the father wanted to marry the bride, against her will, to someone else. On his journey home to the wedding, the youth had lost his way in a forest and, moreover, the Sabbath was drawing close. He saw in despair that it was impossible for him to return to his bride at the agreed time. Suddenly, he was standing in front of a palace, where an old man was sitting in a magnificent room studying the Torah. The old man provided him with

---

* In this sense only, as he also appears in the Bible and the Aggadah, Elijah may be called 'an eternal wanderer'. He can certainly not be identified with the legendary Ahasver who is condemned to wander eternally to atone for his sins; the Ahasver legend seems to be of Christian origin[1]

princely hospitality for the Sabbath, let him attend a festive divine service, then revealed himself as Elijah, showed him the way and enabled him, by means of miracles, to arrive just in time for the wedding.[2]

Another example: Three brothers told Elijah their dearest wishes. The eldest wished for wealth, the middle one for scholarship, and the third for a pious and beautiful wife. Elijah fulfilled all their wishes. After a few years, he visited them again, without revealing his identity. The eldest brother was not prepared to offer hospitality to the stranger in plain, poor clothing. The middle one had been made presumptuous by his immense learning. The youngest and his wife, however, whose existence was poor and simple, received him warmly and generously. Elijah took from the eldest his wealth, from the middle one his scholarship, and bestowed both on the youngest, who was now happy, learned and rich.[3]

And a further example. A pious, learned, rich and charitable man with a happy family life believed that he owed his happiness entirely to his own good qualities and deeds. One day, after losing his way in the desert, he was about to die of thirst, when Elijah appeared to him as an Arab and gave him a pitcher of water on condition that he would transfer to him in exchange half of his 'merits'. The man agreed to this, but drank too much and consequently became very ill. Elijah appeared to him for a second time, in the guise of a physician, and cured him in exchange for the transfer of the other half of his 'merits'. The man grew well, returned home, but grieved and complained about the fact that he had forfeited everything to which his good deeds had entitled him. Then Elijah appeared to him for the third time, revealed himself to him and explained that he had bought his 'merits' from him in order to teach him that what is decisive for man's fate are not good deeds alone, but divine providence and mercy.[4]

That Elijah occasionally enters the open door on the Passover night as an unknown old man and sits down at the family table has already been mentioned (see p. 135). It is also recorded that he has at times appeared on the Day of Atonement in the synagogues of Jerusalem and Safed in order to make up the number of ten worshippers required for public prayers.[5]

While the above-cited and numerous other Elijah tales are usually moulded according to the Aggadic view of Elijah, there is one interesting less known story which is in accordance with the Ḥasidic view of the integrated Elijah-factor. A pious and wealthy Jew asked his rabbi: 'For about forty years I have opened the door for Elijah every *Seder* night waiting for him to come, but he never does. What is the reason?' The rabbi answered: 'In your neighbourhood there lives a very poor family with many children. Call on the man and propose to him that you and your family celebrate the next Passover in his house, and for this purpose provide him and his whole family with everything necessary for the eight Passover days. Then on the *Seder* night Elijah will certainly come.' The man did as the rabbi told him, but after Passover he came to the rabbi and claimed that again he had waited in vain to see Elijah. The rabbi answered: 'I know very well that Elijah came on the *Seder* night to the house of your poor neighbour. But of course you could not see him.' And the rabbi held a mirror before the face of the man and said: 'Look, this was Elijah's face that night.'[6]

These, as most of the other Elijah stories, reveal that the aim of his activity was not merely to balance social injustice or concerned with 'reward and punishment', but also it was almost always to show a Jew the way to the divine and with it also to the truly humane.

And just as the rescue of Persian Jewry related in the biblical book of Esther is ascribed by the Aggadists to Elijah's secret activity, so folk literature contains stories about Elijah's successful intervention to rescue Jewish communities: for instance from pogroms in Bagdad in the tenth century and in Istanbul at the beginning of the sixteenth century,[7] and also at times of blood libel accusations, as in the Yemen at the time of Al-Mansur and in Cracow in the reign of King Casimir IV.[8]

The great veneration felt by the Jewish people for Elijah also found expression in the fact that the synagogues of many communities carry his name, especially if Elijah was reputed to have appeared in them. Furthermore, in the communities of the Near East, synagogues often installed special Elijah rooms, or designated near-by natural caves as 'Elijah's caves'. Places thus dedicated to the trusted, kind helper of the people were visited not only by the local population but also by many pilgrims in the expectation of encountering Elijah there and being accorded his comfort, advice and help. And it may be assumed that many individuals, through religious contemplation and numinous experiences, were indeed comforted and helped.

Particular fame accrued to the Elijah caves in Cairo, in Alexandria, in the vicinity of Jerusalem, near Damascus, Aleppo and Hamath in Syria, and also near Horeb. The cave near Horeb was celebrated through its association with Elijah's overnight stay there and the revelation granted to him; the cave near Damascus through the connection with Elijah's journey there. In Kurdistan, too, several rooms are dedicated to Elijah.

Of religious and historical interest is the Elijah cave on the slopes of the Carmel range, where countless pilgrims have for centuries said their prayers. Its walls bear inscriptions in Hebrew, Arabic and Greek, and many people in need recite psalms there and pray for help. Sick people occasionally spend a night in this cave so as to be cured by Elijah. It is said that the psychically sick especially may expect to be cured there through Elijah's influence.[9]

Thus the contents and variety of folklore convey that through the encounter with Elijah, the simple man of the people is— *mutatis mutandis*—like the Jewish spiritual leaders of all times, made aware of human dependence on the Divine, a knowledge which may lead to man's transformation and a change in his personal fate.[10]

CHAPTER IX

The Elijah-Figure in Christianity

The expectation had been alive in the Jewish people since Malachi's prophecy, that the prophet Elijah would appear before 'the coming of the great and terrible day of the Lord', turn the hearts of the fathers and the sons to God and save Israel from destruction. The redeeming task was also assigned to Elijah later in the sayings of Ben Sira; finally the Jews had the more and more strongly developed conviction that Elijah was the precursor and prophet of the redeemer, of the anointed (Messiah) of the house of David. This decisive role, therefore, which Elijah plays in the Jewish conception of the redemption also found expression in the New Testament.

It is John the Baptist who represents the Elijah-figure in the gospels. According to the gospel of Luke (1: 5–17), the angel Gabriel prophesied to the priest Zacharias that his wife would bear a son who was to be called John (Johanan, i.e. 'God has favoured'):

> he shall be great in the sight of the Lord, and shall drink neither wine nor strong drink; and he shall be filled with the Holy Ghost, even from his mother's womb. And many of the children of Israel shall he turn to the Lord their God. And he shall go before him in the spirit and power of Elias, to turn the hearts of the fathers to the children, and the disobedient to the wisdom of the just; to make ready a people prepared for the Lord.

After the birth of the child, Zacharias prophesies in his thanksgiving the re-establishment of the royal house of David and continues (1: 67–79): 'And thou, child, shalt be called the prophet of the Highest: for thou shalt go before the face of the Lord to prepare his ways; to give knowledge of salvation unto his people by the remission of their sins'.

The gospel of Mark begins with the biblical quotations (1: 2–6): 'Behold, I send my messenger before thy face, which shall prepare thy way before thee', and 'The voice of one crying in the wilderness, Prepare ye the way of the Lord, make his paths straight.'[1]

The four gospels agree in reporting that John the Baptist called in the desert for repentance, a return to God and baptism in the Jordan. Many answered his call, and Jesus, too, let himself be baptised by John (Matt. 3: 1–17; Mark 1: 4–11; Luke 3: 1–22; John 1: 25–34). According to Matthew (3: 4) and Mark (1: 6), John was clothed in a 'raiment of camel's hair, and a leathern girdle about his loins' which corresponds with Elijah's clothing as mentioned in II Kings 1: 8.[2] According to the gospel of John (1: 34), he testified after baptising Jesus that this was 'the Son of God'.

John himself, questioned by priests and Levites from Jerusalem about who he was, answered: 'I am not the Christ.' And to the question if he was Elijah or the prophet,[3] he answered 'No'. He continued: 'I am the voice of one crying in the wilderness, Make straight the way of the Lord' (John 1: 19–23).

Jesus, on the other hand, proclaimed to a crowd of people that John was 'more than a prophet. For this is he, of whom it is written, Behold, I send my messenger before thy face, which shall prepare thy way before thee . . . For all the prophets and the law prophesied until John. And if ye will receive it, this is Elias, which was for to come. He that hath ears to hear, let him hear' (Matt. 11: 7–15; Luke 7: 26–8).

And after the transfiguration of Jesus, his disciples ask him: 'Why say the scribes that Elias must first come?' Jesus answers: 'Elias verily cometh first, and restoreth all things . . . But I say unto you, That Elias is indeed come, and they have done unto him whatsoever they listed' (Mark 9: 12–13).

In the parallel passage in the gospel of Matthew (17: 12–13),

Jesus adds: 'That Elias is come already, and they knew him not'; 'Then the disciples understood that he spake unto them of John the Baptist.'

The synoptic gospels also record that Jesus himself was at first regarded by some as Elijah, by others as the resurrected John or one of the earlier prophets. This is mentioned when Herod asks his entourage who Jesus is (Mark 6: 14–15; Luke 9: 7–8), and again when Jesus himself asks his disciples who people think he is. The disciples themselves, however, according to Peter's declaration, regarded him as the Messiah, and he confirmed this (Matt. 16: 14; Mark 8: 28; Luke 9: 18–21).

At the transfiguration of Jesus in the presence of three chosen disciples on a mountain—according to Christian tradition Mount Tabor—there appear to them, according to the synoptic gospels, first Moses and Elijah who talk with Jesus, according to Luke, about 'his decease which he should accomplish at Jerusalem.' Then a voice out of the clouds proclaims: 'This is my beloved Son: hear him' (Matt. 17: 1–6; Mark 9: 2–8; Luke 9: 28–36). As they are coming down from the mountain, the disciples ask their master whether and when the earthly appearance of Elijah is to be expected, and receive the answer mentioned above—that he has already appeared.

The presentation of John the Baptist as the returned Elijah, or as representing the Elijah-figure, shows that Elijah's return as precursor and attendant of the Messiah was regarded as self evident by scholars and by the Jewish people at that time. This opinion is confirmed in a statement by Justin Martyr, who ascribes to Trypho—representing the Jews who do not regard Jesus as the Messiah—the words: 'For all of us, Jews, expect that the Christ will be a man born of men, and that Elijah [will come] to anoint him. If that one appears to be the Christ, one must know with certainty that he is a man born of men. Yet, since Elijah has not come, I believe that he is not the Christ'.[4]

In any case, in the records of the gospels the essential tasks expected of Elijah by traditional Judaism are performed by John. Most importantly, he calls for repentance and for a return to God, and he prophesies the appearance of one who will come after him, surpass him and bring salvation. The baptism of the penitents, here undertaken by John, had in principle already been indicated —as a symbol of psychic purification and a change of the human heart within the framework of the events of the redemption—by Jeremiah (17: 3) and expressly prophesied by Ezekiel (36: 25). John's asceticism and his stay in the desert and by the Jordan,[5] from the banks of which Elijah ascended, also recall plainly the biblical record of Elijah. The preparation for the redemption in the seclusion of the Judean desert, as practised by the Essenes and the members of the Qumran sect, may be traced back not only to Isaiah (40: 3): 'Hark! one calleth: "Clear ye in the wilderness the way of the Lord" ', but also to the example of Elijah, who in the solitude of the desert was shown the way to the mountain of the revelation.

Just as John undertakes, as far as the people are concerned, the preparation for the redemption which was expected of Elijah on his return to earth, so at the transfiguration of Jesus there appears to him and his disciples the heavenly Elijah, together with Moses. Both the prophets Moses and Elijah were once accorded on the mountain (Horeb) their individual, personality-transcending revelation of God. Moses as the lawgiver and first redeemer of Israel, Elijah as the prophet of the final redemption, are now through their appearance as it were to attest that it is in accordance with Jewish tradition that Jesus was called 'the Son of God'. Malachi, in his last words to Israel (3: 22–3), also referred both to the Law of Moses and to Elijah's return before the 'day of the Lord'. And Jesus himself says, according to Matthew (11: 13): 'all the prophets and the law prophesied until John.'

The gospels of Matthew (27: 46–9) and Mark (15: 34–6) further record that the words of the psalm cited by the crucified Jesus in the hour of his death: 'Eli, Eli, lama sabachtani?' ('My God, my God, why hast thou forsaken me?') were misunderstood by some of those present to mean that Jesus had appealed to the prophet Elijah for help: some exclaimed: 'let us see whether Elias will come to save him.'

From the biblical record of Elijah, the gospel of Luke (4: 24–6) mentions that God sent him at the time of the famine to the pagan widow in Sarepta, for 'no prophet is accepted in his own country.' In the Epistle of Paul to the Romans (11: 2–5), as God once answered Elijah's complaint that he alone was left by saying that a remnant of 7,000 faithful would remain, thus now, too, a remnant has been preserved through God's grace. And the Epistle of James emphasises that Elijah was a human being like other human beings, but that because of his piety his prayers for the drought and later for the rain were answered (Jas. 5: 17–18).

The decisive role attributed to the prophet Elijah in the New Testament appears self evident, as Jesus himself was a Jew and lived among the Jewish people in their own country. But also in subsequent centuries, after Christianity had separated from Judaism and, in spite of widespread persecution by the pagan world, extended and consolidated its hold in the East and in the West, Elijah continued to occupy a prominent, perhaps even the principal, place among all the Old Testament figures.

The early Christian Fathers (first to fifth centuries) regarded Elijah as the greatest and most important of all the prophets: the model of a life of simplicity and moderation close to God which Christians ought to imitate.[6] 'He who chooses monasticism should take as model and patron the great Elijah and look at his mode of life as into a mirror, that he may know what he ought to do.'[7] St Ambrose wrote a detailed treatise, 'Elijah and the Fasting'.[8] On the other hand, the opponents of celibacy and asceticism as St Augustine and others also relied for their arguments on Elijah, who had no misgivings about lodging with the widow in Sarepta, and was fed by the ravens with meat by the Cherith.[9]

The early Fathers regarded Elijah as *'noster princeps'*.[10] Tertullian calls Moses *'informator populi'*, Elijah *'reformator populi'*.[11] For them he was the representative and mediator of the divine spirit, the conqueror of ungodliness and of death.[12] Elijah's ascent, according to general opinion, is the reward for his merits. Among these, some emphasise especially his purity and chastity,[13] others his righteous zeal and the killing of the priests of Baal.[14] 'As Elijah directed all his doing and thinking towards God, he was borne up to heaven in a fiery chariot and remains there until the end of days.'[15]

Elijah's miracles are described exhaustively in patristic literature and are mostly regarded as allegorical references to Christian symbols: e.g. the oil and flour bestowed by Elijah on the widow are seen as the sacraments;[16] her firewood as the wood of the cross;[17] the sacrifice on Mount Carmel as a revival of the divine spirit;[18] the water of the Jordan divided by the prophet as baptismal water.[19] The boy's resurrection was considered to be a reference to the corresponding miracles performed by Jesus.[20] Elijah's ascent alludes to that of Jesus, but it is noted that Elijah was carried up from earth (*rapitur*), while Jesus in his divine character was returning when he entered heaven (*regreditur*).[21]

Exhaustive consideration was given by the early Fathers to Elijah's relation to John the Baptist. Saint Ambrose, Origen and St Augustine interpret the wording of the annunciation of John's birth as meaning that he was not '*Elijah redivivus*': that not Elijah's soul but merely his spirit had passed into the newborn child— rather as Moses' prophetic vocation had been passed on to Joshua. Origen expressly rejects the assumption of the transmigration of Elijah's soul. 'John was Elijah in as much as he was like him, but both maintained their individuality.'[22]

In accordance with this, the dominant patristic opinion is that John the Baptist was Jesus' herald at his first appearance on earth, but that before his final return, on the Day of Judgment, Elijah himself will appear. He will proclaim the return of Jesus, perform miracles and bring about mankind's repentance.[23] Tertullian therefore calls Elijah the 'man at the end of days',[24] and emphasises that he will appear in his own body.

In this view, the two prophetic witnesses mentioned in the Book of Revelation (11: 3) are regarded by some of the early fathers and by many later exegetes as Moses and Elijah. Like Elijah, they destroy the enemy by fire, command the rain not to fall and finally ascend to heaven. Like Moses, they change water into blood.[25]

Prevalent in patristic literature, however, is the assumption that these witnesses are Enoch and Elijah.[26] Thus they also appear in later apocalyptic writings, especially in the Coptic Elijah

Apocalypse, as opponents of the Antichrist. They kill him, and are then themselves killed but resurrected.[27]

The veneration of Elijah as the most important prophet and precursor of the Messiah has also found expression in Christian ritual. In the early Christian liturgy, the description of Elijah's ascent was read from the Bible on Ascension Day. At the consecration of water, Elijah's sacrifice and prayer on Mount Carmel for rain was recited, and in prayers for the dying and the dead he was mentioned as God's life-saving messenger. The Oriental (Syrian) Church introduced as 'Elijah's Fast' a forty-day period of fasting beginning on the Sunday after Whitsun. 20 July was celebrated as 'the Day of Elijah the holy'.[28]

Numerous churches were dedicated to St Elijah and bore his name; in the Oriental Church allegedly as early as the second century, in the Byzantine Church first in the fifth century at the Golden Horn, in the special rites of the Russian Church in the ninth century in Kiev.

Elijah maintained his special place also in the later Christendom of the early middle ages. The theologians point to him and his disciples as the models for the monastic orders. They venerated him above all as a fighter against ungodliness and therefore regarded him also as a patron of the Inquistition. In the last few decades of modern times he has become the protector of pilots.

In popular belief Elijah remained the miracle-worker and helper, guardian against pestilence and deliverer from serious illnesses. In the Near East he was also regarded as the master of rain, storm and thunder, and thus drove out the remnants of the pagan cult of Helios. On the Day of Elijah bonfires were kindled in his honour on the hilltops, and popular celebrations were held.[29]

In the Roman Church, the general official cult of Elijah subsided to become almost exclusively concentrated on Mount Carmel in the Holy Land. Carmel, regarded for centuries in pre-Jewish Canaan as the dwelling-place of the highest storm- and weather-God, later dedicated to the syncretic cult of Baal-Helios, finally the site of God's judgment invoked by Elijah and since

147

then closely connected with his name, became also a Christian site of worship. According to a legend which presumably arose in the early middle ages, the rain-cloud which rose up from the sea after Elijah's prayer on Mount Carmel revealed the mystery of Mary, and it is said that Elijah himself together with his pupils erected a chapel dedicated to the worship of Mary.[30]

Psychologically, the connection established in these legends between Elijah and the cult of Mary can probably be explained by saying that the rain appearing after years of severe drought is to be regarded as a symbol of the Great Mother, the provider of nourishment, the female aspect of God.

As anachronistic as the legend of Mary but more easily understandable is the legendary tradition that the first Christian monastic order developed out of the community of Elijah's disciples and their successors. The first Christian monks had chosen the presumed former meeting-places of the prophet's disciples, the fertile valleys and the caves of Mount Carmel, for their secluded existence.

Historically it seems certain that on one of the highest mountain tops called Muḥraka ('place of sacrifices')—on which Elijah presumably built his altar—and also on the promontory of Mount Carmel, the so-called cape—on which the Baal-Helios cult flourished of old—there existed, as early as the fourth or fifth century, chapels built by the Greek Orthodox Church which were dedicated both to the prophet Elijah and to Mary. These chapels were destroyed later, probably during the Crusades. In their place the Carmelite order, established in the thirteenth century and belonging to the Roman Church, under the protection of St Therese built in the fifteenth century churches, monasteries and convents in which the Elijah tradition in the sense of his spiritual succession was revived. The Carmelite monks and nuns see in the 'prophet and father Elijah' a model of simplicity, of asceticism and of religious devotion and accordingly lead a life remote from the world.

Even today, on the Day of Elijah, a special mass is read in his name in the basilica of St Elias (where he is said to have stayed in the crypt), which is part of the Stella Mare complex on Mount

Carmel. Thousands of the faithful of the various Christian Churches of the Near East assemble there annually for the divine service and the nocturnal feast which follows it.[31]

Apart from this still observed annual Elijah ritual, Elijah's personality does not play an important part in the official Christianity of the last few centuries. The belief in the parousia—the doctrine that at the end of days the Messiah will return in order to establish the kingdom of God, and will be preceded by Elijah as his precursor—disappeared almost completely after about the the beginning of the middle ages, and accordingly has lost most of its significance in Catholic and Protestant theology.*

However, Elijah still remains more than a model of the ascetic life to Carmelite monks. Beyond this, many clergymen, impressed by his religious personality, bring him alive to their congregations in their sermons. Many others have edited publications about Elijah, thus reaching a large circle of interested readers. Some of these are simple renderings of the biblical records of Elijah in modern idiom, some are more or less historically or psychologically based or symbolic interpretations—occasionally taking Aggadic material into consideration. Further, there are comparisons of Elijah or John the Baptist with other personalities, especially Moses and Jesus, and religious-ethical essays in relation to contemporary events.

Moreover, a number of Christian theologians and scholars have concerned themselves with the biblical and also with the Aggadic Elijah, partly in connection with their general researches into Judaism and Christianity,[32] partly within the more specific framework of the subject of the Messiah,[33] or in special monographs on Elijah and John the Baptist.[34] Furthermore, the series 'Études carmélitaines' includes a two-volume work, Élie le prophète, which contains a number of articles dealing with Elijah's role in Judaism, Christianity and Islam, as well as exhaustive discussions of the

---

* For the disappearance of the parousia, see M. Werner, The Formation of Christian Dogma, pp. 40–55, 60, 70, 142. It is officially mentioned today only in this mass read on Mount Carmel. The idea of the parousia has been revived by some recent theologians, and especially by J. Moltmann, who interestingly enough intimates its psychological integration (Theologie der Hoffnung, pp. 184 ff., 204–9)

development of the Christian cult on Mount Carmel and an iconography of representations of Elijah in art.

Many of these scholarly works, besides including the usual analysis of the text, a consideration of the archaeological finds and religious historical comparisons, pay ever-increasing attention to the actuality of the religious content and its significance. Thus H. H. Rowley writes:[35]

> Yet few crises have been more significant for history than that in which Elijah figured, and in the story of the Transfiguration he rightly stands beside Moses. Without Moses, the religion of Judaism as figured in the Old Testament would never have been born. Without Elijah, it would have died. The religion from which Judaism, Christianity and Islam all in various ways stemmed would have succumbed to the religion of Tyre. But it is safe to say that from the religion of Melkart mankind would never have derived that spiritual influence which came from Moses and Elijah and others who followed in their train.

Rudolf Steiner's anthroposophic study of Elijah is also interesting; he tries to see the events described in the Bible from the symbolic and psychological point of view:[36]

> They show the maturing of Elijah, his transformation and the renewed vitality of his ego ... The spirit was incarnate in him, and through him affected mankind ...

> In the most eminent sense it becomes apparent, when we consider the personality of the prophet Elijah and his time, that what constitutes the impulses and the causes in human affairs is by no means exhaustively expressed by what manifests itself and by what finds expression in historic events. In fact, the most important processes in human affairs are those which take place within the souls of men and which from within these souls affect the external world, influence other people and continue to be effective ...

> Thus we can see that the prophet Elijah represents an ascent, an elaboration by mankind of the conception of God to a higher degree, so that we must ascribe to him an important, for mankind epoch-making achievement, if we look at him in the right light. A further examination would reveal that a light is thrown here on to what happened and also on to what was later to lead to the founding of Christendom.

Rudolf Meyer, also theosophically inclined, remarks: 'Elijah is not "guided" by his human personality but by that essence which cannot become part of the personification; by that which surrounds his life.'[37] A well-known Protestant theologian and scholar, M. H. Beek, adopts a similar attitude: 'The Bible is always concerned with profound verities, of greater significance than historic events. I look thus also at the marvellous story of Elijah, who was borne up by God's fiery chariot and horses, because he was too great for death.'[38]

The great veneration felt for Elijah has found expression, however, not only in an abundant literature concerning his personality and his activity but also quite widely in the visual arts. While the main depictions of him in Jewish art are the famous frescoes in the Dura-Europos synagogue showing scenes from the Bible,[39] many examples are to be found in Christian art in the cultures of many countries, especially those of Catholic origin, from the second century onwards. Apart from representations of his features, the principal themes are: Elijah's being fed by ravens, his encounter with the widow, the resurrection of her son, the sacrifice on Mount Carmel, his stay in the desert, the parting of the Jordan and his ascent into heaven. There are murals and reliefs on the walls of catacombs and sarcophagi, and icons, mosaics and paintings in churches, monasteries and convents, on altars, walls, doors, windows and floors; perhaps the most famous example are Giotto's frescoes in the Arena Chapel at Padua. Many more modern works are in museums, for example paintings by Lorenzo Lotto and Corregio, drawings by Rubens and Rembrandt and a woodcut by Hans Holbein.[40]

The passages I have quoted from Christian scholars of our time show that they have recognised Elijah's eternal significance largely in the spirit of the Aggadists, the Kabbalists and even of the Ḥasidic doctrine of the encounter with the Divine through Elijah's mediation. Likewise, the fascination exerted throughout Christian times by the numinous Elijah-personality on many artists has been conveyed to posterity through their works.

CHAPTER X

Elijah in Islam

In the Koran, Elijah (usually called Ilyas or Idris) is at first mentioned briefly, together with Zechariah, John and Jesus: 'and all these We exalted above Our creatures'.[1] A more detailed account of him is given in a later sura (chapter): 'We also sent forth Elias, who said to his people: "Have you no fear of Allah? Would you invoke Baal and forsake the Most Gracious Creator? Allah is your Lord and the Lord of your forefathers." But they denied him, and thus incurred Our punishment, except Allah's true servants. We bestowed on him the praise of later generations: "Peace on Elias!" Thus We reward the righteous. He was one of Our believing servants.'[2]

The traditional commentators on the Koran, especially al-Tabari and al-Thalibi, relate to these verses several versions of the biblical Elijah stories, some with elaborations and additions, some inexactly and incompletely, but in essentials keeping to the original biblical source. They conclude with Elijah's ascent and mention also his transfiguration, emphasised in Jewish Aggadic literature, into a partly divine, partly human being who is capable of appearing on earth.[3]

Sura 18 includes a legend in which there appears a favoured wise servant of God who is not called Elijah in the text but is identified with him in the whole Islamic tradition. The Koran account says:[4]

> Moses said to his servant: 'I will journey on until I reach the land where the two seas meet, though I may march for ages.' But

when they at last came to the land where the two seas met, they forgot their fish, which made its way into the water, swimming at will. And when they had journeyed farther on, Moses said to his servant: 'Bring us some food; we are worn out with travelling.' 'Know,' replied the other, 'that I forgot the fish when we were resting on the rock. Thanks to Satan, I forgot to mention this. The fish made its way into the sea in a miraculous fashion.' 'This is what we have been seeking,' said Moses. They went back the way they came and found one of Our servants to whom We had vouchsafed Our mercy and whom We had endowed with knowledge of Our own. Moses said to him: 'May I follow you so that you may guide me by that which you have been taught?' 'You will not bear with me,' replied the other. 'For how can you bear with that which is beyond your knowledge?' Moses said: 'If Allah wills, you shall find me patient: I shall not in anything disobey you.' He said: 'If you are bent on following me, you must ask no question about anything till I myself speak to you concerning it.'

The next verses relate that this servant [of Mohammed] commits on the journey with Moses several extremely cruel and seemingly pointless acts, so that Moses cannot refrain from asking reproachful questions about them. The guide thereupon explains to him the true content of the events he has just seen, and says, before leaving him: 'That is the meaning of what you could not bear to watch with patience.'

The unnamed servant of Mohammed in this Koran story is regarded as al-Khadir ('the Verdant One') by the earliest canonists Buchari and Sigistani (c. 850), Tabari and Kastellani (c. 900) as well as by all later commentators on the Koran.[5] His family tree is traced back to Noah or Cain, and he is almost unanimously identified with the biblical Elijah. He is the great sage and prophet favoured by God, and as such plays a prominent part in the entire literature of Islam—in the theologically-philosophically orientated as well as in the mystic, legendary and folk writings.

The commentators relate, as antecedent to Moses' encounter with al-Khadir, that Moses once answered 'No' to the question put to him by his people, whether there existed on earth any man wiser than he. Thereupon God had made known to him that he was surpassed in wisdom by God's devout servant al-Khadir, who dwelt 'at the junction of the waters'. He should look for him there and take with him a dried fish as food for the journey and to show him the way. Wherever the fish was revived by contact with water and swam away, there would be the source of life by which he would find al-Khadir.

Further, the commentators relate that after the fish swam away the water was blocked in this place by a rock, and an island was formed there, where al-Khadir sits on a white hide, representing allegorically the bare surface of the earth on which, through contact with his body—according to another version, through his prayer—vegetation sprouts and everything becomes green. Here is the source of life and whoever drinks from it acquires eternal life. Here Moses' encounter with al-Khadir took place.

The site of the meeting of the two seas is usually defined geographically by the commentators as the junction of the eastern and western seas, the Straits of Suez; and is by some also interpreted allegorically as Moses' encounter with al-Khadir, the 'two seas of wisdom'. Moses represents the theological, and al-Khadir the esoterically orientated, mystic wisdom.[6]

While the commentators of the Koran essentially enlarge and elaborate the Moses/al-Khadir legend of sura 18, regarding al-Khadir as the prophet and sage, he is described and venerated as Weli (saint) and mystagogue by the Sufi, the Islamic mystics (Ibn al-Arabi, c. 600, al-Damari, c. 800, Ibn Hagar, c. 850 (years AH), and others)—some regard him as an angel in human shape.[7]

The story of al-Khadir's childhood is described in Sufi literature in the manner of the typical heroic myth: the child of a royal couple, he is born in a cave, suckled by a ewe and later found and raised by a shepherd. It then so happens that as a young man he becomes private secretary at the court of the king, his father. In view of the outstanding abilities of the young man, the king finds out his true origins and appoints his son co-regent. But al-Khadir runs away and wanders about the world until he finds the source of life.[8]

The drinking from the source of life as well as the reviving of the fish signifies in Islamic mysticism the spiritual awakening of the new Adam from the old: 'The members and parts of the human body are in fear and trembling, until the heart is awakened to the real life through the mystic pronunciation of and appeal to the divine name; from the heart there then flows into all parts of the body the sense of security and peace.' Al-Khadir drinks from the source of life and thus acquires eternal life until the end of days.[9] He sits on a throne consisting of light, between the upper and the lower seas.[10] According to some Islamic mystics, he also appears on earth at the time of the apocalypse, is killed by the Antichrist but revived by God.[11]

Generally, al-Khadir is identified by the mystics with the Elijah-figure of Jewish tradition and, like him, is not limited in time and place. Just as he was alive at the time of Moses—according to some authors even at the time of Abraham and subsequently at that of Isaiah—he was also alive at the time of Mohammed; he was present at his funeral and comforted the people over his death.[12] It is recorded that he appeared as Elijah himself to Mohammed on one of his campaigns, as a tall old man with a shining face and wearing glowing white robes. Sharing a meal at a table giving off a green light, bearing an abundance of vegetables, the two prophets had talked to each other. Finally, Elijah had returned to heaven on the wings of angels or on a cloud.[13] The caliphs Omar and Ali had also met al-Khadir, and been taught particularly efficacious prayers by him.[14]

In the same spirit, al-Khadir continues to be represented in Islamic literature as Allah's ambassador. It is his task to initiate and to spread the worship of the true God. Al-Khadir usually dwells, concealed from profane gaze, in holy places, especially in the mosques of Mecca, Medina, Jerusalem and Syria. He does allow himself to be found by pious men striving towards God, listens to their questions and gives them religious instruction. Although he generally appears in the guise of an old man, occasionally he seems to be mature, or a young man. He frequently appears to mystics in visions. The esoteric masterpiece 'Saravis' (c. 1500) is said to have been directly inspired by him.[15]

In the folk literature of Islam, al-Khadir has been wandering about the earth for centuries. He is the counsellor of the pious, teacher of the ignorant, comforter of the unfortunate. He feeds the hungry, protects the persecuted, heals the sick and shows the way to those who are lost.

In most Islamic countries, especially in Iraq, Syria and Egypt, there are mosques and holy places dedicated to al-Khadir where on special days of the year a service in his honour is held and sura 18 is recited. The unshakeable trust in al-Khadir is maintained to the present day by the ordinary man and finds expression in various popular customs intended to enlist his help.[16]

While the Islamic literature of the middle ages in general either points out or assumes that al-Khadir is identical with Elijah, some Koran commentators as well as some mystics mention traditions according to which the figures of the two prophets are not completely identical: they maintain that al-Khadir was an Arab or a Persian, Elijah an Israelite. Both had drunk from the source of eternal life.[17] As one text says: 'Four prophets are alive eternally, two in heaven, Jesus and Idris [Enoch], two on earth, al-Khadir and Elijah, as Lords of water and land.'[18] Mohammed had appointed Elijah as Lord of the land and the desert, al-Khadir as Lord of the sea.[19] The two are such close friends that at times they are called twin brothers on account of their similar activity and because they frequently appear together. They often meet at the border between the world of man and the realm of Gog and Magog.[20] On the Day of Arafa, the great festival of sacrifice, they meet annually in Mecca—according to another version in the month of Ramadan in Jerusalem—where they share a meal at the end of the fast.[21]

The name 'al-Khadir' is regarded in Islamic literature as a surname; the hero's real name is said to have been Balya ben Malkan or, according to another reading, Ilya (Elijah) ben Malkan.[22] Maracci, one of the first Christian scholars of the Mohammedan tradition, remarks: 'Alchedrus [al-Khadir] quem fabulantur Moslemi eundem fuisse, ac Phinehas filium Eleaziri, filii Aaron, cuius anima per metempsychosin emigravit primo in Eliam, deinde ex Elia in S. Gregorium, quem propterea Mahumetani omnes summo honore prosequentur'.*[23]

---

* 'Al Khadir, about whom the Moslems say that he is exactly the same as Phinehas, son of Eleazar who was son of Aaron whose soul through metem-

According to some Arabic authors, 'al-Khadir' was originally the name of an immortal green sea-demon of pre-Islamic Arabian mythology, regarded as the patron of sailors.[24] Later his name was transferred to the immortal Islamic prophet and guardian of the pious who also ruled the seas. His name, 'the Verdant One', meant not only 'eternally living' but also 'animating the world'. According to Omara, as quoted by Friedländer, al-Khadir had been told by Allah at the source of life: 'You are al-Khadir ['the Verdant one'] and wherever you set foot on earth it will become green ... You will become green when you are thus called. Allah gave you immortality'.[25] Wensinck draws attention[26] to the remarkable parallel between this saying and the words of the prophet Zechariah (6: 12): 'Behold, a man [will come] whose name is the Shoot, and who shall shoot up out of his place, and build the temple of the Lord'. Thus the Islamic servant of God is, like the Jewish redeemer, symbolised by newly flourishing life. And Omara's words, which mean that 'the Verdant One' will be verdant only when so recognised by man, correspond to the Jewish attitude that the possibility of redemption must actually become a reality in man.

Islamic literature unequivocally shows that the identification of al-Khadir with Elijah—they are at times called twin brothers—is derived in the first instance from the Koran story of Moses' encounter with the pious servant of Allah. Now it is apparent that the second part of this story, the experiences on the journey Moses took with the servant of God,[27] resembles in almost every detail the Jewish Aggadah about the journey of R. Joshua ben Levi with his friend the prophet Elijah (see p. 55). And here as there it is shown that even the personality of a religious leader who is close to God is not capable of understanding completely the divine conduct of world events. This can be done only by one who has transcended his human boundaries and become the messenger and mouthpiece of God.

------

psychosis first passed to Elijah and then from Elijah entered into Saint Gregory, and the Moslems therefore accord him the greatest honour'. The name 'Gregory' ought obviously to be corrected to Saint George, who, as the dragon-killer, is also a prototype of the hero-archetype

That this second part of the Koran story is identical with the rabbinic Aggadah has been pointed out by I. Goldziher,[28] M. Lidzbarski,[29] K. Vollers,[30] I. Friedländer,[31] and A. J. Wensinck.[32] Beyond this, they have compared this [the search for the junction of the seas, the miracle of the fish, the source of life and the figure of the servant of God] to themes from the Epic of Gilgamesh, the Greek legend of Glaucus and the so-called Roman d'Alexandre.[33] They examined the motifs, their transformations and migrations and the change of the hero's name to which these lead. Although the results of their researches differ in details, they are in complete agreement in maintaining that the Islamic al-Khadir corresponds in every respect to the Jewish Elijah. Thus for instance Vollers says:[34]

> If we examine the Jewish [rabbinic] tradition about the biblical Elijah, we notice with surprise that almost all the statements made about the Elijah of the Hagadah [Aggadah] are those familiar to us in the Islamic tradition from Chidher [al-Khadir]. As Elijah is to this day simply called *the* prophet, Chidher is also *the* prophet to the Moslems . . . Like Chidher, Elijah is not confined within the limits of the human lifespan, but survives all generations and ends only with the end of the world and the coming of the Messiah, or his annunciation through the Antichrist.

> As the Jews discuss whether Elijah is to be regarded as a human being or as an angel, so do the Moslems debate about Chidher. As Elijah is the patron of the mystics and Kabbalists, so Chidher has an equally high position with the Islamic mystics, which is already known to us. Elijah's encounters with pious men, scholars, the oppressed and the persecuted are as numerous as Chidher's appearances.

> We are unlikely to find it difficult to decide which has to be regarded as the original and which as the derivation.

> We may thus state without hesitation that the Islamic Chidher is to a large extent the Elijah of the Jewish tradition under a new name.

Compare Friedländer:[35]

> Not only can the various Khadir anecdotes be traced back to precisely corresponding Elijah legends, but the basic conception of Khadir as an omnipresent counsellor and helper in need is an

exact counterpart of the rabbinic conception. The Mohammedan scholars are quite aware of this identification when they repeatedly state that Khadir is like Elijah.

It is particularly remarkable that some Islamic commentators and mystics not only identify al-Khadir with the biblical and Aggadic Elijah, but beyond this speculate about the mystery of this immortal. Ibn Hagar's comments: 'al-Khadir whom Moses met was only the al-Khadir of that period . . .' and 'every period has its al-Khadir',[36] implies an acknowledgment of the archetypal meaning of the al-Khadir-Elijah-figure. The legend cited above about his childhood and youth also characterises al-Khadir plainly as a prototype of the hero-archetype (see p. 154). The interpretation of the fish revived at the meeting of the seas as 'the awakening of the new Adam from the old'[37] corresponds to the symbolism of human transformation and transcendence represented in detail by depth psychology.

Sura 18 has been extensively analysed by C. G. Jung. He sees Moses as 'the man on the quest' for 'the place of the middle', in which transformation takes place; Joshua as Moses' 'shadow' who fails 'to recognize a moment of crucial importance'. The fish, 'their nourishment', represents 'a content of the unconscious' which has to be assimilated and 'by connection with its origin, the water of life, becomes revived.' The sea, turned to solid ground as an island, is the place of the middle personified by al-Khadir. 'He is the "Long-lived-One" who continually renews himself, like Elijah.' Al-Khadir symbolises 'not only the higher wisdom but also a way of acting which is in accord with this wisdom and transcends reason.' Moses looks up to him as such and accepts his instructions.[38]

Questioned by the editor of *Élie le prophète* (see p. 149)[39] about the significance of Elijah, Jung emphasised in his answer that Elijah is a living archetype. If constellated it may raise a new religious attitude, an immediate relationship with God. And in his *Civilization in Transition*, Jung calls Elijah a 'divine-human personality . . . or Anthropos . . . the dogmatized figure of Christ, as well as of Khidr, the Verdant One'.[40]

CHAPTER XI

Elijah in Contemporary Judaism

What part is played by the Elijah-figure in the history of the Jewish people in the last century? The emancipation of the Jews in Western Europe, their assimilation to the culture of their host-people which this brought about, the 'Enlightenment' among the Jewish population of the Eastern European states, the mass emigration to America in the nineteenth century—then in the twentieth century the beginning of the national Zionist movement, the systematic Jewish settlement of Palestine after World War I, the Holocaust and finally the establishment of the State of Israel, were a chain of radical changes which affected the religious and cultural attitude and political structure of the Jewish people more than anything else that had happened in nearly two thousand years.

In eighteenth-century Ḥasidic doctrine the Elijah-figure, as has been shown, was above all regarded as a psychic factor intrinsic to the individual, as the longing of the Jew to extend his experience of God, and at the same time as divine illumination and guidance for those striving for it. The first two or three generations of leaders of the Ḥasidic movement took this 'path of Elijah' to their individual enlightenment and salvation. The elite among their followers earnestly sought it and consciously let their rabbi lead them towards this goal. The great majority of Ḥasidim, however, were able to project only their own unconscious Elijah-factor on to the spell-binding personality of their rabbi and to follow his explicit instructions (see pp. 130–1, 196–7).

In later Ḥasidic literature, from the second half of the nineteenth century onwards, there is hardly a mention of Elijah as an intrinsic psychical factor. The *zaddik* himself was less a spiritual leader than one who advised his followers on individual problems. The mass of religious Jews, both Ḥasidim and Mitnagdim [their religious opponents], saw in Elijah once more exclusively the inspired fighter for God in the past, and above all the personal prophet and precursor of the general Messianic redemption at the end of days. Accordingly, relevant contemporary religious literature emphasised the biblical and Aggadic representation of Elijah. Only a few religious leaders as well as a few Jewish writers also stressed the symbolic and timeless meaning of the Elijah-figure and its actual relevance to their own problems.

R. Samson Raphael Hirsch (1808–88)—founder of the Western European neo-orthodoxy which strove for a synthesis of a strictly traditional religious attitude and the general spirit of the age—describes in detail the struggle of the prophet, in whom 'the spirit of Phinehas' came to life, against the worship of Baal. He interprets Elijah's theophany at Horeb as a divine justification of Elijah's own 'storm, earthquake and fire' in contrast to his 'small voice of silence'. 'God first sends Elijah through His blazing light, so as to shake the foundations and put out the light of the earth.' 'Elijah is not the Messiah, but precedes him, and as long as Elijah is there, the Messiah will not come.'[1] However, in his commentary on the Torah, R. Hirsch speaks of Elijah's future reappearance so as to bring about 'the covenant of peace', the final complete harmony of man, world and God. He will show the way to it 'through healing the breach between the generations' and 'through re-awakening the old spirit of Horeb of man's sub-mission to the divine command'.[2] The striking interpretation of Elijah's theophany in the sense of the apocalyptic version of the process of the redemption corresponds to R. Hirsch's own zealous struggle against the superficially rationalising Jewish reform movement of his time and shows his vital attitude to the biblical and Aggadic Elijah.

A far more comprehensive part is played by Elijah in the out-standing theosophy of R. Abraham Kook (1865–1935), the last of the Jewish mystics, who has left voluminous records. According to him, it is possible to attain the experience of the unity of the divine universe through meditation, as this unity is eternally real and opposites exist only in the human view. In the framework of this conception, Elijah plays a decisive part. He represents the possibility of becoming conscious of this unity, and activates it at first in the individual and later in the collective:

> As Elijah embraces [within himself] the holiness of the world of making, he can perfect the world of man until it is in complete harmony with the higher worlds. Just as he saw before his ennoblement the evil in everything in the world, and therefore wanted to extirpate with ardent zeal the spirit of uncleanliness, so he recognised after his ennoblement the divine sparks in the world of man and leads them upwards to the 'spirit of harmony' . . .[3] Elijah unites within himself completely the essence of the human and the angelic and therefore he can bring about the redemption.[4]

He can awaken in the sinner his hidden desire to return. Even the human being who goes through a psychic deterioration has experienced a flash of Elijah's light.[5]

The small voice of silence with which God spoke to Elijah represents the model of the meditation in which unity can be attained: 'To him who is quietly thinking, engrossed in his quietness, the worlds of the spirit and of making are revealed.' 'Listen to the voice of the internal dialogue' and 'if you honour silence... then from the spirit of silence will issue the stream of speech... and with it peace to the near and to the far'[6]; i.e. a spontaneous direct relationship between man and man will be attained.

But the longing for union with the Divine, inherent in the Jewish people, which is activated by Elijah, if it is to be durable ought to be linked with the acceptance of the Torah tradition and the observance of its commandments. Therefore Nadab-Abihu, who in their religious enthusiasm exceeded the divine commandment, had to be reincarnated in Phinehas-Elijah. 'The stormy-powerful awakening spirit of youth has to unite for spiritual and practical activity with the deliberate-cautious spirit of age, so as to hasten the redemption and create the basis for . . . the coming of both Elijah and the Messiah.'[7]

In another work, R. Kook explains the 'union of fathers and sons' through Elijah as follows:[8]

The altar of God which has been destroyed will be rebuilt with twelve stones, corresponding to the twelve tribes of Jacob, by Elijah, the zealous angel of the covenant. He will bring about peace, through turning 'the heart of the fathers to the children and the heart of the children to their fathers', by means of the light of the Torah mysteries penetrating the community of the Jewish people. All its activities, hopes and plans appear in different forms, holy and secular, as construction and destruction, but all of them together contribute to the building, within and without, both to the individual and to the collective one, far beyond the threshold of the consciousness of those who are doing this work and far beyond their own limited aims . . . 'at the end of days you will understand'.

When the divine love [in man] reaches its highest degree, it is transformed into zeal for God in utter purity. And then it is no longer a force derived from the supreme conception of God but becomes instead an effective [active] force. The very essence of everything is transformed into love and spreads to embrace every manifestation of life, all thoughts and deeds . . . Divine zeal is inherent in the Jewish community in general. 'Zealous God is his name and there is no other God beside him.' And thus eternal life is implanted in the Jewish community. The measure of the greatest, essential, active love is the measure of life. And 'death has no power over whosoever is zealous for God.' The individual personality is the measure for [his relationship to] Elijah: the power of its love and the depth of its understanding, the extent of its strength and its holiness correspond to the measure of the personal and individual Elijah-revelation [which it experiences] . . . But in the Jewish community generally, it is Elijah's soul and the mighty strength of Phinehas, the zeal which is the great negation, with which the people reject every alien influence. But Elijah is also the angel of the covenant. Even if not every individual has yet appropriated him, he comes because of the general appropriation of the Elijah-potential by the collective, before the dawn of the great day of God.[9]

R. Eliyahu Dessler (d. 1951), for many years the spiritual leader of the largest *yeshivah* in Israel, repeatedly included brief, pregnant references to Elijah's significance in his speeches to his pupils. He emphasised especially that Elijah abandoned his egocentricity as symbolised by his belt made of the skin of the ram which had been sacrificed in place of Isaac;[10] furthermore, that through his transformation Elijah overcame the opposites within himself and thus became the precursor of the redemption. The 'Giluy Eliyahu' of pious individuals would in itself mean their spiritual illumination in our world today.[11] But in order to attain the Messianic age, especially after the immeasurable sufferings of the Jewish people in our time, Elijah's call for the return to God would after all have to be heeded.[12]

Noteworthy also is the essay 'Elijah at the gates', by J. Hadari. He mentions Elijah's positive transformation and his significance for Judaism. That during the revelation at Horeb Elijah stood 'in the entrance of the cave' and that the Aggadists frequently met him 'at the entrance', indicates, according to Hadari, that Elijah always appears at the beginning of a new spiritual or historical period. Thus the biblical Elijah lived at the changeover from oral to recorded prophecy; also, Malachi's mention of him means not only the conclusion of Israelite prophecy, but at the same time the changeover from the written Torah to the oral tradition. Similarly, Elijah had appeared to the scholars of the oral doctrine [Tannaim] at the time of the completion of the Mishnah, and to the later scholars [Amoraim] when they began and when they completed the record of their doctrines in the Talmud. With this view of 'Elijah at the gates', Hadari tries to do justice also to the symbolic meaning of the Elijah-figure.[13]

In an interesting remark, Rabbi J. Soloveitchik emphasises the significance of Elisha as Elijah's pupil and successor to the present difficulties of the devout Jew. The settled, socially rooted Elisha becomes the pupil and successor of the lonely religious fighter Elijah and develops within himself the synthesis of devout prophecy and close relationship with the people and political activity. 'Is the modern man of faith entitled to a more privileged position and a less exacting and sacrificial role?'[14]

The Jewish, like the Gentile, scholars of the last century at first considered the biblical Elijah predominantly with the help of the usual scholarly methods: criticism and interpretation of texts, a representation of the historical and religious contexts, taking into consideration ancient manuscripts and archaeological finds. In particular they endeavoured, with Elijah as well as with all other biblical figures, to distinguish the historical from the legendary. There are such representations of Elijah by J. Morgenstern,[15] with special emphasis on the inner connection between Elijah's appearance and the first written utterances of the biblical prophets; by Martin Buber,[16] especially from a mythic-religious view; and a particularly detailed account by Lea Bronner, essentially based on a comparison with the mythological material of the Ugaritic texts.[17]

There are numerous philological, archeological and religious-oriented comments on the biblical description of Elijah in the lectures by H. Gevaryahu, F. Melzer and I. Yeivin given within the framework of the Israeli Society for Bible Studies. They also discussed Elijah's transformation, to be explained by God's reprimand to him at Horeb and the termination of his prophetic mission. At the same time it was pointed out that Elijah had already proved on Mount Carmel his love for the people by the building of an altar out of the twelve stones symbolising the tribes of Israel as well as through his humble desire for rain. The chairman, M. Silberg, concluded 'Elijah appears when someone finds himself in an apparently inescapable dilemma . . . and as he will, according to Malachi, presage the general salvation, he is also able to presage to the individual . . . for he is a presager by his nature.'[18]

Concerning the Aggadic Elijah, there is an older scholarly treatise by S. Kohn,[19] who calls him the 'defender of the faith at all times' and divides his Aggadic representations into three periods: from Malachi to the end of the Mishnah, Elijah has a purely Messianic significance; from then to the completion of the Talmud he also takes a hand in earthly temporal events; finally up to the end of the fifteenth century, there is the 'mystic degeneration of the Aggadah'.*

---

* Kohn was typical of the Jewish historians of his time in his complete failure to appreciate and respect Jewish mysticism. Only G. Scholem's comprehensive scholarly researches into Kabbalist literature[20] and the editing and publishing by him and his pupils of hitherto mostly unknown manuscripts made scholars aware of the outstanding significance of the Jewish mystics for the history of religion. Scholem's impressive modern presentation of Kabbalist teachings, moreover, influenced many Jewish and Gentile circles

Scholem emphasises Elijah's significance as mystagogue in the Kabbalah. In particular, he points out that mystic inspirations received from Elijah, as the generally recognised 'bearer of divine tidings', were respected even if their content at times did not seem to accord with the traditional view.[21]

A systematic scholarly representation of Elijah in the Aggadah from the viewpoints of content and literary history is provided by M. Ish-Shalom in the introduction to his critical edition of the *Seder Eliyahu Rabbah ve-Seder Eliyahu Zutta* (see p. 57 and n. 123). An interesting essay, 'Elijah in the Aggadot of Israel', was published by M. Guttmann first in the Hebrew journal *He-Atid* and later, with additional material, in *Mafteah ha-Talmud*, an encyclopaedic work he originated. It is particularly noteworthy that Guttmann is probably the first scholar to draw explicit attention to the Aggadic view of Elijah as a timeless personality.

I. Heinemann, in *Darke ha-Aggadah*, calls one of the Aggadic methods 'condensation', i.e. 'the tendency to illustrate the ideologies pervading Jewish history through identifying their representatives.' As example, he mentions the identification of Elijah with Phinehas, through which his timelessness is emphasised.[22] This 'condensation' comes close to the psychological view of Elijah as archetype.

R. S. Jacobsohn also considers the Aggadic Phinehas-Elijah in the light of 'condensation'. In another study he emphasises the basic difference between Elijah and all other prophets, but makes no attempt to analyse what is exceptional in Elijah, because 'one should not dare to explain rationally the enigma of this unique mysterious personality.'[23]

Shorter scholarly essays concerning the biblical and the Aggadic Elijah were published by Robert Zion[24] and M. W. Levinsohn.[25] Eliezer Margaliot systematically compiled a comparatively rich choice of biblical, Aggadic and to some extent Kabbalist quotations concerning Elijah's character, his activity and his mission in the future.[26] The affinity of Elijah's character with that of the prophet Jonah, and also the spiritual relation between Elijah and the prophet Hosea, both mentioned by the Aggadists, are presented by J. Bacharach on the basis of extensive biblical material[27] (see p. 19 n. 28, 72, 94).

Of particular interest is an essay on Elijah written by Israel Cohen. The writer explains the blatant difference between the zealous-avenging biblical Elijah and the benevolent and helpful Aggadic one by saying that the Jewish people could not bear the negative picture of the biblical Elijah and therefore created a new, positive Elijah-figure. The possibility of fitting this transformation into the framework of tradition had been provided by his ascent to heaven, which made credible his mission as the guardian angel of the Jewish people. This view in certain respects comes close to the depth-psychological explanation of his transformation.[28]

Several modern, not traditionally religious, Hebrew poets and novelists have also written on the Elijah-figure: Jacob Kahan in particular should be mentioned here. In the year of the great Russian pogroms (1905) he believed that he recognised Elijah in a stranger whom he met in a European city. After weeks of violent emotions caused by this experience he wrote *The Vision of the Tishbite*. In the wealth of its metaphorical apocalyptic events, Elijah constantly stands out in his tragic relationship with God and man; at the end, however, he proclaims the dawn of a new aeon of harmony and peace.[29] The same author wrote a moving description of Elijah's flight into the desert, his loneliness and despair, his remorse over the murder of the prophets of Baal and finally his journey to the mountain of God. From the divine words there, 'go, turn back', which follow 'the small voice of silence', the writer makes Elijah understand 'that there is for him no other way and no choice of action; that this is the life which God has determined for him on earth.'[30]

The theme of Elijah's wanderings in the desert and the revelation which followed appears in different versions by other writers. Hillel Bavli, like Jacob Kahan, makes Elijah accept his fate.[31] P. Ginzburg has God put an end to Elijah's mission as a prophet to punish him.[32] To A. Me'iri, Elijah remains obdurate.[33] S. Frug, on the other hand, sees Elijah as emerging transformed from the revelation.[34]

While most of the works mentioned represent Elijah's personality in its individual ambiguity, M. Shoham (1893–1937) in his play *Zor vi-Yrushalayim* (*Tyre and Jerusalem*) presents the biblical events of Elijah's time with a profundity and transparency which show the religious, anthropological and psychological significance of the struggle between Judaism and paganism. In particular, in a confrontation between Elijah and an itinerant sage from Tyre, the author reveals the polar contrast of sensual-fetishist idolatry and the spiritual-humble relation to the Divine in monotheism. We have, accordingly: on the one hand unlimited enjoyment of the moment, but connected with egocentricity, striving for power and unbridled passion; on the other hand, humane simplicity and unselfishness, but at the same time seriousness and the grave pressure of constant awareness of the divine demands. In Elisha, Shoham portrays these opposites arising as a psychical conflict within the individual. In contrast to the biblical representation, he appears in the drama as a prince at the royal court, participating in its unbridled debauchery, and in bondage to the seductive and tyrannical queen. Like her, he hates Elijah, and is ready to carry out her planned revenge on him. But he becomes more and more fascinated by Elijah's outstanding prophetic personality. In a hard inner struggle, he feels himself against his will surrendering to the Divine. Nevertheless, he hesitates to become Elijah's successor. Only when Elijah gives him to understand that human reluctance to accept God's summons is an essential mark of the prophet's nature, Elisha is ready to proclaim God's word. It is remarkable that Shoham later writes to a friend,[35] that though the paganism of Tyre was in its time subdued by Jerusalem, the struggle between the paganism of power and the Judaism of the spirit still continues to be carried on, and that Elijah, 'who is regarded by the Jewish people as the hero for all times', has not yet proclaimed 'the great and terrible day of the Lord'.

It may be said that in the nineteenth and the early twentieth centuries, some Jewish religious leaders emphasised the necessity of orientating themselves by the Elijah-personality with regard to contemporary events or within a comprehensive framework of a Jewish theosophy. Poets and novelists were moved by

Elijah's personality both as individuals and in their national consciousness, and strove to give new creative expression to his numinous activity. Jewish scholars, too, like their Gentile colleagues of the last decades, began to deal not only with the scientific methods of research but also with the contemporary religious significance of the texts under consideration. But beyond this there was no general constellation of the Elijah-archetype, neither among the overwhelming majority of the Jewish leadership nor among the Jewish people as a whole. The constantly growing general desire for freedom in the twentieth century expressed itself essentially in abandoning what till then had been the traditional criteria and in a striving for increased social and political rights. It caused Jewry to assimilate to the predominantly scientific-positivistic and artistic, non-religious cultural values of the surroundings, and also to support the liberal and socialist movements or the efforts for universal peace. Its realisation was expected to lead to the collective liberation and the individual salvation assumed to be contained within it. The yearning for redemption has been mostly projected on to ideologies. In one of his poems, A. Shlonski deplores that nowadays the Jewish people content themselves with a substitute for the Messiah and do not open the door when Elijah knocks.[36]

In the twentieth century, with the awakening and the growth of the Zionist national movement, emphasis was placed on the wish for a return to the homeland and its reconstruction, the revival of the Hebrew language and the striving for national independence. For a large group of traditionally religious Jews, this was inseparably linked with the hope for the spiritual regeneration of the Jewish people, though only a few people seemed to follow Rabbi Kook in assigning the central role in it to Elijah's intrinsic significance.

Then the Holocaust befell the Jewish people. In his profoundly moving epic poem, in which pain, helpless rage, hate and despair after the horrifying extermination of six million Jews by the German National Socialists are condensed and find mythic-mystic expression, Uri Zevi Greenberg mentions the prophet Elijah: he sees him as the only Jew whom the ruthless murderers were unable to persecute—'since he was not flesh and blood, but the spirit of the Jewish people', mourning and lamenting by the graves of those who have been murdered, whom he loved and who had waited in vain for his coming.[37]

In a later, gruesomely vivid poem, A. Shlonski shows the figure of Azazel (Satan), dancing wildly in a drunken frenzy to the music of his saxophone, merging into one person with the prophet Elijah who is quietly blowing the ram's horn (*shofar*). At the end of this painfully stirring vision, the poet envisages the diabolical aspect of this hybrid figure maintaining the upper hand.[38] It represents human ambivalence under extreme tension; the sad longing for transcendence and unity in desperate conflict with the unquenchable thirst for Dionysian drunkenness. Psychologically, it indicates a striving for the redeeming extension of consciousness as against uninhibited decline into the unconscious. The poet seems to regard as inevitable in Jewish, as in general contemporary, life the turbulent dissolution of the human personality.

The helplessness of the victims exposed to the abysmal horrors of the Holocaust, their despair about humanity and their cry for divine help and for redemption is expressed particularly effectively in the novel by Eli Wiesel, *The Gates of the Forest*, in a dialogue with Elijah. A young Jew trying to hide from his persecutors in a cave in the forest is joined by another fugitive, a stranger and yet somehow familiar to him, who relates that one night Elijah, the prophet whose task is to proclaim the coming of the Messiah, appeared to him. When, in desperation, he pointed out to him the indisputable urgency of immediate redemption in view of the Holocaust, Elijah had answered that he too was wandering about in despair. But then he told him the secret: 'The Messiah is not coming; he is not coming because he has already come. The Messiah is everywhere, ever present.' But it is precisely his presence, Elijah said, which gave the moment its apocalyptic horror. 'He has a name, a face and a destiny.' On the day when these three are one, the present time will be linked to God. He, Elijah, has no right to tell him more. And no rebellion against God will help. 'All you achieve by this is to open yourself to him . . . Later you'll see the light and perhaps it will pervade you.

For the present let it suffice you to know that the Messiah is already among men.' Then the persecuted remembered that his father used to say: 'The Messiah is that which makes man more human.'[39]

Elijah, in this novel, proclaims that the turbulent apocalyptic days of our time with all their sufferings are the 'heels of the Messiah' and have to be accepted in humility. Only through the 'Messiah in man himself'—man becoming really human—will redemption come about. That means that he has to unite his name [the name 'Messiah', i.e. man's longing for salvation], his face [his appearance, his becoming conscious] and his destiny [his vocation, the activation of his psychic potential]. This will be the union of man within himself, with his fellow-men and with the Divine.

The Holocaust, understandably enough, enormously strengthened the drive and struggle for national independence and gave it an irresistible impetus.

Since the establishment of the State of Israel, non-religious circles and also a considerable number of traditionally religious people took as the heroic figures of the Jews Joshua, the biblical conqueror of Canaan, and the leaders and kings who followed him and who established and extended the Jewish realm. These models, which do not correspond to the archetype of the hero personally undergoing adventures and tests, then tended to be projected on to contemporary war heroes and state leaders.

The Elijah-factor, on the other hand—the human urge towards individual psychic development and transcendence, so far as personal ambition does not completely repress it—is more or less adequately projected as in the Gentile world onto father-figures or outstanding personalities. Sometimes Elijah himself or an old man associated with him appears to a Jewish dreamer to give help or advice.

Within the psycho-therapeutic framework there occurs the transference to the analyst as spiritual guide. When, in Freudian psychoanalysis, the analysed person succeeds in adapting to reality in the sense of accepting his individual fate, this may be regarded as the integration of a partial function of the Elijah-factor. The Jungian individuation process may lead the human soul beyond this to the consciousness of the divine immanence in the human soul and to the relationship of dialogue between it and the ego, which approximately corresponds to the Elijah-factor (see pp. 195–6).

A surprising change in the attitude to religion occurred at the time of the Israeli–Arab war in 1967, with its decisive victory for the Israelis and above all with their conquest of the Old City of Jerusalem. It seems that the younger, non-religious generation which had been born and had grown up in the country, and who generally felt themselves to be a newly established Israeli nation, became conscious of belonging to the historical Jewish people. This aroused in many feelings of being related to the Jewish tradition, and frequently released also hitherto repressed individual religious emotions.[40] In traditional religious circles and especially amongst the young people, the Western Wall of the Temple compound, once again accessible to them, became and has remained ever since the central site for traditional prayers and beyond this a place exerting an almost magical attraction.

Most of the rabbinic leaders see the Holocaust, the establishment of the State, the mass immigration from the Diaspora and the Israeli victories which they regard as miracles, as the dawn of the 'Messianic Age', a historical process which appears to be almost apocalyptic (see pp. 62–3).[41] Corresponding to the traditional ideas of the redemption, such overwhelming events will lead, through the constellation of the Elijah-archetype, to a return, a realisation of the human dependence on the higher divine power and to a positive direct relationship between man and man, which form the basis of a new Messianic world order (see pp. 76–7).

Yet one cannot ignore, however, that for many traditional-religious people in Israel carried away by enthusiasm over the great victory, the attachment to the soil of the Promised Land and its holy places acquired clearly mythic features.[42]

The descent into the depth of the mythic may bring about a revitalising psychic transformation, but it also harbours the danger of a stumble into chaos. Seen mythologically, only a well-equipped hero may dare to descend and, defeating the voracious dragon lurking in the depths, gain the hidden treasure. Psychologically, this means that only the Great Individual with a strong and at the same time resilient ego, confronted with the deepest layers of the collective unconscious can, coming to terms with it, become transformed and mature. Collectives faced with the mythic world are very much in danger of being swallowed up by the fearful chaos of inhumanity.

Whether, through the activation of the 'inner Elijah' in a few Great Individuals, an intensive striving for *devekut*—adhesion to the Divine—has already begun to develop, and whether then, through an intensified constellation of the Elijah-archetype, the Jewish collective will find the way to *teshuvah*, is beyond the knowledge of those at present alive.

CHAPTER XII

Elijah, Prototype of the Hero-Archetype, in the Development of Judaism: Summary and Conclusions

The historical personage of the prophet Elijah as described in the biblical Books of Kings shows clearly the traits of the heroic figure [hero-archetype] as it exists in innumerable variations in the imagination of all peoples, finding expression in their oral and written traditions, in legends, myths and religions.

The hero's way of life manifests a basic trait in the structure of the human psyche: the dynamics of man's unconscious striving for the fullest possible activation of his psychic potential, and of his painful struggle with infantile inhibitions, anxieties and feelings of guilt which oppose his individual self-realisation. Through being victorious in his struggles, mostly with the help of a higher power, he renews his ego and transcends its limitations, accepts the world and returns to it in order to act as a guide to his fellow-men.[1] As with the heroes of all the more highly developed religions who are in search of God and are God's fighters, the inner development of Elijah and his spiritual striving for a personal experience of God find direct expression most frequently in biographical data and spiritual adventures. His stormy experiences in the outer world, his struggle against Baal and Astarte, against Ahab and

Jezebel, and against his own people, correspond to the struggle he wages within against his own weak ego, vacillating between hubris and disintegration, threatened by both. He strives partly unconsciously, partly almost consciously, for an extension of his consciousness and for a comprehensive experience of the Divine. His inner struggle ends in victory with the gradual perception of the positive-female aspect of God, which reawakens his psychic energies, provides them with a direction and changes his personality. The revelation of 'the small voice of silence', preceded by the appearance of ambiguous natural phenomena, indicates to Elijah that in God all opposites are united, that his various manifestations, often incomprehensible and terrifying, have to be accepted, and that the divine Being itself can be felt only as *mysterium tremendum et fascinans* (see pp. x, 14). Elijah's ascent to heaven means his union, his 'at-one-ment' with the universal creative spirit, God the father, who had revealed also his female aspect.*
With this, Elijah's potential of becoming as a man the son of God is realised with the help of divine grace. He became the Great Individual, a hero who stands out from his people. His close disciple Elisha, who saw the ascent of his master, is aware of this meaning of the event (see p. 31). Besides this, Elijah's ascent in his spiritual and physical unity symbolises the wholeness of his personality, and may also hint at his future return to earth.

The patriarchs of the Jewish people in search of God were heroes who followed Him; especially Jacob, who became 'Israel', a fighter for God (Gen. 32: 29), and whose sons, the tribes which united to form the people, called themselves *bne Israel* (sons of Israel). Then came Moses, who delivered them from Egypt and was their leader, through whom they received the revelation on Horeb and were instructed to become 'a kingdom of priests, and a holy nation' (Exod. 19: 6). The particularly transparent biblical representation of Elijah's personal struggle, his transformation and transcendence supplemented the still living memory of the

* The union of the hero with the father-God, is, according to Joseph Campbell, equivalent to the *coniunctio mystica*. In this, he experiences the female and the male as two parts of a whole; the former makes him understand that the 'father'-God precedes the separation of the sexes; i.e. he is androgynous. 'The father himself is the womb of the new-born'[2]

precedent of the patriarchs and the demand on the individual and the collective to be aware of the hero's path to divinity. This made Elijah become the personification of the archetypal hero and was decisive for the spiritual-religious development of the individual Jew and of the Jewish people (see pp. 29–31).

In the realm of history, the spiritual leadership of Israel devolves directly upon Elisha, who in the beginning continues the master's activities in his spirit and accordingly represents some aspects of the Elijah-archetype.

The direct effect of the Elijah-archetype is manifested for the first time in Malachi. Its impact is particularly strong because it is documented not in a historical report but in the climax and summary of his prophetic addresses to Israel which are at the same time the conclusion of the biblical Books of the Prophets. In view of the critical religious and social situation which existed at that time, and fearing an imminent divine judgment, Malachi visualises the return of Elijah, the son who had gone back to his heavenly father, who will now be able to show his brothers the way to God and to each other (see pp. 33–6). Elijah as the archetypal figure of the hero is as it were completed through Malachi's prophetic words inasmuch as he makes him return to the world after his transcendence in order to save his people. This prophecy gave significance and meaning to a presumably already widely held vague belief in Elijah's return: he became the precursor of the redemption.

About three hundred years later, Ben Sira mentions that some day Elijah will gather the dispersed tribes of Israel and also that he may bring about the salvation of the individual (see p. 39). Both these tasks of Elijah share the momentum towards a fundamental change, a change including return and renewal.

According to the character of the Elijah-archetype, it constellates mainly in situations of crisis in which, in accordance with the peculiarity of the Jewish people, the spiritual and the national aspects are always mingled. It was particularly strongly active during the almost permanent crisis which lasted for more than two centuries: a time of internal dissensions, the threatened and finally the actual loss of national independence and the destruction of the Temple. In order to ensure the continuation of the Jewish people as God's champion independently of the existence of the state and the national sanctuary, the spiritual leaders assured with equal care the written standardisation of the biblical laws and their practical interpretation, and also sought—as Aggadists—to consolidate and deepen the direct spiritual relationship of the individual and the collective to the Divine. This was accomplished by the 'encounter' of the Aggadists with the biblical Elijah, and their reflections and understanding of him were here of particular importance. The mysterious, archetypal motive of Elijah's ascent to heaven became clear to them. His change, in their view hardly begun on earth and only hinted at in the Bible (see pp. 50, 75-6), appeared to them as completed by his transformation which took place in heaven. They saw him transformed by means of direct divine illumination, saw his awareness of God extended, his personality made harmonious (see p. 77). Participating in the Divine to a larger extent than human beings can generally achieve, but without merging with it, related equally to both God and man, he becomes the mediator between macrocosm and microcosm, the correspondence of which was formulated by the Aggadists: 'everything which God created above he also created below'. This *correspondence* is led by Elijah towards a *union.*[3] He is God's messenger, a spiritual guide; he helps the individual and the collective in need, teaches the Torah, guarantees the covenant throughout the generations (see pp. 52-4, 58) and at the time of redemption will play the decisive role in leading the people unanimously back to God (see pp. 62-7, 65, 67). Then he will support the Messiah with advice and by authoritatively interpreting the laws of the Torah (see p. 68). He will also resurrect the dead (see p. 68).

The Aggadic identification of Elijah with personalities of the biblical past, his very presence at their own time, their conviction that 'he will meet the devout of every generation' and the expectation that he will one day play a decisive role in the national and universal redemption, raised Elijah's personality out of its specific historical context (see pp. 75-6). Through their awareness that he existed beyond time, the Aggadists became conscious of the essence of Elijah's archetypal significance: he represents man struggling with himself, man striving for the Divine who, redeemed, with his help, becomes the divine instrument through which the collective is brought closer to its spiritual and physical deliverance.

The masters recorded their comprehension of the biblical Elijah out of their experience of 'meeting him'. Both the mythic-mystic and the popular Aggadah had an extraordinarily profound and lasting effect on the Jewish people. Their statements concerning Elijah's personality and his part in redemption gradually became consolidated in a doctrine of redemption—though significantly enough not one that was unequivocal. Its character became increasingly universal and eschatological. Although, regarded realistically, in the course of the subsequent centuries of the Diaspora final redemption seemed to lie in the distant future, an unshakeable belief in it was kept alive by the constant expectation of Elijah as the precursor of the Messiah. This also finds expression in the Midrash cited above concerning the birth of the Messiah on the day on which the Temple was destroyed, and his fate: in the destruction also lies the germ of rebirth. The new-born is not yet able to develop and is scattered across the sea, into the distance, the infinite; but Elijah lives to bring about the future return of the redeemer (see p. 63).

The image of an ever-helpful Elijah, which also found lasting and manifold expression in a continually growing folklore centred upon him (see chapter VIII), made the people aware of divine assistance in times of national crises and also especially in personal hardship and desolation. Elijah's capacity at any time to release the individual from spiritual distress may be seen also as an indication that the collective can achieve redemption to begin with in the individual and with his help.

The Elijah-archetype made its impact beyond the circles of observing Jews and even beyond the Jewish people. The association of Elijah and Messiah was taken so much for granted by the whole people that, when Jesus appeared, his pupils and disciples regarded John the Baptist as the returned Elijah. In the Christian church itself the Elijah-figure continued for centuries to play a not inconsiderable role (see chapter IX). Islam shaped the personality of al-Khadir, their most important prophet after Mohammed (see chapter IX), in the image of the Aggadic Elijah.

The Elijah of the Aggadah has certain aspects in common with Hermes—God's messenger in Greek mythology—a spiritual leader who also symbolises the reconciliation of opposites, totality and immortality.[4] The most decisive of the differences between him and Elijah is that the latter was originally completely human. In this Elijah also differs from the evangelical figure of Jesus, whose very conception was divine and who after his resurrection did not become God's messenger but himself became God and—according to the early church—will be reincarnated and return to the world of man only at the time of final, general redemption (see p. 146). Elijah, especially in view of his human origin and his task as God's messenger, is comparable rather with the Bodhisattvas who, like the incarnations of Buddha, are manifestations of an archetypal Buddha but do not enter completely into *nirvana*; they remain in the world in order to assist the redemption of their fellow-men. However, whereas the Bodhisattva[5] does not expect the final deliverance of mankind to be men's *identification* with the Divine as Hinduism does,[6] but considers *nirvana* to be the complete self-extinction of all phenomenal existence,[*][7] the redemption to which Elijah will lead mankind means its existence in the real world in which its *likeness* to God is implemented to the full.

As the depth of the Aggadah, which appeals above all to man's emotionality, gives rise to Jewish mysticism, so Elijah, the Aggadic spiritual guide, becomes the mystagogue of the Kabbalists.

Erich Neumann has pointed out that every archetype is capable

---

[*] In certain schools of Buddhism, however, especially in the Mahayana, man's salvation does not require resorption in *nirvana* but the changing of men's psychic attitude to experience the identity of *nirvana* and *samsara*, the phenomenal world (Stcherbatsky, op. cit., pp. 186–7, 205; Glasenapp, op. cit., pp. 112, 121; Watts, op. cit., p. 69; Humphreys, op. cit., p. 128). Similarly in Hinduism men can overcome the opposites of the Absolute Being (Brahma) and its manifest phenomenal world (*maya*) by reaching cosmic consciousness through deep meditation (*On the Bhagavad Gita*, pp. 437–50; Zaehner, op. cit., pp. 50 ff.). See also pp. 187–8 below.

The similarity of Elijah to the Persian figure of Saoshyant is mentioned by W. Bousset, 'Die Religion des Judentums', p. 513 n.

of affecting a person numinously-dynamically, blurring or dissolving his 'images' of God, man and the world; but if the ego stands firm, the psychic energy which has been released can again become luminous, i.e. it can generate new images.[8] In this sense, the transforming impulse which brought forth the Kabbalah seems to be the dynamic of the Elijah-archetype, the breath of his spirit (ruaḥ). The biblical Elijah was buoyed up by the spirit, commanded fire and water, both symbols of the spirit; he revived the dead youth with his breath, was himself borne up to heaven in a whirlwind, and the Aggadists expect him to resurrect the dead. The Kabbalists themselves regard the ruaḥ as the middle and thus the mediating part of the soul, between what is completely divine in man and that part of his soul which is bound to his body (see pp. 91, 94). It is this ruaḥ-dynamic of the Elijah-archetype which released the psychological process that affected the Kabbalists. It became apparent that every Jewish mystic, when descending into the depth, unconsciously or consciously followed the hero's path of the biblical-Aggadic Elijah; he became aware of the 'Giluy Eliyahu'—or this was how he designated his numinous experience. Like their master, the Kabbalists returned after their mystical experiences of God to the world of their fellowmen and of Jewish tradition.

They then became significant and leading figures to their contemporaries and to posterity, through both esoteric circles of disciples which formed about them, and their written records. Here, they only very occasionally tried to describe their immediate mystical experiences (see p. 87). They tended to record the results of their meditations upon their encounter with the numinous: their changed image of God, their enlarged view of the holy scriptures, of tradition, and of religious rites and symbols.

While in a literal interpretation of the Bible, God appears above all as the creator and ruler of the world and has almost always a personal character,* he becomes, in mysticism, the en-soph, the infinite absolute Being out of whose 'nothingness'

---

* The fact that in Judaism in general the Divine is conceived in personal aspects is expressed in the Midrash: 'On the Red Sea God appeared to the children of Israel as a hero; on Mount Sinai as an old man' . . .[9]

emanate the *sefirot* and the 'worlds' which are formed by them (see pp. 104–5). In them, the various aspects of the godhead manifest themselves by degrees, and the world of man makes its appearance in the lowest hypostasis. Furthermore the whole of the Torah is seen by the Kabbalists as a living organism in which the Divine expresses himself[10] and which is, as it were, his name.[11] Corresponding to the body and soul of the organism, the Torah has besides its literal meaning a hidden, intrinsic, symbolic or allegorical one[12] which the mystics endeavour to understand and which Elijah may reveal to them.

And just as the Kabbalah traces the biblical image of God back to the primordial existence and the manifestation of the Divine, so in the human sphere there reappeared as the goal of redemption the original Adam, the earthly equivalent of the *adam kadmon*, the highest inner divine emanation.

In the Aggadic conception, the first human being, Adam, created in God's likeness, was androgynous.[13] The separation of Adam's female components brought into our world the first pair of opposites, so decisive for human destiny. Accordingly, the mystics see every human soul before it leaves the divine realm as both masculine and feminine. Only on earth, in its physical incorporation, does the androgynous soul divide into two souls, one male and one female, which enter respectively a male and a female body. Divine providence can ordain that because of his spiritual merits a man may marry the woman whose soul was once united with his own.[14]

Adam's original sin was seen by the mystics as the separation of the *shekhinah*, the divine immanence here on earth, experienced as feminine, from the higher transcendental stages of the emanation, designated as masculine; they felt this separation to be most significantly symbolised by the plucking and especially by the eating of the fruit from the tree of knowledge,[15] or else by the separation of the tree of knowledge from the tree of life. With this, the divine incarnation in man, in its original comprehensive meaning, was suspended but remained latent. Some Aggadists had intimated that Elijah was free from sin, as was Adam before the Fall (see pp. 46, 102–3). In the Kabbalah, Elijah achieves the perfection of the first human being and is transformed into the angel Sandalphon (see pp. 97–100). He rules in the lowest manifestation of the divine emanation, the 'world of making' (see pp. 97–9, 105), and through his connection with the higher transcendental *sefirot* he is able to bring about, by means of his male *sefirah* Yesod, the redeeming *coniunctio mystica* of Tiferet and Malkhut (*shekhinah*).[16]

Luria's doctrine of reincarnation, which stipulates a general transmigration of souls (metempsychosis) for the purpose of restoring in all men the original purity of soul of the first human being, regards Elijah-Sandalphon as the one who in the course of his life on earth has brought to perfection his original soul, derived from Adam-Cain, through being joined by sparks from other souls. As one who has been redeemed, he becomes the angelic example and guide to the not yet redeemed (see p. 106).

Thus in the Kabbalah, Judaism undergoes a certain mythical revival, but this is not a regression into the archaic. On the contrary, the new-born images and symbols even in the written conceptions of the Kabbalists—above all in the Zohar, Cordovero's works and especially in those of Luria's school—proved to be numinous and inspiring for generations to come. The living relationship of the traditional Jew to the biblical God of Israel was remoulded, strengthened and incorporated in the dynamics of the infinite godhead and became a decisive factor in the redemption of the *shekhinah*, Israel and mankind (see pp. 106, 180). This was once again the effect of the Elijah-archetype: a going back to the origins, transformation and renewal, and a return into the contemporary world.

Then at the beginning of the eighteenth century, when the Jewish masses had been thrown into despair by the most cruel persecutions and the tragic collapse of the pseudo-Messianic movement of Shabbetai Zevi, the Elijah-archetype became constellated once more. This led an important group of mystics to an unexpected experience. It did not lead, to begin with, to a transformed image of God and the world, as happened at the changing of the biblical to the Aggadic Elijah, and the Aggadic one to the mystical. The Ḥasidic mystics experienced consciously in themselves the dynamics of a creative change and understood its significance. They were clearly aware of the presence of Elijah within the psyche which, in their abstract 'Giluy Eliyahu', a few earlier mystics had intuitively surmised (see pp. 108–9). They became fully aware that the transformation—and redemption—aspect of the heroic Elijah-archetype was the tendency of the soul to self-awareness, the 'pattern' of a psychic process. They understood that this process may lead one to overcome the 'opposites' and to experience the unity of God, mankind and the world, and may even bring about a structurally altered conscious psychic attitude which suspends the boundaries between the observing subject and the observed object (see pp. 124–5). They saw the effect of Elijah, the 'precursor of redemption', both in the intense yearning for an awareness of God and in the suddenly apparent illumination with its existentially gripping experience. Thus transformed, their psychical attitude could lead directly to Da'at, personal redemption. Instead of an extended *image* of God, they achieved an existential *experience* of God, the highest degree of *devekut*, in which the ego is aware of itself in unison with the Divine (see pp. 127–8).

In the religious sense the *shekhinah*, the divine immanence in mankind, was thus released from 'exile' and made accessible to the influx of the transcendent godhead. The Ḥasidic mystic had experienced for himself the *coniunctio mystica*. Psychologically this would mean that the knowledge of the unity of all existence is not projected on to an archetypal prototype but is realised in the site of its origin, the human soul.

The psychic integration of the process of redemption and the decisive part played in it by Elijah-Da'at as conceived by Ḥasidism was, at least in its definition and special emphasis, new to traditional Judaism, and pointed indubitably to an intuitive depth-psychological knowledge by the Ḥasidic leaders.

Gershom Scholem has pointed out, with reference to Aron Marcus,[17] that the Maggid of Meseritz and his school coined the concept of '*kadmut ha-sekhel*', which corresponds to the unconscious of contemporary depth psychology.[18] S. Hurwitz later provided a thorough interpretation of the Ḥasidic utterances concerning the unconscious in their context. They represent the unconscious as knowledge belonging to the second *sefirah* of the divine emanation (Ḥokhmah) and generally concealed from the individual, though it may be revealed to him in his *binah*, corresponding to the third *sefirah*. The unconscious is here accorded an active, the consciousness a predominantly passive role. Hurwitz further points out that according to R. Ze'ev Wolf of Zhitomir, the union of the unconscious with the conscious, i.e. of the Ḥokhmah called 'father' with the Binah called 'mother', is 'the secret of the two higher *parẓufim*' (aspects of the emanation), in which the masculine influences the feminine, namely by means of the *sefirah* Yesod which is active within it, and represents in the mystic figure of God the *membrum virile*. This is the '*unio mystica*' which is considered by the classic Kabbalah as a suprapersonal divine event but in the Ḥasidic view also as the union of human opposites. 'Apparently', Hurwitz concludes, 'the Maggid was intuitively aware that the *coniunctio* takes place in the depth of the human soul.'[*][19] Rivka Schatz pointed out that individual redemption in the Ḥasidic sense means an extension of the consciousness, and mentioned among other quotations in support of this one of the statements by Menahem Nahum of Tchernobil cited above, which also describes the psychic Elijah-factor and the Da'at connected with it. She rightly emphasised that the equation of psychic experiences with theosophical conceptions by the Maggid of Meseritz are not to be taken 'psychologistically', as if the divine emanation did not exist in its own right and had to be regarded purely as a human experience.[20]

The Maggid's relevant doctrines were formulated by his pupils and have come down to us in a sometimes garbled or ambiguous form. They seem to converge upon this: in contemplation, the Ḥasidic mystic experiences the divine nothingness, its turning into the all-embracing divine Being and his own participation in it. The Divine thinks within him and speaks through his mouth. Human will and divine will become one (see p. 128).

---

[*] The Ḥasidic conception of the unconscious as male and consciousness as female may be understood in a religious sense: that the active Divine reveals itself to the more passive human soul

Compare Neumann's remarks about the creative individual: 'he comprehends that the image of God is like himself "changing"... only the source, the point at which the stream originating in darkness enters the light and becomes *both at once*, is the turning point of transition and transformation... that which is transformed and gushes forth as a well is not the opposite of the divine... but its mouth and expression.' That man's creativity is brought about by his being created in the image of God the creator is mentioned in the *Zohar Ḥadash* and intimated in Rashi's commentary to Genesis.[21]

The Ḥasidic mystic sees everything emanating from the godhead as 'divine sparks', which constitute the existence of all creation and are therefore in contact also with the divine soul of man.

The religious experience of the highest degree of *devekut*, the revelation of the Divine as eternal, infinite 'nothingness' and the awareness that this nothingness is the origin of the universe of which the individual himself is a part, means that man in deep meditation may experience the divine Being and at the same time himself as one of its manifestations. In psychological terms, the human consciousness knows, when it approaches the deepest layers of the collective unconscious, that it is unknowable; but at the same time the consciousness experiences that it is born from this inexhaustible origin, and that its ego is developed and may be transformed by it, and it surmises that it will be reabsorbed by it at the time of death. It is obvious, however, that the transcendental experience of the mystic cannot be explained exactly through our present psychological knowledge and its terminology (see p. 124). The Divine apparently reveals himself out of the collective unconscious, but is not identical with it.

The crucial transformation, experienced as a rebirth of man's personality, corresponds to a symbolic view of Elijah's resurrection of the dead. This is intimated by the talmudic phrase: 'the day of the rain is as great as the resurrection of the dead' (see p. 47*). The rain, which Elijah withholds and then grants, effects renewal. With an allegory of death and rebirth, of passing away and a new beginning, Ḥasidic literature repeatedly points out that it is essential for the seed to decompose in the earth so that a new plant may sprout from it.[22] The fertilisation from above by the rain from heaven, and the decomposition below in the earth, are essential for the regeneration, corresponding to Elijah creatively uniting earth and heaven. Psychologically the resurrection would mean that the human being with his egocentricity, his fears, inhibitions and anxieties must cease to be so that he may be reborn through spiritual enlightenment and also with new, stronger roots in life on earth.

Higher degrees of *devekut* can, at least in the beginning, be achieved only in solitude and in meditation. In Jewish mystic circles, the isolation from the world took place mostly by temporary retreat, similar to Elijah's solitude in the desert. And meditation corresponds to the hearing of the 'small voice of silence', as Elijah experienced. Psychologically this means that the consciousness adjusts to listen to and to observe the unconscious, in order to become aware of its contents and to understand them.

This highest degree of *devekut* cannot be maintained (see p. 128), just as it is impossible to make manifest the eternal in its perfection here on earth. Ḥasidic mysticism represents the relationship man-God as fluctuating, just as Elijah ascends and descends and just as the divine ray of light in Luria's Kabbalah continually alternates between emanating creatively and streaming back again. In monotheism, an I-Thou relationship to a personal God can be achieved, but the mystic may draw beyond this close to the Divine until he experiences union with it—not as identity but as participation in the essentially inaccessible. Then he may continue to return once more to the relationship of dialogue and then draw close again towards a union.

But Ḥasidism demands, besides a relationship of dialogue with God, also a relationship of dialogue with the world around us, using the biblical saying: 'In all thy ways acknowledge Him' as a basis for the instruction that one should recognise that everything one encounters in life addresses oneself personally (see p. 119).

The relationship of dialogue with God on the one hand and with the world and man's activity in it on the other, forms at the same time a unity, like every polarity of opposites. For the dynamic tension of opposites is also the means of moving beyond them towards a higher 'third' transcending and embracing them; analytical psychology calls the higher 'third' of the opposites conscious and unconscious 'transcendent function' or 'uniting symbol'.[23] This psychological phenomenon accords with the Ḥasidic saying: 'Da'at decides between two [opposites] and unites them' (see p. 125).

It seems that regarding the polarity of the relationship of dialogue with God and with the world, the 'third' transcending and embracing is the highest *devekut*, the experience of the unity of God, mankind and the world. It could be said that the 'ascending Elijah' leads towards the unity, the descending one back towards the polarity of the relationship of dialogue, on the one hand with God and on the other with the world.

In any case the essential is the dynamics, the moving towards the goal, but the possibility of redemption is contained in the present. The Aggadah says: 'If the children of Israel after crossing the Red Sea had said not "the Lord shall reign" but "the Lord reigneth", their redemption would have been immediate.'[24] This corresponds to the Ḥasidic emphasis on the fact that in Malachi it does not say 'I will send you Elijah' but 'I send you Elijah': he is always present. The constant presence of Elijah the redeemer means psychologically his psychic integration.

Redemption in the Ḥasidic sense accordingly may culminate in achieving a state of consciousness approximating to the *samadhi, nirvana* and *satori* of Eastern religions, to the doctrines of Plotinus[25] and his neo-Platonic successors and to the experiences of Western mystics.[26] The Zohar intimated this state of consciousness in the saying that the *shekhinah* had spoken out of the mouth of Moses.[27] Luria's theosophy comes very near to that of the *Bhagavad Gita* in his distinction between the absolute divine Being and its manifestations. Their reunification is experienced by the Ḥasidic ascent from the I to Nothingness, like the contemplative method recommended in this Hindu text.[28]

Psychologically this state of mind can be designated as the achievement of 'cosmic consciousness'. On this theme, the

Canadian psychiatrist Richard M. Bucke[29] published a detailed study based on his personal experience and the biographical data and the writings of some historical personalities.* He believed, besides, that in the course of further psychic development the whole of mankind would gradually achieve this state of consciousness. This prediction seems to be noteworthy in view of the recent results of investigations of extra-sensory phenomena,[30] the growing understanding that science cannot be objective but is an 'interplay' between man and nature,[31] and that energy and matter are not absolute opposites.[32]

There is a remarkable, far-reaching parallel between the Ḥasidic conception of personal redemption and the results of contemporary researches in depth psychology, especially that of C. G. Jung's school. They share the knowledge that the unconscious is the matrix of consciousness, that the progressive extension of consciousness is due to the integration of previously unconscious material, and that human consciousness is developed by the perception of opposites. Finally, they know that there is in the psyche an inherent striving for wholeness through the reunion of opposites. This tendency can, by a psychic maturation process, lead to the understanding that the ego is dependent upon a higher psychic authority (the Self)[33] and this may bring about a decisive transformation of man, called individuation.

This parallelism between the Ḥasidic and the depth-psychological conceptions raises the following questions: what view does depth psychology take of the transformation undergone by the Elijah-figure in the course of Jewish history, first seen as biblical and historical, then recognised as an archetype, and finally psychically integrated in Ḥasidism. And further: what role is played by the Ḥasidic psychic Elijah-factor and its inherent Da'at-knowledge in individual redemption, and to what extent does this correspond to the maturation process in analytical psychology?

From a general point of view, the Elijah-figure corresponds to

* K. Walker has the same opinion: 'We are all immersed in the Universal Mind and we derive from this common source similar, if not identical, ideas' (*The Unconscious Mind*, p. 57)

the phenomenon of man's transformation, his striving for unity. This becomes apparent with the biblical Elijah in the effect of the revelation of the 'small voice of silence' which he had at the threshold of the cave, in the extension of his image of God, in his transcendence, in the symbolism of fire, rain and whirlwind which is connected with it. With the Aggadic Elijah it becomes apparent in his changed attitude to mankind, in his becoming God's messenger, in his being charged with guiding the way to God, preparing for universal redemption and in resurrecting the dead. In mysticism, he transmigrates to God's image as it was incarnated in Adam, or to the angel Sandalphon, and he can bring about the *coniunctio mystica*. In Ḥasidism the Elijah-factor leads man to psychic unity by full harmonic activation of his potential and the experience of union with the Divine.

If for the sake of illustration, some psychic instances may be taken out of their dynamic context, the Elijah-factor corresponds first of all to the sudden new experience arrived at intuitively, the illuminating flash of insight and the emotion usually caused by it, the 'aha-phenomenon' with which one registers that consciousness has been extended. With the biblical and Aggadic Elijah-figure, these functions are intimated by his characteristically sudden, unexpected appearances in difficult historical or personal situations, and by the unforeseen changes effected in them through Elijah's pronouncements or his intervention.

If what is revealed by the extension of consciousness is of vital importance to the one concerned, the emotional experience is particularly strong and activates the function of feeling, the opposite of the function of thought. The comprehending thought is joined by the awareness of the decisive value of the new experience.[34] This affects the whole personality of the individual. He becomes 'committed'. This corresponds to the Aggadic Elijah as the 'breaker through' (see p. 66 fn.), and especially to the effectiveness of the psychic Elijah-factor in the Ḥasidic view of the union of the opposites above and below, soul and body, thought, speech and action. It corresponds also to the Aggadic view of the transformed Elijah who has become complete and who, as the guarantor of the covenant symbolised by the circumcision, strives to unite the masculine with the feminine, Logos with Eros, by direct contact (see pp. 58–9).

The striving for unity of the Elijah-factor is not, however, restricted to the registration of single new awarenesses. Beyond this, the Elijah-factor is the general human striving for unity, at first unconscious but gradually becoming more and more conscious.

This corresponds to the striving of the psyche, empirically established by C. G. Jung and his school, to make its partly opposing basic functions fully conscious, to activate them both in an extravert and in an introvert direction and to achieve as far as possible a harmonious balance between them. This striving for unity emanates from the 'Self' which is superior to the ego and embraces it. It represents the potential wholeness of the human personality and also includes its share in the collective unconscious. On the basis of Jung's manifold empiric-analytic experiences and exhaustive research into the psychology of religion, the Self as a symbol of wholeness seems to be identical with the image of God in human experience.[35] The tendency of the Self to guide the human ego towards wholeness by the 'transcendental function' and the simultaneous striving for wholeness by the ego[36]—which Neumann calls centroversion or automorphism—correspond to the Elijah-function which is also reciprocal in its effect: to the divine will to manifest its own image in mankind and to the human yearning for transcendence to the Divine. This dynamic relationship between the ego and the Self, which he calls 'the ego-Self axis',[37] corresponds to the effect of the psychic Elijah-function as described in Ḥasidic literature. It is the integration of the Elijah represented in the Bible and Jewish tradition, the guide back to God. What had once been mankind's paradisic unconscious 'participation mystique' becomes through Da'at-knowledge effected by the Elijah-factor the conscious experience of unity.

The psychic maturation—the activation of the entire psychic potential and the comprehension of the meaningfulness of one's own fate—which Jung called the 'individuation process', can happen spontaneously or be induced and directed analytically.[38]

The spontaneous development, which may transcend the usual state of consciousness, occurs especially with the 'Great Individuals', whose creativity is, so to speak, turned inwards. It finds expression in their whole personality, in the spontaneity and adequacy of their relationship to other people, and of their reaction to external events; it has a direct effect upon their environment. These 'Great Individuals' are the true prototypes of the hero-archetype. In the religious sense they are the 'saints'. They represent the universal man created in God's image, in his individual wholeness. Close to these 'Great Individuals' are the great artists, whose works may reveal temporary experiences of the unity of all reality. Through them their contemporaries and posterity can participate in their creativity and may derive a similar experience of unity.[39]

The analytic-synthetic individuation process, from which the concept of self-awareness mentioned above was empirically derived, begins with making conscious the human 'shadow'. It is the sum of the dark elements in the personality which the ego condemns as negative values and therefore represses and tends to project on to his fellow-men. Furthermore, it may contain important but neglected parts of his potential. Man has to recognise and dissolve his projections whereby his aggression can be considerably reduced, and has as far as possible to assimilate his shadow and activate his entire potential.[40] The harmonisation of Elijah's personality, as intimated in the Bible and carried out by the Aggadists, corresponds to the integration of his shadow.

A particularly prominent role is played by this problem, which is essentially that of evil and sin, in the deterministic Ḥasidic doctrine of R. Mordecai Josef Leiner of Izbice (see p. 119, n. 6) and his spiritual successor, R. Zadok ha-Kohen of Lublin (see p. 121 and n. 18). As everything that happens is ultimately God's will, the freedom of the human will is questioned; not only do disastrous natural events happen with God's consent, but so does everything that men do, even if it is sinful. But nevertheless, men should act as though they had freedom of will (see p. 119, n. 12). As a biblical example, R. Leiner analyses the deeds of Phinehas-Elijah during the wandering of the Israelites in the desert,[41] and

R. Zadok stresses Elijah's transgression on Mount Carmel against the prohibition of offering a sacrifice elsewhere than in the Temple.[42] The Talmud mentions that Moses, Elijah and Hosea reproached God with forcing men to sin by endowing them with evil instincts.[43] But R. Zadok challenges men to accept the paradox of this situation. He explained that the 'return to God out of love, which changes sins into merits'[44] mentioned in the Talmud, means that the sinner may repent with his whole heart of his transgression, but at the same time understand that this was God's will.[45] The religious meaning of this is that the image of God has become incarnate in man in its awe-full as well as in its benevolent aspect, that man's evil instinct may also serve the purpose of God, and that the will of God must be accepted as decisive.

As the Aggadah says: 'Man has to bless [God] for the evil as well as for the good, for it is said (Deut. 6: 5): "And thou shalt love the Lord thy God with all thy heart, and with all thy soul, and with all thy might." "With all thy heart" [means] "with both your inclinations, the good and the evil" . . . "with all thy might" [means] "whatever measures He metes out to thee, thank Him in a mighty measure." '[46] Even more extreme is another saying: 'even a sinful deed may be blameless at the right time.'[47]

Psychologically this means that it is essential to accept the shadow so that the polarity of good and evil in man's deeds can— no less than that of the good and bad occurrences in his life—be transcended to the understanding of their true meaning.[48]

The confrontation with the shadow in the analytical individuation process is followed by one's becoming conscious of the contra-sexual elements in the soul, *anima* or *animus*. When the *anima* has been integrated by men after having been projected on to the beloved, it is experienced and realised as a psychic factor, as the feminine-receiving capacity of one's own soul. With this, one becomes receptive to the collective unconscious and capable of establishing genuine relationships.*[49]

---

* This representation refers to the psychology of the male. The female individuation process leads, through introjection of the *animus-* projection, to the development by the woman of her own male soul-components. Through the constellation of the positive aspect of the 'Great Mother', the original female receptiveness to the collective unconscious may be restored

In the biblical representation of Elijah the *anima*, the image of the feminine soul, is not projected onto a human being. Elijah experiences the *anima* in the figure of the angel which awakens and refreshes him (see pp. 24, 25fn.). The cave in the mountain in which he spends the night may also be seen symbolically as representing the 'feminine in the masculine'. The *integration of the anima* becomes apparent when the feminine aspect of God is revealed by Elijah's hearing and understanding the 'voice of silence', his transcending human limitations and his ability to establish genuine relationships after his return to earth.

With regard to human eroticism, the Talmud says: 'He who finds the woman who corresponds to him is kissed by Elijah.'[50] The Kabbalah speaks about the division and the eventual reunion of the masculine-feminine soul of human beings (see p. 181). Furthermore, in the *coniunctio mystica* between divine transcendence and immanence, Elijah symbolises the *membrum virile*, while he is also the messenger of the *shekhinah* (see pp. 129, 97, 99). This, too, corresponds to the reciprocal function of the Elijah-factor mentioned above (p. 124).

In the continuation of the analytical individuation process, before the experience of the Self and leading to it, the archetype of the wise old man is constellated. In fairytales and legends, as well as in the specific hero myth, the wise old man, according to Jung, 'represents knowledge, reflection, insight, wisdom, cleverness, and intuition on the one hand, and on the other, moral qualities such as goodwill and readiness to help, which make his "spiritual" character sufficiently plain.'[51] He always appears when the hero is in a hopeless and desperate situation from which only profound reflection or a lucky idea—in other words, a spiritual function or an endopsychic automatism of some kind—can extricate him: it 'comes about spontaneously in the psychic space outside consciousness when conscious thought is not yet—or is no longer—possible.'[52] He is 'the superior master and teacher, the archetype of the spirit, who symbolizes the pre-existent meaning hidden in the chaos of life.'[53]

Concerning the archetype of the spirit, Jung says:

spirit is always an active, winged, swift-moving being as well as that which vivifies, stimulates, incites, fires and inspires. To put it in modern language, spirit is the dynamic principle, forming for that very reason the classical antithesis of matter—the antithesis, that is, of its stasis and inertia.[54]

A transcendent spirit superimposed itself upon the original, natural life-spirit [of man] . . . [it] became the supranatural and transmundane cosmic principle of order . . .[55]

The hallmarks of spirit are, firstly, the principle of spontaneous movement and activity; secondly, the spontaneous capacity to produce images independently of sense perception; and thirdly, the autonomous and sovereign manipulation of these images. This spiritual entity approaches primitive man from outside; but with increasing development it gets lodged in man's consciousness . . . He himself did not create the spirit, rather the spirit makes *him* creative, always spurring him on . . . So much, indeed, does it permeate his whole being that he is in gravest danger of thinking that he actually created the spirit and that he 'has' it.[56]

It is obvious that the Elijah of the Bible and of the tradition derived from it is the Jewish version of the wise old man, the redeemed redeemer, into which the victorious 'hero' developed, and at the same time he is the Jewish prototype of the arche-type of the spirit and presents it in its various aspects.

The Hebrew word *ruaḥ* means both 'wind' and 'spirit'. In the biblical record, Elijah is 'borne up' by the *ruaḥ*'. That means within the immediate context, first: he appears and disappears suddenly and unexpectedly, as if blown by the wind. But it also indicates that the divine spirit has taken hold of him, and shows his stormy and relentless zeal for it. The biblical Elijah is possessed by the spirit, at times almost obsessed by it. Hardly ever is he able to serve the spirit consciously, except when he resuscitates the dead youth with his breath. In the theophany on Horeb, the divine spirit is revealed to him in the 'small voice of silence'. His further transformation is symbolised by the whirlwind, which bears him up to the primordial spirit.

In the Aggadic view, driven by the spirit which he serves consciously only from time to time, the human prophet is then transformed through his ascent into an angel, a spiritual being.

As a member of the 'heavenly family' he represents the spirit, the aspect of the godhead turned towards the world of man. As *homo maximus*, in whom the divine incarnation has realised itself completely, he becomes a messenger and a mediator to mankind. As such he can also soar above the earth as an eagle—this also being a symbol of the spirit—observing it or passing over it with four wing-beats. As the precursor of the Messiah he brings about the 'breaking through' to redemption.

In the Kabbalah, Elijah is the inspirator of the mystics, revealing to them the secrets of heaven and the hidden spirit of the Torah. His soul, derived from the *ruaḥ* of Cain, the first son of mankind, restores the soul of Adam to its original wholeness.

In the final stage of the depth-psychological individuation process, the wise old man represents the sum of the experiences gained in the analytical process, makes man aware of the meaning of his fate and may permit him to know the meaning of man's fate in general.

The decisive significance of awareness of the meaning is stressed by P. W. Pruyser: 'Thus religion mediates between various perspectives on human affairs; it acknowledges the uniqueness and worth of individuals, it upholds the regularities of nature, it accepts the value of corporate realities from the family to the state and mankind at large. Each perspective creates its own meanings, but the religious perspective aims at encompassing all perspectives and adding a *meaning-of-meanings*.'[57]

The appearance of the old wise man in the dreams or in the active imagination (see p. 171) of the analysand shows that he is able to internalise his spiritual guide who will lead him to be aware of the dependence of his ego on the Self. He will guide him to wholeness by the union of opposites and may enable him to transcend his boundaries and to share in the character of the cosmic, the eternal.

This corresponds to the integration of the Elijah-factor by the Ḥasidic mystics, to their Da'at-awareness of the reality of the unity of God, man and the world. It means their redemption.

The two questions posed above (p. 188) as to the depth-psychological meaning of Elijah's transformation in the history of Jewish thought and as to the meaning of the Elijah-factor in the process of psychic maturation itself can now be answered.

Psychologically, the gradual development of the biblical into the Ḥasidic Elijah corresponds to man becoming more and more conscious of the manifestations of the spirit-hero archetype. At first seized and driven numinously-dynamically by the archetype, man is gradually confronted with the images and symbols which correspond to his inner psychic instances. Finally, consciousness of the inner psychic dynamic striving towards wholeness is reached, and the ego is ready to give way to it. It is precisely this dynamic that has developed and transformed the Elijah-figure in the course of Jewish history, which, as the inner 'Elijah-factor', can arouse and guide the personal striving for redemption demanded by early Ḥasidism.

It may be regarded as certain that the psychic guidance by the Ḥasidic rabbis—especially by the pupils of the 'Great Maggid' himself—induced in numerous individuals a genuine psychic maturity, which brought them close to *devekut* in the sense of conscious participation in the Divine. The initial projection of the inner Elijah-function on to the rabbi, and the processes of transference between him and those whom he led, would basically correspond to the relationship between analyst and analysand. The nature and aim of individual redemption in the Ḥasidic sense appear to be comparable, *cum grano salis*, with the synthetically and prospectively oriented depth-psychological individuation process (see p. 190).*[58]

In the last century, however, the Ḥasidic leaders mostly ceased to be spiritual guides to their followers in this sense, and turned instead into advisers on specific religious questions and personal problems. Both the Ḥasidic and other traditionally religious circles saw Elijah almost exclusively as the future precursor of the redemption of the collective, and do so even today. Only a few,

---

* It is interesting that, on the initiative of R. Abraham Kalisker and R. Menahem Mendel of Vitebsk (*c.* 1850), Ḥasidic circles in Tiberias gathered regularly for discussion sessions of self-criticism. These talks may be compared with the customary group psychotherapy of today; J. G. Weiss, 'R. Abraham Kalisker's concept of communion with God and men', *Journal of Jewish Studies*, 6, 1955

out of their individual religious experience, achieved a profounder and larger view of the Elijah-personality, as becomes apparent in their researches, poetry or religious and philosophical conceptions (see pp. 160-1). An intensive constellation of the Elijah-archetype, such as formerly appeared among the Jewish people in times of crises and radical changes, has so far not occurred in the century of assimilation to the non-religious surroundings, of the Holocaust and the national Jewish movement. But the drawing near to the deeper layers of the collective unconscious which is noticeable among the Jewish people, especially the youth, at the present time, may lead to a change, to spiritual renewal and conscious striving for the realisation of the unity of all that exists (see pp. 171-2).

By the fascination which the biblical Elijah-personality exerted, Elijah became the prototype of the hero-archetype for the Jewish people. Their spiritual leaders, in confrontation with him, emphasised sometimes one, sometimes another trait of his personage, corresponding to the situation of the collective as well as to their own religious attitude. The changing emphasis was developed in reciprocity with the Jewish spiritual stirrings and strivings: it adjusted itself to them and at the same time decisively influenced their direction, always aiming to strengthen and deepen the relationship between men, the world and the Divine towards unification.

The Jewish version of the—in itself universal—hero-archetype is apparent first in the prominence of the divine initiative, which at critical historical and personal moments brings about a change, generally signifying return, transformation and renewal. Furthermore, most important for the predominantly patriarchal Judaism, it leads to the awareness of the immanent female aspect of God as a prerequisite for redemption. Finally, in Ḥasidism the Elijah hero-figure is integrated. It becomes an inner psychic factor: the dynamic relationship between God and man. By being aware of his role therein, man achieves his individual redemption.

The Jewish imprint on the hero-archetype, however, makes its universal significance also apparent. For the national liberation expected of Elijah is linked with the redemption of mankind. And the psychic integration of Elijah, *the awareness of all existing phenomena as manifestations of the Divine, has in itself a universal character*. It means at the same time that the individual can find his redemption even while living in the as yet unredeemed world.

The essential significance of the archetypal hero Elijah was gradually revealed: in the beginning by the record of the biblical prophet and finally by the psychic integration of his inherent meaning for man. The features of Elijah, an ever-living figure in Jewish history, were formed and transformed during centuries in the souls of great individuals and of the collective, in their religious experiences and attitudes, their despairs, their hopes and their dreams, which converged in their striving for nearness to God and close relationship with their fellow-men.

The changing but at the same time stable features of the ever-lasting Elijah have been the predominant dynamics in the development of Judaism.

Notes

Introduction and Acknowledgments

1   pp. 188 ff., 194–5, 384–6
2   p. 47
3   Erich Fromm, *Psychoanalysis and Religion*, pp. 22–4; *The Anatomy of Human Destructiveness*, pp. 224 ff., 233 ff.
4   op. cit., pp. 384–6
5   op. cit., chapters 3, 4, 5, 6
6   ibid., p. 54; E. R. Goodenough, *The Psychology of Religious Experiences*, pp. 8, 17, 27; P. W. Pruyser, *A Dynamic Psychology of Religion*, pp. 336–9; Fromm, *The Anatomy . . .*, p. 226; M. Buber, *On Judaism*, p. 221
7   Buber, *The Eclipse of God*, pp. 40, 42–5, 128–9; *On Judaism*, pp. 214–15; Fromm, *The Anatomy . . .*, pp. 234, 266
8   James, op. cit., pp. 67, 327; Otto, op. cit., pp. 21–2, 194, 197, 204–6; G. Allport, *The Individual and his Religion*, pp. 61–2, 139; Fromm, *Psychoanalysis and Religion*, p. 95; Henri Bergson, *The Two Sources of Morality and Religion*, pp. 230–2, 238–9
9   p. 389
10 pp. 50 ff.
11 *Dynamics of Faith*, pp. 1, 4–5, 9; see also Émile Durkheim, *The Elementary Forms of the Religious Life*, pp. 417 ff.
12 op. cit., pp. 230–2; for the mutual relationship between static and dynamic religion, see ibid., pp. 238–9
13 op. cit., p. 142. Allport agrees generally with James's and Otto's conceptions, but lays more emphasis on man's 'religious intentions' and especially on the innumerable individual variations of the expression of his religiousness

Chapter I   The Biblical Record of the Prophet Elijah

1   The edition of the Old Testament I have used is *The Holy Scriptures, according to the Masoretic Text*, of the Jewish Publication Society, Philadelphia, 1917

2 This assumption corresponds chronologically with the remark in the Babylonian Talmud (Baba Batra 15a) that the Books of Kings were compiled by Jeremiah

3 Archaeological and anthropological findings, as well as depth-psychological considerations, lead to the conclusion that most prehistoric peoples inclined to a primitive monotheism. See W. Schmidt, *Ursprung der Gottesidee*, vol. 1, pp. 135 ff., 207 ff., 246, 767 ff.; H. Kuehn, 'Das Problem des Urmonotheismus', p. 34 (p. 1670), and *On the Track of Prehistoric Man*, pp. 66, 69–70; E. Neumann, *The Origins and History of Consciousness*, p. 282; K. T. Preuss, *Die geistige Kultur der Naturvölker*, p. 60; E. Fromm, *Psychoanalysis and Religion*, p. 24. See also pp. ix, x above.

4 The depth-psychological aspect of free will lies beyond the scope of this work. For the deterministic doctrines of several Hasidic rabbis, see pp. 119, 121, 191–2

5 See J. Kaufmann, *Toldot ha-Emunah ha-Yisraelit*, vol. 1, pp. 709–37

6 Exod. 3 : 14. The tetragram of God's name proclaims his vital activity, his immutable fidelity towards himself and his autonomy which is above earthly existence, yet which reveals itself in the world (O. Grether, *Name und Wort Gottes im Alten Testament*)

7 Kaufmann, op. cit., pp. 301 ff., 685 ff.; M. Buber, *Torat ha-Neviim*, pp. 67–76

8 I Kings 16 : 31; Flavius Josephus, *Antiquities*, 8. 316 ff. (trans., vol. 5, p. 743)

9 I Kings 16 : 32. Concerning the *ashera*, see also Judg. 6 : 25–7

10 II Kings 9 : 22; see also Buber, pp. 69 ff.; L. Bronner, *The Stories of Elijah and Elisha*, p. 133

11 Flavius Josephus, *Antiquities*, VIII. 319 (in trans., vol. 5, p. 743)

12 For a detailed consideration of Elijah's origin, see Robert Zion, *Beiträge zur Geschichte und Legende des Propheten Elijah*, pp. 6–8

13 B. Jacob, *Im Namen Gottes*. The Church Father St Jerome traces Elijah's name back to Helios. This might seem reasonable mythologically; philologically, however, it is untenable (Zion, op. cit., p. 5)

14 See n. 24 below

15 A. Alt, *Kleine Schriften zur Geschichte des Volkes Israel*, vol. 2, p. 137

16 H. H. Rowley, *Men of God*, pp. 37–67; W. Haussig, *Götter und Mythen im vorderen Orient*, pp. 250–64, 271–3, 429; A. Jirku, *Der Mythos der Kananäer*, pp. 14–26, 52 ff.; W. F. Albright, *Archeology and the Religion of Israel*, pp. 156–7

17 The fire descending from heaven is interpreted by most exegetes as a stroke of lightning. But it has to be noted that whenever consumption of sacrifice by heavenly fire is mentioned in the Bible, this is called '*esh*' ('fire') and not '*barak*' (lightning')

18 In view of the political division of the Israelite tribes at this time into the two rival kingdoms of Judea and Israel, Elijah's emphasis on their religious unity was of particular significance

19 To consider the pouring of the water as magic to induce rain, as is done by many Bible scholars, is not admissible. Neither is it a symbolic action like the water-offering at the feast of Sukkot. It is not rain that is expected during the contest, but fire

20 *Akedat Yizhak*, vol. 4, *Bamidbar*, pp. 117b ff. For the psychological explanation of Elijah's cruelty, see pp. 22–3 below

21 BT Berakhot 58a. Similarly Rashi's commentary on the biblical verse, and M. Buber and F. Rosenzweig in their translation (*Die Schriftwerke, Bücher der Geschichte*, vol. 2, p. 406)

22 I Kings 19: 5–8

23 It seems that Elijah understands, through his immediate encounter with Elisha, that the tasks imposed on him (the anointing of Hazael and Jehu) are to be undertaken not by him but eventually by Elisha; see also R. David Kimḥi (Redak) on this passage

24 According to F. C. Fensham, the epitheton '*zevuv*' of Baal may not mean 'fly' but, corresponding to the Ugarite root of the word, 'fire' ('A possible explanation of the name *Baal-Zevuv*', *Zeitschrift für alttestamentliche Wissenschaft*, 79, 1967, pp. 361–4). Concerning the punishment by fire sent from heaven, see n. 17 above

25 This is according to the text: that Elijah was carried up through the storm *in* the chariot follows from Elisha's subsequent exclamation

26 II Kings 2: 12. See also the Septuagint, R. I. Abrarvanel (*Perush al Nevimi Rishonim*, p. 608) and Rudolf Kittel (*Bücher der Könige*, vol. 1, p. 189) on this passage

27 For the relationship of Jonah to Elijah, see pp. 72, 94–5

28 BT Shabbat 129a; Keritot 10a; Niddah 21a, b

29 *The Origins and History of Consciousness*

30 The dependence of his fate on the female (which is man's condition in the matriarchal world) is brought about through his relatively low consciousness of his maleness and ensuing feeeling of psychic and social inferiority; E. Neumann, *The Great Mother*, pp. 212, 226, 303–4; see also M. Grant, *Myths of the Greeks and Romans*, pp. 146 ff.

31 S. Mowinckel, *He That Cometh*, p. 85

32 The Septuagint interpolates, as she threatens Elijah with death, 'If you are Elijah, I am Jezebel' (I Kings 19: 2)

33 See p. 191

34 According to some traditional commentators on the text, e.g. Gersonides (Ralbag), however, Elijah was divinely commanded to do so

35 BT Baba Batra 74b; M. r. Gen. 98, 23; M. Tehillim 120. 4

36 Aggadic literature explicitly calls the angels sexless; Kabbalistic literature occasionally distinguishes between giving-male and receiving-female angels (2 Zohar 256b; R. Naphtali Bacharach, *Emek ha-Melekh* 169a). In any case, the angel here appearing to Elijah is to be regarded as a positively female aspect of God

37 The forty days during which Elijah wandered in the desert correspond to the forty years during which the Israelite people wandered in the desert and to the forty days and nights during which Moses received divine revelations on Horeb

38 The vertical (the mountain) symbolises spirituality, the relationship to the 'self'; the horizontal the relationship to man and the world

39 C. G. Jung, *Mysterium Coniunctionis*, pp. 494 ff.; Rank, *The Art and the Artist*, pp. 40–1

40 Concerning the meaning of Elijah's theophany in the history of religion, see U. Mann, *Theogonische Tage*, pp. 411–16

41 A Hebrew play on words says: '*mekom ha-turfah hu mekom ha-trufah*' ('the site of shame is the site of healing')

42 J. G. Frazer, *The Golden Bough*, p. 104; C. Kerényi, *The Gods of the Greeks*, pp. 191–2, 199

43 Frazer, op. cit., p. 104

44 C. Kerényi, *The Heroes of the Greeks*, pp. 64 ff., 73–4, 140, 203

45 'Torah' literally means 'instruction', which, of course, contains many laws. But the JPS translation of 'Torah' as 'law' does not fit the context of this psalm

46 *Patterns in Comparative Religion*, p. 108

47 *Maitri Upanishad: Second Prapathaka*, cited from K. Walker, *Diagnosis of Man*, p. 138; see also C. G. Jung, *Psychology and Alchemy*, p. 366

48 See also Jung, *Mysterium coniunctionis*, pp. 205–6, and see pp. 78, 100, 110 below

49 *The Myth of the Birth of the Hero*, pp. 65–6

50 *Prometheus: Archetypal Image of Human Existence*, pp. xviii ff. and *The Heroes of the Greeks*, pp. 2, 3, 10 ff., 13

51 *Symbols of Transformation*, pp. 345 ff. and 'Approaching the Unconscious', in *Man and His Symbols*, p. 68

52 *The Origins and History of Consciousness*, pp. 178, 197, 221–2, 306, 318–19, 375–81, 415

53 'Ancient myths and modern man', in *Man and His Symbols*, pp. 101, 111, 112; J. L. Henderson and Maud Oakes, *The Wisdom of the Serpent*, pp. 41 ff., 61

54 *The Eternal Ones of the Dream*. The well-known anthropologist and psychoanalyst writes in the conclusion (p. 250) of his extensive observations and studies of primitive tribes in Australia: 'Man at this low stage of culture may be completely dependent on nature yet in his myths he is the growing child and in his dreams of eternity he creates his own world. And like the Saviour God of Christendom, Malpunga the phallic hero and all the other eternal ones of the dream have a claim to the proud sentence "I am the Path, the Truth and the Life"'

55 *The Hero with a Thousand Faces*; especially part I, chapters 1–4 and part 2 pp. 245, 255–60, and 'The Historical Development of Mythology', in *Myths and Mythmaking*, p. 20

56 A. S. Rappoport, *Myth and Legend of Ancient Israel*, vol. 1, pp. xv–xvi; W. F. Otto, *Die Gestalt und das Sein*, pp. 86–7; Patai, *Myth and Modern Man*, p. 73

57 C. Kerényi, *The Heroes of the Greeks*, p. 203; M. Grant, *Roman Myths*, p. 57

58 Corresponding in Jewish mysticism to the cloak which is the covering with which the 'transcendent divine light' surrounds the one who has been chosen; see p. 107 n. 130

59 See Kittel, *Die Bücher der Könige*, to this passage, and also similar interpretations by Jewish exegetes, e.g. Ibn Ezra and Abrarvanel

60 e.g. R. David Kimḥi on this passage

61 Mal. 3: 22–4; the Septuagint reads 'Elijah the Tishbite' and 'the heart of man to his fellow-men'

62 But then Rashi mentions that the discussion about this verse from Malachi in the BT (Menaḥot 110a) comes to a different conclusion. Rashi's opinion agrees with that of Maimonides (*More Nevukhim* 1. 36; *The Guide for the Perplexed*, p. 83). Solomon Ibn Gabirol says in *Keter Malkhut*: 'Thy glory is not diminished by those who worship others than Thee, for the goal of all of them is to attain to Thee' (*The Kingly Crown*, ch. 8, p. 31); see also R. Ḥayim of Volozhin, *Nefesh ha-Ḥayyim* III, para. 9

63 When the Bible describes revelations experienced by individuals there often occurs a sudden change from the visionary appearance of an angel to the sound of God's voice, e.g. from the burning bush (Exod. 3: 2–4)

64 See p. 60

65 Concerning the historical constellation, which explains the expectation of the angel of the covenant and Elijah at the time of Malachi, see B. de Vries, 'Eliyahu ha-Navi ba-Eskhatologia ha-Mikrait'

Chapter II   The Elijah-Figure in the Apocrypha

1 In *The Apocrypha and Pseudepigraphia of the Old Testament* (ed. Robert H. Charles), vol. 1, p. 74

2 ibid., p. 82

3 ibid., p. 119

4 ibid., pp. 499–501 (slightly altered)

5 The original Hebrew text of verse 11a is difficult to read: according to Smend's correction mentioned by Charles, the opening word 'asher' ('who') has been changed to 'ashre' ('blessed'). The Greek and Syrian translations made about 150 years after Ben Sira have been found to be inexact, and the emendations of the verse based upon them do not correspond to the original Hebrew text (ibid., remarks 1 and 11)

6 ibid., vol. 2, p. 255

7 ibid., p. 263

8 ibid., p. 161

9 ibid., p. 521

10 ibid., p. 590

11 ibid., pp. 576–7. About the origin and contents of this apocalyptic book, see ibid., pp. 542 ff.

12 Elijah and Enoch are frequently also mentioned together in a similar context in the later apocalyptic and in Kabbalist writings; see pp. 40–1, 47–8

13 ibid., p. 235

14 ibid., pp. 31–2

15 Concerning the ascent of Moses, see ibid., p. 407; Philo Judaeus, *De Sacrificiis Abelis et Caini*, 3.8 (quoted from H. A. Wolfson, *Philo: Foundation of Religious Philosophy*, vol. 1, p. 403); M. R. James, *The Lost Apocrypha of the Old Testament*, pp. 43 ff. For the ascent of Isaiah, see Charles, op. cit., vol. 2, pp. 155–6. Ezra's ascent is mentioned in IV Book of Ezra (Charles, op. cit., vol. 2, p. 621)

16 *Oracula Sybillina* II: 187–9; II: 245–9 (quoted from E. Hennecke, *Die neutestamentlichen Apokryphen und Apokalypsen*, vol. 2, pp. 505–7)
17 *Questiones et Solutiones in Genesis*, I: 86 (quoted from Wolfson, op. cit., vol. 1, p. 403)
18 *De Praemiis et Poenis*, 28: 163; 29: 16 (quoted from Wolfson, op. cit., vol. 2, pp. 411, 414–15)
19 *Dialogue with Trypho*, 8: 4 (also 49: 1), quoted from *An Early Christian Philosopher: Justin Martyr's 'Dialogue with Trypho'*, ed. J. C. M. van Winden, p. 123. See also p. 143 below

Chapter III   Elijah in Aggadic Literature

1 See pp. 57–8
2 M. r. Gen. 71. 12
3 M. r. Gen. 99. 12
4 M. r. Gen. 71. 12; M. r. Exod. 40. 4
5 M. r. Exod. 40. 4
6 M. r. Gen. 73. 5
7 M. r. Gen. 71. 3
8 M. r. Gen. 73. 5; *Pesikta Rabbati*, pt 13, p. 54a
9 *M. Tehillim* 43. 1; *Pesikta Rabbati*, pp. 13 a–b
10 M. r. Lev. 33. 4; M. r. Num. 21. 3; *Sifre Bamidbar Pinḥas* 131; *Pirke de-R. Eliezer*, ch. 29, p. 213 (see also pp. 69, 72ff. below)
11 *Seder Eliyahu Rabbah*, p. 97; *Seder Eliyahu Zutta*, p. 199; M. r. Gen. 71. 9
12 BT Baba Meẓia 114, a, b; *M. Mishle* 9. 3, p. 62
13 For a thorough discussion of the different opinions held by the Aggadists concerning the tribe to which Elijah belonged, see Robert Zion, *Beiträge zur Geschichte und Legende des Propheten Elijah*, pp. 9 ff.
14 *Sifre Devarim*, pt 342, p. 393; *Avot de-R. Natan*, ch. 37, version B; *Seder Olam Rabbah*, vol. 2, ch. 20, p. 333; *Yalkut Shimoni*, vol. 2, 224, p. 761
15 Concerning the Aggadic concept of the Ẓaddik, see pp. 46, 129
16 M. r. Gen. 77. 1; *M. Shemuel* 29. 2, p. 135
17 M. r. Deut. 10. 3
18 M. r. Gen. 21. 5; M. r. Lev. 27. 4; see also pp. 46, 102 below
19 M. r. Exod. 8. 3; *M. Tanḥuma*, vol. 1, Va'era 8, p. 74
20 JT Sanhedrin 10. 2; *Yalkut Shimoni*, vol. 2, I Kings 207, p. 756
21 M. r. Gen. 33. 6
22 Similarly *M. Tehillim* 78, 5, p. 346
23 Most of the Jewish exegetes, especially R. David Kimḥi, R. Abrarvanel and Gersonides in their commentaries to the biblical text, also emphasise Elijah's arbitrary proclamation of the drought
24 See also *Yalkut Shimoni*, vol. 2, 1 Kings 209, p. 757. Malbim in his biblical commentary mentions that it was apparent from Elijah's prayer that he himself felt that God had punished him
25 *Mekhilta de-R. Yishmael*, Introduction to part Bo, p. 2; *Avot de-R. Natan*, ch. 47, version B, p. 85. In contrast to Elijah, Elisha is repeatedly reported to have performed miracles for individuals

26 Ahab's subsequent repentance after Elijah's threat, i.e. after the crime against Naboth, is described in detail in JT Sanhedrin 10. 2, p. 21a

27 *M. Tehillim* 117. 2, p. 480

28 *M. Tehillim* 68. 9, p. 318

29 M. r. Num. 23. 9; *M. Tanhuma* (ed. S. Buber), Bamidbar p. 165

30 *Pesikta Rabbati*, pt 4, p. 13b

31 *M. Aggadat Bereshit* 76, p. 148

32 M. r. Num. 18. 10; *M. Tanhuma* (ed. S. Buber), Bamidbar, p. 96

33 BT Berakhot 31b–32a; *Yalkut Shimoni*, vol. 2, 116, p. 758; see also pp. 191–2 below

34 *M. Aggadat Bereshit*, pp. 148–9

35 M. r. Exod. 44. 1; *M. Aggadat Bereshit* 70, p. 155

36 M. r. Lev. 31. 4; *Pesikta de-R. Kahana*, pt 28, pp. 427–8

37 *Seder Eliyahu Zutta*, ch. 8, p. 186; see also *Yalkut Shimoni*, vol. 2, 217–18, p. 759

38 M. z. Shir ha-Shirim 1. 6

39 M. r. Shir ha-Shirim 1. 39

40 *Seder Eliyahu Zutta*, p. 186; *Yalkut Shimoni*, vol. 2, 218, p. 759

41 *Mekhilta de-R. Yishmael*, Introduction to part Bo, p. 2

42 Especially R. J. E. Halevy, *Dorot ha-Rishonim: Tekufat ha-Mikra*, p. 15 n. 2

43 *Pesikta Rabbati* 183a

44 *M. Tanhuma*, vol. 1, Pekude 3, p. 133; Seder Yezirat ha-Valad (*Ozar Midrashim*, vol. 1, pp. 243 f.)

45 JT Berakhot 5.1

46 *Seder Eliyahu Rabbah*, ch. 5, p. 23

47 M. r. Exod. 8. 2; *M. Tanhuma*, vol. 1, Va'era 8b, p. 74

48 *Masekhet Derekh Erez Zutta*, ch. 1, p. 18; *Yalkut Shimoni*, vol. 2, 367, p. 842

49 BT Sukkah 5a; *Mekhilta de-R. Yishmael*, p. 65b

50 The Jerusalem Targum renders II Kings 2: 11 as 'he ascended as if to the sky'. See also Philo (cited in ch. II n. 17 above). R. D. Kimhi says to this passage: 'Elijah's body was destroyed in the sphere of the fire and his spirit returned to God.' See Ramban's commentary to Lev. 11: 5 and A. J. Heschel, *Torah min-ha-Shamayim*, vol. 2, pp. 53–6

51 *Seder Olam Rabbah ha-Shalem*, vol. 2, ch. 17, pp. 275–6

52 Flavius Josephus, *Antiquities*, 9. 28 (trans., vol. 6, p. 17)

53 BT Baba Batra 121b; *Seder Olam Rabbah ha-Shalem*, vol. 1, ch. 1, pp. 46–7. According to the Talmud passage cited, Ahijah, called Elijah's teacher, is David's treasurer mentioned in I Chr. 11; 36

54 *Avot de-R. Natan*, ch. 38, version B, p. 52a (103)

55 BT Hagigah 15b; Gittin 6b; Baba Mezia 59b; *M. Tehillim* 18. 2, 104. 25

56 BT Megillah 15b; Hagigah 15b; Baba Mezia 59b

57 BT Pesahim 53b, Baba Mezia 85b, 86a

58 M. r. Lev. 34. 8; M. r. Ruth 2. 14; *Yalkut Shimoni*, vol. 2, 604, p. 1042

59 *Seder Olam Rabbah*, vol. 2, ch. 17, p. 276

60 *Yalkut Reubeni la-Torah*, vol. 2, Addenda p. 8

61 BT Berakhot 4b

62 *M. Tehillim* 8. 7
63 Targum Kohelet 10. 20
64 N. Leibowitz, *Iyunim be-Sefer Shemot*, pp. 212 ff.
65 BT Berakhot 58a, Nedarim 50a, Sanhedrin 113a, Ḥullin 6a (Tosafot); *Pesikta de-R. Kahana*, pt II, pp. 196–7.
66 BT Berakhot 6b; *Yalkut Shimoni*, vol. 2, 601, p. 1041
67 BT Shabbat 109b
68 BT Ta'anit 21a, Sanhedrin 109a, Avodah Zarah 17b
69 BT Avodah Zarah 18b
70 M. r. Bereshit 83. 3
71 Mr r. Esther 10. 2; *Pirke de-R. Eliezer*, ch. 50, p. 407; *Aggadat Esther* 4. 13
72 M. r. Esther 7. 9; M. Esther (*Oẓar Midrashim*, vol. 1, p. 55)
73 *Sifre de-Aggadeta*, p. 17a (33), p. 51a (101)
74 BT Baba Meẓia 85b
75 *M. Tehillim* 9. 9
76 BT Kiddushin 40a, Sanhedrin 108b
77 BT Berakhot 58b, Ta'anit 21a, Avodah Zarah 18b
78 BT Shabbat 109a–b, Gittin 70a; JT Kilayim 9. 4, Ketubot 12. 3; M. r. Gen. 33. 3
79 *M. Tanḥuma*, vol. 2, pt Ha'azinu 8, pp. 123–4; *Asseret ha-Dibrot* (*Oẓar Midrashim*, vol. 2, p. 453)
80 JT Sotah (p. 198a); M. r. Deut. 5 (end); *Bet ha-Midrash*, vol. 1, pp. 62ff.
81 M. r. Bereshit 33. 3; *M. Tanḥuma* (Yelamdenu), vol. 1, pt Vayeḥi, p. 57
82 *M. Tanḥuma* (ed. S. Buber), Bereshit, p. 20
83 BT Ketubot 61a, Nedarim 50a, Baba Meẓia 114b
84 M. z. Ruth, 1. 20, 4. 11; *Yalkut Shimoni*, vol. 2, 607, p. 1043
85 R. Nissim ben Jacob, *Ḥibbur yafeh me-ha-yeshuah*, pp. 58 ff.
86 *Yalkut Shimoni*, vol. 2, 601, p. 1041
87 Alef Bet de Ben Sira (*Oẓar Midrashim*, vol. 1, p. 39)
88 *Avot de-R. Natan*, ch. 13, version B, p. 16 (31); *Pirke de-R. Eliezer*, ch. 1, p. 1
89 BT Sanhedrin 109a
90 BT Nedarim 50a
91 M. r. Lev. 9. 9; M. r. Deut. 5. 15 etc.
92 BT Berakhot 3a, Yevamot 63a, Sanhedrin 113 a–b
93 BT Baba Meẓia 85b
94 BT Yoma 19b, Sanhedrin 97b
95 BT Shabbat 33b
96 See also pp. 108ff.
97 BT Ta'anit 29a, Nedarim 50a etc.
98 JT Berakhot 9. 3 (p. 74a); *M. Tehillim* 18. 12, 104, 25
99 BT Yevamot 63a; *Seder Eliyahu Rabbah*, chs 9–10, p. 51
100 *Masekhet Derekh Ereẓ Rabbah*, p. 1
101 BT Ḥagigah 15b; Yemot ha-Mashiaḥ (*Midreshe Geulah*, p. 332); see p. 51 n. 56 above
102 BT Megillah 15b, Gittin 6b
103 BT Baba Meẓia 59a, b

104 BT Ḥagigah 15b
105 BT Baba Meẓia 114a, b; *Seder Eliyahu Rabbah*, ch. 2, p. 8, ch. 8, p. 91; *Seder Eliyahu Zutta*, ch. 1, p. 167; *M. Shemuel* 5. 2, p. 57
106 BT Eruvin 43a
107 BT Shabbat 13a, b; see also *Encyclopedia talmudit*, vol. 2, pp. 6 f.
108 BT Ketubot 62b, Baba Meẓia 114a; *M. Tanḥuma*, vol. 2, pt Vayelekh 2, p. 122; *Avot de-R. Natan*, ch. 13, version B, p. 15b (30)
109 BT Berakhot 3a, 29b; Ḥagigah 9b; Ketubot 67a, 105b; Sanhedrin 113a; JT Terumot 1.4
110 BT Baba Meẓia 83b, Baba Batra 7b, Sanhedrin 98a, Makkot 11a; JT Terumot 8 (p. 47a); M. r. Gen. 94 (end)
111 JT Demai 2. 1 (p. 8b), Sheviit 9. 6 (p. 27b)
112 M. r. Gen. 35. 2; *M. Tehillim* 36. 8, p. 252
113 BT Ketubot 77b; *M. Tehillim* 36. 8
114 BT Sanhedrin 98a.
115 ibid.
116 R. Nissim ben Jacob, *Ḥibbur yafeh me-ha-yeshuah*, pp. 6 ff.; *Oẓar Midrashim*, vol. 1, p. 211
117 *Bet ha-Midrash*, vol. 1, p. 48
118 BT Ketubot 77b
119 BT Ta'anit 22a
120 BT Baba Kamma 60b. For Elijah and the angel of death, see p. 95 below
121 BT Shabbat 104a, 108a (Rashi's comment), Yevamot 102a
122 Mishnah, Baba Meẓia 3. 4–5, etc. For further details concerning Elijah's legal authority and duties, see M. Guttmann, *Mafteaḥ ha-Talmud*, entry 'Eliyahu'; E. Margaliot, *Eliyahu ha-Navi*, p. 145; *Encyclopedia talmudit*, vol. 2, pp. 6 ff.
123 *Seder Eliyahu Rabbah ve-Seder Eliyahu Zutta*, M. Ish-Shalom (ed.)
124 BT Ketubot 106a
125 *Pirke de-R. Eliezer*, ch. 29, pp. 213–14
126 G. Róheim, *The Eternal Ones of the Dream*, pp. 68, 72–3; Richard Thurnwald, 'Primitive Initiations- und Wiedergeburtsriten', in *Eranos-Jahrbuch 1939*, p. 390–1. See also K. Kohler, *Jewish Theology*, p. 49
127 Mishnah Eduyot 8. 7 (abbrev.)
128 Maimonides, *Mishneh Torah*, vol. 4, pt Melakhim, ch. 12
129 BT Sanhedrin 97b–98a. The two possibilities are intimated by R. Saadia Gaon (*c.* 900) in *Emunot ve-Deot*, pt Redemption, chs 5 and 6 (in trans., Treatise VIII, chs 5 and 6, pp. 301–12)
130 See pp. 59–60 for Elijah's task according to Mishnah Eduyot, and also pp. 65–6
131 Pirke ha-Mashiaḥ (*Midreshe Geulah*, p. 292); M. Konen (*Oẓar Midrashim*, vol. 1, p. 256)
132 M. r. Gen. 5. 1; 8.1
133 *M. Ḥaserot vi-Yterot*, p. 43 and Rashi's comment to Numbers 26: 42
134 *Pirke de-R. Eliezer*, ch. 40, p. 315
135 *M. Bereshit Rabbati*, pp. 130–1; *Midreshe Geulah*, p. 304. Variations without naming Elijah are in JT Berakhot 2. 4–5, and M. r. Ekhah 1. 59. See also p. 178 below

136 M. Konen (*Oẓar Midrashim*, vol. 1, p. 256); Pirke ha-Mashiaḥ (*Midreshe Geulah*, pp. 307–8)
137 BT Sanhedrin 97a
138 M. r. Exod. 18. 9
139 BT Eruvin 43a–b, Pesaḥim 13a
140 JT Pesaḥim 3, 6
141 M. r. Gen. 2. 4, 8. 1
142 M. r. Gen. 2. 4
143 M. r. Num. 14. 14; *Sifre le-Sefer Devarim*, pt 41, p. 87
144 Mishnah Sotah 9. 15; JT Shekalim 3.3
145 *Yalkut Shimoni*, vol. 1, 930, p. 639
146 *Pirke de-R. Eliezer*, ch. 43, p. 344
147 Psalms 3. 6; *M. Tehillim* 3. 7, p. 39
148 *M. Tehillim* 43. 1, p. 267
149 M. z. Shir ha-Shirim 7. 4
150 *Mekhilta de-R. Yishmael*, pt 16. 33, p. 51b. Elijah's task to anoint the Messiah is mentioned by Justin Martyr, *Dialogue with Trypho*, 49. 1 (p. 123)
151 *Pesikta rabbati* (ed. M. Ish-Shalom), pt 35, p. 161 (trans. Braude, vol. 2, pp. 674–5); see also D. Flusser, *Jesus*, p. 40
152 M. z. Shir ha-Shirim 5. 2 (p. 26); *Yalkut ha-Makhiri*, Isaiah 11. 4; Pirke ha-Mashiaḥ (*Midreshe Geulah*, p. 328)
153 The concept of 'a new Torah' is originally derived from Isa. 2: 2–4. For the development of this concept, see G. Scholem, *On the Kabbalah and its Symbolism*, pp. 77 ff.
154 Perek Eliyahu, Sefer Zerubavel, Maase Daniel, Tefillat R. Shimon bar Yoḥai, Pirke Mashiaḥ (all in *Midreshe Geulah*)
155 BT Sukkah 52a; JT Sukkah 5. 2
156 See also the detailed psychological study by S. Hurwitz, *Die Gestalt des sterbenden Messias*
157 Zerubbabel was high priest in the time of Ezra
158 Maase Daniel (*Midreshe Geulah*, pp. 128 ff.)
159 Sefer Eliyahu (*Midreshe Geulah*, pp. 31–48); *Bet ha-Midrash*, vol. 3, 3, pp. 65 ff. The Sefer Eliyahu, composed in Persia in the sixth century, is presumably derived from an original Hebrew manuscript of the first century. The Christian Coptic Elijah Apocalypse is also based on this manuscript (see p. 147 n. 27 below)
160 M. z. Shir ha-Shirim 2. 8, p. 26
161 M. r. Kohelet 4. 1
162 Mishnah Sotah 9. 15; M. z. Shir ha-Shirim 7. 14
163 BT Berakhot 31a, Ta'anit 7a; M. r. Gen. 13. 4
164 BT Sukkah 52b
165 ibid.
166 Gen. 14: 18; BT Nedarim 32b; Flusser, *Melchizedek and the Son of Man*, pp. 23 ff.
167 BT Sukkah 52b, according to Rashi on the text
168 Targum Jonathan Deut. 30. 4; Targum Ekhah 4. 22; Targum Kohelet 10. 20
169 *M. Mishle* 19. 22, p. 87

NOTES TO PAGES 70–79

170 *M. Tanḥuma* Shemot, vol. 1, p. 83
171 *M. Tehillim* 107. 1
172 M. r. Ekhah 1. 57
173 M. z. Shir ha-Shirim 2. 8, p. 26
174 ch. 15, p. 102
175 ibid., ch. 40, p. 315
176 *Pesikta Rabbati*, pt 4, p. 113; *Yalkut Shimoni*, vol. 2, 209, p. 757
177 M. r. Deut. 3. 16–17
178 Tosefta Sotah 4. 7b; BT Sotah 13a
179 BT Ḥullin 7b; R. D. Kimḥi on 2 Kings 2: 9
180 BT Sotah 47a, Sanhedrin 107b
181 Jonah chs 1 and 4. See pp. 19 above, 72, 94 below
182 *Pirke de-R. Eliezer*, ch. 33, p. 240; *Yalkut Shimoni*, vol. 2, 209, p. 757
183 M. Maase Torah *(Bet ha-Midrash*, vol. 2, p. 95)
184 *M. Tehillim* 8. 7
185 *Seder Eliyahu Rabbah*, ch. 18, pp. 97–8. For the significance of the Messiah
      ben Joseph, see pp. 66–7 above
186 *M. Tanḥuma* (ed. S. Buber), vol. 2, Bamidbar, p. 62
187 M. r. Gen. 60. 3; *Seder Eliyahu Rabbah*, ch. 12, p. 55
188 e.g. Targum Jonathan to Exod. 6: 18; *Yalkut Shimoni*, vol. 1, p. 535
189 *Pirke de-R. Eliezer*, ch. 29, p. 213
190 *Yalkut Shimoni*, vol. 1, p. 535
191 *Pirke de-R. Eliezer*, ch. 47, p. 371; see also p. 74 below
192 *Sifre le-Sefer Bamidbar*, pt 48b, p. 131
193 Likkutim mi-Shoḥer Tov *(Bate ha-Midrashot*, vol. 1, p. 296)
194 There is a detailed representation in V. Aptowitzer, *Bet ha-Mikdash shel
      Ma'alah al pi ha-Aggadah*. For the relationship between Metatron and
      Sandalphon-Elijah, see pp. 98ff. below
195 Jerusalem Targum to Num. 25. 12
196 V. Aptowitzer, *Die Parteipolitik der Hasmonäer*, pp. 96 ff.
197 *The Book of Direction to the Duties of the Heart*, p. 241

Chapter IV   Elijah in Jewish Mysticism

  1 BT Ḥagigah 11b ff.
  2 M. r. Gen. 68. 10; M. r. Exod. 33. 4
  3 In the *Sefer Yezirah* is the first mention of the emanation of the ten
     sefirot by which, together with the twenty-two letters of the Hebrew
     alphabet, the world was created. The book seems also to be connected
     with Hekhalot and Merkavah mysticism
  4 For Elijah in the *Sefer ha-Bahir*, see pt 48, p. 22
  5 The most outstanding mystical books of the Ḥaside Ashkenaz are the
     Sefer Ḥasidim (Book of the Devout), presumably composed by R. Judah
     the Ḥasid and R. Eleazar of Worms, and *Ḥokhmat ha-Nefesh (The Science
     of the Soul)*, ascribed to R. Eleazar; it contains the doctrine of the
     archetypes based on the above mentioned macrocosmic-microcosmic
     parallelism (see p. 79 above)

6 *Major Trends in Jewish Mysticism*, pp. 156–204
7 BT Shabbat 32b
8 *Zohar Ḥadash* 59c; *Tikkune ha-Zohar* 1a
9 1 Zohar 100b (*Midrash ha-Ne'elam*); 3 Zohar 242a; *Zohar Ḥadash* 49b; *Tikkune ha-Zohar* 19a, etc.
10 1 Zohar 151a, 217a
11 1 Zohar 24a; *Tikkune ha-Zohar* 21a
12 3 Zohar 144b; *Tikkune ha-Zohar* 21a
13 Iggeret R. Sherira Gaon, p. 37
14 *Sefer Ḥasidim*, p. 731
15 *Oẓar ha-Geonim*, Ḥagigah 14b (vol. 4, p. 14)
16 *Ma'arekhet ha-Gedolim*, item 'ha-Ravad'; cf. G. Scholem, *Reshit ha-Kabbalah*, pp. 60 ff., 101 ff.
17 *Sefer ha-Peliah*, Hakdamah (Introduction)
18 S. Dresnitz, *Shivḥe ha-Ari* 33. 2; R. Naphtali Bacharach, *Emek ha-Melekh*, 2, Introduction, p. 10a
19 ibid., 3, Introduction, p. 11a; R. Ḥ. Vital, Hakdamah to *Eẓ Ḥayyim* 4b, 5a
20 Bacharach, op. cit., 3. Introduction, p. 11a, b
21 R. Ḥ. Vital, *Eẓ Ḥayyim*, Introduction, pp. 9–10
22 See p. 116
23 R. Ḥ. Vital *Sha'are ha-Kedushah*, pt 3. 7
24 ibid.
25 R. Luria Ashkenazi, *Likkute ha-Shas*, p. 55a
26 R. Ḥ. Vital, *Sha'are ha-Kedushah*, pt 4
27 R. Ḥ. Vital *Sha'ar ha-Kavvanot* 50a
28 R. Joseph Karo, *Maggid Mesharim*, pp. 76–7
29 ibid., p. 5
30 ibid., p. 13
31 R. Moses Cordovero, *Derishat be-Inyane Malakhim* (in R. Reuben Margulies, *Malakhe Elyon*, appendix)
32 R. Livai of Prague, *Neẓaḥ Yisrael*, ch. 28
33 *Sifra de-Ẓeniuta*, Introduction, p. 5
34 S. Ginzburg, *R. Moshe Ḥ. Luẓẓatto u-Vne Doro*, vol. 1, pp. 31, 39, 40. For the relationship between Metatron and Elijah, see pp. 99–100 below
35 ibid., vol. 2, p. 408
36 *Zohar Ḥadash* 59c, d
37 *Zohar Ḥadash* 23d
38 1 Zohar 151a
39 3 Zohar 221b
40 3 Zohar 242 a, b
41 *Zohar Ḥadash* 62b
42 2 Zohar 119a
43 *Zohar Ḥadash* 62c
44 *Tikkune ha-Zohar* 23b–24a
45 ibid., 17a, b
46 3 Zohar 238a
47 p. 13
48 ibid., p. 120

49 1 Zohar 209a (abbrev.)
50 1 Zohar 209b (abbrev.); Num. 25. 12
51 1 Zohar 81a, b; see p. 194 below
52 H. Vital, *Sefer ha-Likkutim*, p. 1b; *Emek ha-Melekh*, ch. 49, p. 29a; see also pp. 91 above and 194 below
53 *Tikkune ha-Zohar*, Introduction, p. 3b
54 ibid.
55 ibid.
56 *Zohar Hadash* 23b
57 This verse relates to Elijah in the Aggadah (M. r. Num. 12. 13 and *Pesikta Rabbati*, pt 5)
58 An unknown mystical work often cited in the Zohar and also mentioned in some Midrashim
59 2 Zohar 197a, b (abbrev.)
60 3 Zohar 88b
61 2 Zohar 150a; 3 Zohar 88b; see also G. Scholem, *Von der mystischen Gestalt der Gottheit*, pp. 249 ff.
62 1 Zohar 101a; 3 Zohar 126b, 152a
63 *Zohar Hadash* 75d, 76a
64 3 Zohar 238a
65 Rivka Schaerf-Kluger, *Satan in the Old Testament*
66 *Sifre le-Sefer Devarim* 6. 5, p. 55 (see p. 192 below). According to 2 Zohar 150a, it is the angel of death who exchanges the physical garment of the souls of the dead for the ethereal one in which they may ascend to heaven
67 2 Zohar 201b
68 pt 48, p. 22
69 R. M. Cordovero, *Pardes Rimonim*, gate 24, ch. 14, pp. 161a, b
70 This passage cited by Cordovero is included with commentary by J. Tishby in his edition of the manuscript 'She'elot u-Teshuvot le-R. Moshe de Leon be-Inyane Kabbalah'. According to Tishby, this passage does not necessarily conflict with the view of the Zohar, which he sees also implying in several passages that Elijah had always been an angel. The Aggadot of R. Azriel (ed. J. Tishby, p. 66) and also the Midrash Konen (*Bet ha-Midrash*, vol. 4, p. 27) relate the Aggadic saying, that only one single angel approved of the creation of man, not to Elijah but to the angel Boel who therefore was called Raphael and appointed 'the healer'. But R. Azriel also mentions the view that the other archangels, Michael and Gabriel, 'came from the generations like Enoch and Elijah', i.e. they were originally human beings. Concerning the conflict between de Leon's opinion and the Zoharic view of the Elijah-figure discussed by Cordovero, see also R. Margulies, *Malakhe Elyon*, p. 16 n. 25, and A. J. Heschel, *Torah min-ha-Shamayim*, vol. 2, p. 53
71 *Sefer ha-Kanah*, p. 68a; R. Menahem Azariah da Fano, *Aseret Ma'amarot* 4. 19. That Elijah's girdle was made of the skin of this ram is mentioned earlier in *Pirke de-R. Eliezer*, ch. 31, p. 229
72 Cordovero, op. cit., sha'ar 24, ch. 13, pp. 160b–161a
73 1 Zohar 151a, b
74 1 Zohar 46b; see also n. 70 above

75 op. cit., sha'ar 24, chs 12, 13, 14, pp. 160–1
76 *Emek ha-Melekh*, p. 178c
77 ibid., p. 37a
78 BT Sanhedrin 38b. Because of this formulation, Metatron is sometimes called 'the lesser YHVH' or 'the little YHVH' (e.g. III Enoch, 12: 5; M. Bereshit rabbati, pp. 28–9). The Talmud passage cited above, however, argues against the deification of Metatron. See also E. Urbach, *Ḥazal: Pirke Emunot ve-Deot*, pp. 118–19, nn. 14, 15
79 3 Zohar 189a, b
80 BT Avodah Zarah 3b
81 M. r. Num. 12. 15
82 Jerusalem Targum to Gen. 5: 24
83 H. Odeberg (ed.), pt 1, pp. 79 ff.
84 Cordovero, op. cit., sha'ar 16, ch. 4
85 *Zohar Ḥadash* 42d, 68d–69a; R. Ḥ. Vital, *Sefer ha-Likkutim*, p. 7b
86 2 Zohar 94b; Cordovero, op. cit., sha'ar 16, ch. 4
87 3 Zohar 227a; *Tikkune ha-Zohar* 23a; Cordovero, op. cit., sha'ar 16, ch. 4
88 *Zohar Ḥadash* 42d; *Emek ha-Melekh*, pp. 169b, 178c; R. Natan ben Shelomo, *Megale Amukot*, ch. 218
89 Cordovero, op. cit., sha'ar 16, ch. 4
90 Comment of R. Ḥayat on *Ma'arekhet ha-Elohut*, p. 169
91 3 Zohar 189a, b; *Emek ha-Melekh* 81b; for a comprehensive characterisation of Metatron, see *M. Bereshit Rabbati*, pp. 27–9
92 BT Ḥagigah 13b; 1 Zohar 167b
93 *Sefer Temunah*, pp. 56 ff. (written in the thirteenth century, probably based on earlier sources). About this remarkable book, see G. Scholem, *Ursprung und Anfänge der Kabbalah*, pp. 407 ff.
94 *Zohar Ḥadash* 38d
95 *Emek ha-Melekh* p. 94. See p. 74 n. 193 above
96 *Tikkune ha-Zohar* 23a
97 M. Konen (*Oẓar Midrashim*, vol. 1, p. 254); R. Ḥ. Vital, *Sefer ha-Likkutim* (Sha'ar ha-Pesukim, pt 2)
98 Masekhet Aẓilut (*Oẓar Midrashim*, vol. 1, p. 67); *Emek ha-Melekh*, pp. 169b, 179a, 180d; R. Natan ben Shelomo, *Megale Amukot al ha-Torah*, p. 44
99 *Sefer Temunah*, p. 56a; for further details about Sandalphon-Elijah, see R. Reuben Margulies, *Malakhe Elyon*, pp. 148–54, text and notes
100 1 Zohar 37b; 2 Zohar 206a; I. Lange (ed.), MS. Moscow, Günzburg 82, concerning R. Judah's comment on Num. 24. 17
101 J. Dan, *Torat Ḥaside Ashkenaz*, p. 220
102 R. J. Karo, *Maggid Mesharim*, pp. 42 ff. For Karo's view of Metatron, see R. Z. Werblowsky, *Joseph Karo, Lawyer and Mystic*, p. 270
103 *Sefer ha-Likkutim* (Sha'ar ha-Pesukim, pt. 2, Likkute Shir ha-Shirim, p. 69b)
104 Masekhet Aẓilut (*Oẓar Midrashim*, vol. 1, p. 68)
105 R. Menahem Azariah da Fano, *Aseret Ma'amarot* 3. 22. In the Zohar, Metatron himself is represented as having two aspects: a higher and a lower, old and young, or mercy and strength; as such, they are compared

to the two cherubim (*Zohar Ḥadash* 42d, 85b). For further details about
Elijah-Sandalphon, see R. Margulies, *Malakhe Elyon*, p. 148
106 *Emek ha-Melekh*, p. 169a
107 *Avodat ha-Kodesh*, pt ha-Yiḥud, ch. 16
108 1 Zohar 13a, 93a
109 2 Zohar 190a
110 R. N. Z. J. Volozhin, *Ḥumash Ha'amek Davar*, vol. 4, p. 111a (225)
111 3 Zohar 27b–28a
112 3 Zohar 215b
113 3 Zohar 217a
114 3 Zohar 57b (abbrev.)
115 R. Ḥ. Vital, *Sefer ha-Gilgulim*, chs 3 and 4 (Likkutim)
116 ibid., chs 1 and 2; see also G. Scholem, *Von der mystischen Gestalt der Gottheit*, pp. 194 ff.
117 *Sefer ha-Gilgulim*, chs 3 and 4
118 The supreme parts of Adam's soul had passed on to Enoch-Metatron
119 *Sha'ar ha-Gilgulim*, Introduction, pp. 31–2
120 ibid.
121 From the transcendent parts of the soul originating with Nadab and Abihu, sparks are passed on, at Elijah's ascent, to Elisha, who received his own original soul from Joseph. *Sefer ha-Gilgulim*, ch. 35; *Sha'ar ha-Gilgulim*, ch. 32
122 *Sefer ha-Gilgulim*, ch. 31; see p. 52 above
123 ibid., ch. 32
124 C. G. Jung, *Psychological Types*, pp. 330 ff.
125 *Sha'ar ha-Gilgulim*, ch. 38
126 *Tikkune ha-Zohar*, p. 3b; R. M. Cordovero, *Pardes Rimonim* 16. 1; R. Ḥ. Vital, *Eẓ Ḥayim*, section 7, sha'ar 3
127 For the symbols of Adam's sin, see p. 181 n. 15
128 *Emek ha-Melekh*, pp. 42b, c, 51b (abbrev.); R. Natan ben Shelomoh, *Megale Amukot*, ch. 111
129 BT Berakhot 59a; see also J. Campbell, 'The living waters are the tears of God', in *The Hero with a Thousand Faces*, p. 146
130 *Sefer ha-Gilgulim*, ch. 35; see p. 103 above
131 See also R. Z. Werblowsky's extensive study, *Joseph Karo, Lawyer and Mystic*, chs 11 and 12, and Epilogue
132 See G. Scholem, *Major Trends in Jewish Mysticism*, pp. 139–40; see also p. 98 above

Chapter V Elijah in the Sabbatian Movement

1 G. Scholem (ed.), 'Iggeret Nathan ha-Azati al Shabbetai Ẓevi ve-Hamarato', *Koveẓ al-Yad*, 1966, p. 423 ff.; see also pp. 113–14 above
2 Nathan refers by this to the saying of the sages that Elijah will come to make peace (Mishnah Eduyot 8. 7)
3 Mal. 3: 24
4 'Iggeret Nathan', p. 455

5 The description of the character and attitudes of Shabbetai and Nathan and their relations as Messiah and prophet is based on G. Scholem, *Major Trends in Jewish Mysticism*, pp. 287 ff. (see now his *Sabbatai Ṣevi*). The historical background follows the account in S. Dubnow, *History of the Jews*, vol. 4, pp. 51 ff. See also the interesting psychological study of Shabbetai by S. Hurwitz, 'Sabbatai Zwi', *Studien zur analytischen Psychologie C. G. Jungs*, vol. 2, pp.239 ff.

Chapter VI   Elijah in Ḥasidism

1 R. Ephraim of Sudlikov, *Degel Maḥane Efrayim*, p. 77b (based on Psalm 69: 19)
2 ibid., p. 16a
3 *Toldot Ya'akov Yosef*, p. 74a, b, based on passages cited from Psalms 118: 5 and 4: 2
4 ibid., pp. 40a, b, 86b
5 R. Solomon of Lutzk, *Likkute Amarim* (*Maggid Devarav le-Ya'akov*), p. 12a
6 R. M. J. Leiner, *Me-ha-Shiloaḥ*, vol. 1, pp. 14a, 17b, 25b; vol. 2, pp. 7b, 38a (see also pp. 191–2 below). See also J. Weiss, 'Spät-jüdische Utopie religiöser Freiheit', in *Eranos-Jahrbuch 1962*; Rivka Schatz, 'Autonomia shel ha-Ruaḥ ve-Torat Moshe', *Molad*, 21, 1961
7 R. Ze'ev Wolf of Zhitomir, *Or ha-Me'ir*, pp. 39a, b, 40b
8 *Likkutim Yekarim*, p. 17b. Meditation on the prayer structure means contemplating the combination of the creative forces of the letters into words. For a discussion of Ḥasidic contemplative prayer, see Rivka Schatz-Uffenheimer, *ha-Ḥasidut ke-Mystikah*, chs 6, 7, 10; R. Louis Jacobs, *Hasidic Prayer*, ch. VI
9 *Likkutim Yekarim*, p. 28a; R. Menahem Nahum of Tchernobil, *Sefer Meor Enayim*, p. 106
10 *Likkutim Yekarim*, p. 20a
11 *Likkute Amarim*, p. 31b (62); *Or Torah*, p. 15b (30); *Likkutim Yekarim*, pp. 17b, 20a, 21a; *Sefer Meor Enayim*, pp. 106, 155–6, 215
12 *Toldot Ya'akov Yosef*, p. 131; R. Ephraim of Sudlikov, *Degel Maḥane Efrayim*, p. 63; *Likkute Amarim*, p. 39b; *Likkutim Yekarim*, pp. 15a, 24a; *Or Torah*, p. 58a (115); *Meor Enayim*, p. 166
13 *Toldot Ya'akov Yosef*, p. 154 d (see pp. 51 n. 53, 71 n. 178 above)
14 R. Solomon of Lutzk, *Divrat Shelomoh*, p. 13b; *Likkute Amarim*, Introduction; *Likkutim Yekarim*, p. 24b
15 Ed. S. A. Horodezki
16 *Likkutim Yekarim*, p. 24b
17 *Sippure Eliyahu ha-Navi*, various tales in vols 1 and 2
18 R. Zadok ha-Kohen of Lublin, *Peri ha-Ẕaddik*, vol. 4, p. 27
19 *Or Torah*, p. 52b (104); *Likkutim Yekarim*, p. 31b
20 R. Menahem Mendel of Lubavitch, *Derekh Miẕvotekha*, p. 31b
21 R. Zadok ha-Kohen, *Peri ha-Ẕaddik*, vol. 1, p. 159, and *Dover Ẕedek*, pp. 98–100. R. Zadok regards Adam's sin too as God's will (*Dover Ẕedek*, pp. 47, 97). See pp. 118–19 above and 191–2 ff. below

22 R. Barukh of Medziboz, *Sefer Bozina de Nehora* (quoted from M. Buber, *Or ha-Ganuz*, p. 103) also in *Tales of the Hasidim*, vol. 1, p. 257
23 R. Solomon of Lutzk, *Divrat Shelomoh*, p. 13b
24 1 Zohar, 59b
25 R. Naḥman of Bratzlav, *Likkute Moharan*, p. 81b
26 *Or Torah*, p. 56a (111)
27 R. Menahem Nahum of Tchernobil, *Sefer Meor Enayim*, p. 69 (abbrev.), also p. 135
28 This means that the Elijah-factor exists in every individual even if he is not aware of it; see the quotation of the same author, pp. 22–3
29 *Meor Enayim*, pp. 166–7
30 ibid., pp. 162–3
31 ibid., p. 135
32 R. Mordecai of Tchernobil, *Likkute Torah*, p. 47a.
33 In M. Buber, *Or ha-Ganuz*, p. 236, also in *Tales of the Hasidim*, vol. 1, p. 257
34 *Divrat Shelomoh*, p. 23a
35 *Eser Orot*, p. 60; see also p. 55 above
36 S. Mowinckel, *Die Erkenntnis Gottes bei den alttestamentlichen Propheten*; R. A. Steinsalz, 'Mashma'ut ha-"Yediah" ba-Tanakh', *Sinai*, 60, 1967, pp. 1–3
37 e.g. R. M. Cordovero, *Pardes Rimonim*, sha'ar 3, ch. 8; *Meor Enayim*, pp. 178, 278
38 *Likkutim Yekarim* 24a; *Sefer Meor Enayim*, pp. 232, 260–3
39 R. Shneor Zalman of Liady, *Likkute Amarim* (*Sefer Tanya*), p. 14
40 *Meor Enayim*, p. 261; R. Meshullam Fabish of Zharabaz, *Derekh Emet*, p. 28; also *Likkutim Yekarim*, p. 24a
41 *Meor Enayim*, pp. 63, 279; *Yismaḥ Lev* (in *Meor Enayim*), p. 342
42 *Meor Enayim*, pp. 63, 96
43 *Yismaḥ Lev* (in *Meor Enayim*), pp. 304–5; R. Menahem Mendel of Vitebsk, *Peri ha-Arez*, pp. 9a (17), 17a (33)
44 ibid., pp. 14b (28), 28a (55); R. Ephraim of Sudlikov, *Degel Maḥane Efrayim*, p. 47
45 R. Aaron of Starosselje, *Avodat ha-Levi*, vol. 2, Likkutim, p. 20
46 R. Jacob Joseph of Pulnoye, *Toldot Ya'akov Yosef*, pp. 63–4
47 ibid., p. 70; *Ketonet Passim*, p. 8b
48 R. Jacob Joseph of Pulnoye, *Ketonet Passim*, p. 8c; *Zofnat Paneaḥ*, p. 121
49 R. Jacob Joseph of Pulnoye, *Toldot Ya'akov Yosef*, p. 39b; *Ben Porat Yosef*, p. 62c; *Sefer Meor Enayim*, pp. 84, 97–8, 178; *Yismaḥ Lev*, ibid., p. 339
50 The possibility of experiencing the unity of subject and object is repeatedly intimated in Ḥasidic literature, especially in *Meor Enayim* and *Likkute Amarim* (*Sefer Tanya*)
51 *Shir ha-Shirim*, p. 190
52 See the diagram on p. 104
53 M. r. Exod. 15. 13; M. r. Num. 2. 2; M. *Tanḥuma* (ed. S. Buber), vol. 2, p. 72; see also pp. 77, 106 above
54 *Likkute Amarim* (*Sefer Tanya*), p. 14; R. A. Steinsalz, *Hokhmah–Binah–Da'at be-Shitat Ḥabad*

55 See p. 79 n. 2, and *Avot de-R. Natan*, ch. 31, version A, p. 91
56 R. J. Gikatilla, *Sha'are Orah*, p. 80a; *Tikkune ha-Zohar*, Hakdamah , p. 6a
57 *Likkute Amarim*, p. 12a (25); *Likkutim Yekarim*, p. 21b
58 *Yismah Lev* (in *Meor Enayim*), pp. 338–9, 341–2
59 *Likkutim Yekarim*, p. 22a. Various expressions of the same thought can be found in *Likkute Amarim*
60 *Or Torah*, p. 52b (104); R. Menahem Mendel of Vitebsk, *Peri ha-Arez*, p. 14b (28)
61 *Likkutim Yekarim*, pp. 23b, 24a; R. Ze'ev Wolf of Zhitomir, *Or ha-Me'ir*, p. 7b; R. Meshullam Fabish of Zharabaz, *Derekh Emet*, p. 28
62 *Meor Enayim*, p. 288b
63 ibid., pp. 178 a, b
64 *Likkutim Yekarim*, p. 11a; *Meor Enayim*, p. 105
65 *Likkute Amarim*, p. 23a (45); *Or Torah*, p. 16b (32); *Likkutim Yekarim*, p. 12b
66 BT Ḥagigah 13a; see also p. 99 above
67 See also Rudolf Mach, *Der Zaddik in Talmud und Midrasch*; BT Kiddushin 72b
68 M. Shemuel, 29, 2
69 M. r. Gen. 77a
70 BT Sanhedrin 12b
71 Pt 44, p. 21
72 R. J. Gikatilla, *Sha'are Orah*, p. 15; see also *Meor Enayim*, p. 109, based on Targum Onkelos to 1 Chr. 29: 11
73 *Or Torah*, p. 4b (8); *Likkutim Yekarim*, p. 37a
74 *Meor Enayim*, p. 244; for greater detail, see pp. 109 ff. and 286. It is also said: The Zaddik connects the higher worlds with the ones below (R. Menahem Mendel of Vitebsk, *Peri ha-Arez*, p. 25b)
75 *Noam Elimelekh*, pp. 26 b, d
76 *Or Torah*, p. 4b (8); *Likkutim Yekarim*, p. 37a
77 *Or Torah*, Rimze Tehillim, p. 44a (87); *Likkutim Yekarim*, p. 35a
78 R. Israel of Koznitz, *Avodat Yisrael*, on Avot, p. 8a
79 *Likkute Moharan*, pp. 100, 104. For Hasidic points of view on the *zaddik*, see also *Derekh Ḥasidim*, ed. J. Kenig, pp. 333 ff.; G. Scholem, *Von der mystischen Gestalt der Gottheit*, ch. 3
80 *Likkute Amarim*, p. 32a (63)
81 *Ketonet Passim*, p. 25b
82 ibid., p. 27b

Chapter VII Elijah in Liturgy and Ritual

1 The Talmud, in connection with this, points out the special significance of the afternoon prayer, as the Bible records that Elijah prayed on Mount Carmel at this time of the day (BT Berakhot 6b)
2 BT Berakhot 3a
3 *Divrat Shelomoh*, beginning of the passage Va'ethanan
4 'In worship man ascends to the Divine; in myth the divine descends to

16

him and becomes incarnate' (W. F. Otto, *Die Gestalt und das Sein*, pp. 86-7)

5 Particulars are in E. Margaliot, *Eliyahu ha-Navi*, pp. 135 ff.
6 For details, see S. Z. Kahane, 'Eliyahu ha-Navi be-Moẓae Shabbat', *Yeda-Am*, 7 (25), 1961, pp. 9ff.
7 For the development of the custom of 'Elijah's cup', see R. J. Avida, *Koso shel Eliyahu ha-Navi*

Chapter VIII   Elijah in Jewish Folklore

1 See J. Campbell, *The Hero with a Thousand Faces*, p. 63
2 *Maaseh-Book* (ed. Gaster), p. 341 (abbrev.)
3 ibid., p. 313 (abbrev.)
4 *Sippure Eliyahu ha-Navi*, vol. 1, p. 172 (abbrev.)
5 Quoted from *Enzyclopedia Ivrit*, vol. 3, p. 541
6 For this story I am indebted to Dr S. Z. Kahane of Tel-Aviv, who heard it told in a Ḥasidic circle
7 *Sippure Eliyahu ha-Navi*, vol. 1, pp. 299 ff.
8 ibid., pp. 292 ff.
9 J. Braslawsky, 'Me'arot Eliyahu ha-Navi mi-Kahir ad Ḥalab', *Yeda-Am*, 7(25), 1961, p. 49 ff.
10 Further folk literature is quoted in J. Bergmann, *Legenden der Juden*; H. Schwarzbaum, *Studies in Jewish and World Folklore*; L. Newman, *The Hasidic Anthology*

Chapter IX   The Elijah-Figure in Christianity

1 The first quotation is a combination of Mal. 3: 1 and Exod. 23: 20, the second is Isa. 40: 3
2 The Hebrew expression '*baal-sear*' is sometimes interpreted in Jewish tradition as meaning 'the hairy one', but usually as clothed in a hairy hide
3 'The prophet' refers to the prophet resembling Moses mentioned in Deut. 18: 15
4 Justin Martyr, *Dialogue with Trypho*, 49. 1, also 8. 4 (p. 123). See also p. 42, and ch. II n. 19 above. For John as the returned Elijah, see also the detailed studies by A. Schlatter, *Johannes der Täufer*, pp. 16-55, and J. Schütze, *Johannes der Täufer*. For contradictions in the New Testament regarding the Elijah-John identification, see the particularly interesting study by J. A. T. Robinson, *Elijah, John, Jesus: an Essay in Detection*, pp. 263-81. See also W. Bousset, 'Die Religion des Judentums', in *Handbuch zum Neuen Testament*, pp. 232-3
5 For the similar relationship of Elijah and John with the river Jordan, see N. Glueck, *The River Jordan*, p. 244-5
6 Clement I, Letter 1, 17. 1; Clemens Alexandrinus, Paedagogus 3, 38. 1; 2, 112. 3; St Gregory of Nyssa, Homilia, Cantus Canticorum 7 (quoted from *Reallexikon für Antike und Christentum*, vol. 4, p. 1150)
7 St Athanasius, Vita Antonii, ch. 7 (ibid.); St Ambrose, Letter 63 (quoted from A. Ohlmeyer, *Elias, Fürst der Propheten*, pp. 207-8)

8 St Ambrose, Expositionis evangelii secundum Lucam libri decem (*Reallexikon*, p. 1150)

9 St Augustine, Commentary to Gen. 9: 6 (quoted from M. Wormbrand, 'Eliyahu ha-Navi ba-Masoret ha-Noẓrit', *Yeda-Am*, 7 (25), 1961, p. 40, and Ohlmeyer, op. cit., p. 205)

10 St Jerome, Epistula 58. 5 (*Reallexikon*, p. 1150)

11 Adversus Marcionem 4. 12. (in Ohlmeyer, op cit., p. 203)

12 St Cyril of Jerusalem, Catena 16. 28; St Isidore of Pelusium, Epistula 1. 297; Basil of Seleucia, Oratio 11 (all quoted from *Reallexikon*, vol. 4, p. 1150)

13 Nilus (the Monk), Epistula 181 (ibid., p. 1150); St Peter (Chrysologus), Oratio 43. (ibid., p. 1150); St Ambrose, Expositio in Lucam 1: 36 (ibid., p. 1154)

14 Basil of Seleucia, Oratio 11. 4 (ibid., p. 1154)

15 Aphraates (quoted from Wormbrand, op. cit., p. 40)

16 Prosper of Aquitaine, De Promissionibus et praedictionibus Dei 2. 29, 63 (*Reallexikon*, p. 1151)

17 St Augustine, Contra Faustum 12. 34 (Ohlmeyer, op. cit., p. 209)

18 St John Chrystosom, De Sacerdote (ibid., p. 106)

19 St Ambrose, Expositio in Lucam 1. 36 (*Reallexikon*, p. 1153); St Augustine, Contra Julianum 1. 3. 10 (Ohlmeyer, op. cit., p. 177)

20 St Cyril of Jerusalem, Catena 18. 16 (*Reallexikon*, p. 1153)

21 St Ambrose, Expositio in Lucam 4: 96 (ibid.)

22 Origen, Commentary to Matt. 3: 1–2 (ibid.); St Ambrose, Commentary to Luke 1: 17 (Ohlmeyer. op. cit., pp. 195–6); St Augustine, De civitate Dei 20. 29 (ibid., p. 191); see also D. de Saint-René, 'In spiritu et virtute Eliae', in *Élie le prophète*, vol. 2, pp. 190 ff.

23 Justin Martyr, *Dialogue with Trypho*, 49. 2; Origen, Commentary on John 2: 39; 4: 7; St Hippolytus, Christ and Antichrist, pp. 46–7; St Augustine, De civitate Dei 20. 29 and Quaestiorum evangeliorum libri duo 2. 21 (*Reallexikon*, p. 1154)

24 De carnis resurrectioni (Wormbrand, op. cit., p. 41)

25 St Hilary, About Matthew, ch. 20 (Ohlmeyer, op. cit., p. 201)

26 Tertullian, De testimone animae, ch. 35 (Ohlmeyer, op. cit., p. 201); see also St Hippolytus and Irenaeus (W. Bousset, *The Antichrist Legend*, pp. 27, 58)

27 The Elijah-Apocalypse is based on a Jewish work, revised, presumably by a Christian hand, in the seventh century to include the Messiah who had already appeared and the figure of the Antichrist; G. Steindorff, *Die Apocalypse des Elias*, pp. 1–24, 150–69; P. Riessler, *Altjüdische Schriften ausserhalb der Bibel*, pp. 114–25; Bousset, op. cit., pp. 27, 58, 203–8; see also p. 68 n. 159 above

28 *Reallexikon*, pp. 1156 ff.; *Lexikon für Theologie und Kirche*, vol. 3, pp. 808–10; Ohlmeyer, op. cit., pp. 211–19

29 *Reallexikon*, pp. 1156–7; *Lexikon*, pp. 808 ff.

30 C. Kopp, *Elias und das Christentum auf dem Carmel*; *Élie le prophète*, vol. 2, pp. 34–133; Ohlmeyer, op. cit., pp. 117–18, 211

31 *Élie le prophète*, vol. 2, pp. 134–50; Ohlmeyer, op. cit., pp. 215–16,

219–22; personal communications from Father Élie, Prior of the Carmelite monastery on Mount Carmel

32 F. Weber, *Die jüdische Theologie auf Grund des Talmud und verwandter Schriften*, pp. 337–9, 352–4; H. Strack and P. Billerbeck, *Kommentar zum Neuen Testament aus Talmud und Midrasch*, vol. 4, pt 2, pp. 767 ff.

33 H. Gressmann, *Der Messias;* S. Mowinckel, *He That Cometh*

34 G. Fohrer, *Elias*. See also p. 143 n. 4 above

35 *Men of God*, p. 64–5

36 From 'Der Prophet Elias im Lichte der Geisteswissenschaft', in *Wendepunkte der Geistesgeschichte*, pp. 96–116

37 *Elias, die Zielsetzung der Erde*, p. 41

38 *Auf den Wegen und Spuren des Alten Testamentes*, p. 189. W. Nigg, another well-known theologian, also emphasises the historical as well as the metahistorical significance of Elijah (*Drei grosse Zeichen*, pp. 79–83)

39 The Dura-Europos synagogue, supposedly built *c*. 100 CE, was abandoned in 256; see *Encyclopedia Judaica*, vol. 6, pp. 257 ff., and for the Elijah frescoes, pp. 290, 294, 296. See also L. Réau, 'Iconographie', in *Élie le prophète*, vol. 1, p. 231

40 'Elijah in the Arts', *Encyclopedia Judaica*, vol. 6, pp. 640–2; *Lexikon der christlichen Ikonographie*, vol. 1, pp. 607–12; *Reallexikon*, pp. 1158 ff.

Chapter X Elijah in Islam

1 Sura 6. 86 (p. 433)

2 Sura 37. 123–33 (pp. 174–5)

3 This chapter is based on two articles by A. J. Wensinck: 'Ilyas', *Encyclopaedia of Islam*, ed. B. Lewis *et al.*, vol. 3, p. 1030, and 'Al Khadir', in the edition by M. Houtsma *et al.* (*EOI*), vol. 2, pt 2, pp. 681–5; on I. Friedländer, 'Al Khadir', *Encyclopaedia of Religion and Ethics* (*ERE*), vol. 7, pp. 693–5, and on K. Vollers, 'Chidher', *Archiv für Religionswissenschaft*, 12(1), 1909, pp. 234–84

4 61–83 (pp. 96–8, abbrev.); Vollers, op. cit., pp. 238–9; *EOI*, vol. 2, pt 2, p. 861; *ERE*, vol. 7, pp. 693–5

5 Vollers, op. cit., pp. 240, 248; *EOI*, vol. 2, pt 2, pp. 863, 864, 865. The name of the prophet al-Khadir (or al-Hadir) means 'The Verdant One'; in popular language he is often called 'Hidher', 'verdant'

6 Vollers, op. cit., pp. 241–52 (abbrev.); *EOI*, vol. 2, pt 2, p. 863

7 Vollers, op. cit., pp. 253, 256, 257; *EOI*, vol. 2, pt. 2, pp. 863, 864

8 Vollers, op. cit., pp. 254–5

9 ibid., p. 254; *EOI*, vol. 2, pt 2, p. 863

10 Vollers, op. cit., p. 260

11 ibid., pp. 255, 257; *EOI*, vol. 2, pt 2, p. 862

12 Vollers, op. cit., pp. 256, 265; *ERE*, vol. 7, p. 695

13 Vollers, op. cit., pp. 263–4; *EOI*, vol. 2, pt 2, p. 865

14 Vollers, p. 252

15 ibid., pp. 256, 257, 260; *EOI*, vol. 2, pt 2, pp. 864, 865; *ERE*, vol. 7, p. 694

16 Vollers, op. cit., p. 261; *EOI*, vol. 2, pt 2, p. 864; *Élie le prophète*, vol. 2, pp. 269 ff. The story of al-Khadir's sale as a slave is very similar to one about Elijah (see p. 53 above). See also I. Obermann, 'Two Elijah stories in Judeo-Arabic transmission', *Hebrew Union College Annual*, 23, 1950–1, pp. 387 ff.

17 Vollers, op. cit., p. 248; *EOI*, vol. 2, pt 2, p. 864

18 Vollers, op. cit., p. 260

19 ibid.; *ERE*, vol. 7, pp. 694–5

20 ibid. (Here and elsewhere Elisha is confused with Elijah)

21 Vollers, op. cit., pp. 262–3; *EOI*, vol. 2, pt 2, p. 864

22 Vollers, op. cit., p. 258; *EOI*, vol. 2, pt 2, p. 863

23 Prodromi to sura 18. 57 (quoted from *EOI*, vol. 2, pt 2)

24 *EOI*, vol. 2, pt 2, p. 864; *ERE*, vol. 7, p. 695

25 I. Friedländer, *Die Chadirlegende und der Alexander Roman*, p. 145, based on British Library Add. Manuscript 5928

26 *EOI*, vol. 2, pt 2, p. 864

27 Sura 18, 72–83 (pp. 99–100)

28 *Abhandlungen zur arabischen Philologie*, vol. 2, 1

29 'Wer ist Chadir?', *Zeitschrift für Archaeologie*, 2, 1892, pp. 104–16

30 op. cit., pp. 239, 271–2

31 'Zur Geschichte der Chadirlegende', *Archiv für Religionswissenschaft*, 13, 1910, pp. 92–110. A summary of Friedländer's studies on al-Khadir is given in *ERE*, vol. 6, pp. 693–5

32 *EOI* vol. 2, pt 2, p. 864

33 I. Friedländer, 'Alexander's Zug nach der Lebensquelle und die Chadir-legende', *Archiv für Religionswissenschaft*, 13, 1910, pp. 161–246. The legend of Alexander the Great's march in quest of the source of life is related also in the Babylonian Talmud, Tamid 31b

34 op. cit., pp. 271–2. He also deals with the relationship of Elijah (or al-Khadir) to Christianity, especially with the Apocalypse of John and with parallels in eastern religions (pp. 274–6)

35 'Zur Geschichte der Chadirlegende', p. 97, also in *Die Chadirlegende und der Alexander Roman*, pp. 255 ff.; see also Obermann, op. cit.

36 Vollers, op. cit., p. 260; also *ERE*, p. 695

37 Vollers, op. cit., p. 254; see also p. 154 above

38 'Concerning Rebirth', In *The Archetypes and the Collective Unconscious*, pp. 137–41 (abbrev.)

39 Vol. 2, pp. 15–16

40 pp. 327–8

Chapter XI   Elijah in Contemporary Judaism

1 S. R. Hirsch, 'Phineas-Eliyahu', in *Judaism Eternal* (ed. R. I. Grünfeld), vol. 2, pp. 291–300

2 Vol. 4 (24), 12–13

3 *Orot ha-Kodesh*, vol. 3, pp. 365, 366 ff.

4 ibid., p. 366

5 ibid., vol. 3, p. 362
6 ibid., pp. 274, 275
7 ibid., p. 360; see also pp. 102–3 above
8 *Orot*, p. 44
9 *Orot ha-Kodesh*, vol. 3, p. 364
10 *Mikhtav Me-Eliyahu*, vol. 2, p. 200
11 'Koveẓ Maamarim', vol. A, p. 123, 6 and 7
12 *Mikhtav Me-Eliyahu*, vol. 1, p. 209
13 'Petaḥ shel Eliyahu', *Bi-she'arayikh*, 9, 1972, pp. 26–33
14 'The man of faith', *Tradition*, 7 (2), 1965, p. 67
15 *Amos Studies*, vol. 1, pp. 291–317
16 *Torat ha-Neviim*, pp. 67–76. He also published *Elijah: ein Mysterienspiel*, a play about the biblical Elijah
17 *The Stories of Elijah and Elisha*. In his recently published book, *Ancient Prophecy in Israel*, B. Uffenheimer thoroughly analyses the historical and religious background of the biblical Elijah-Ahab record, and concludes that the historical Elijah is excessively glorified in the text by ascribing to him miracles and magic power. At the same time, he does emphasise the profound meaning of the prophet's hearing the divine 'voice of silence' as representing the crucial transformation of the zealous and militant Israelite prophets before Elijah's time to the later warning and guiding ones (pp. 233–4)
18 Ḥ. Gevaryahu, 'Iyunim be-Sefer ha-Melakhim: Eliyahu ha-Navi'
19 'Elijah in der Legende', *Monatsschrift für Geschichte und Wissenschaft des Judentums*, 12, 1863, pp 241 ff.
20 *Major Trends in Jewish Mysticism*
21 *On the Kabbalah and its Symbolism*, pp. 15, 19–20
22 p. 30
23 *Binah Ba-Mikra*, p. 173; *Ḥazon ha-Mikra*, pp. 411 ff.
24 *Beiträge zur Geschichte und Legende des Propheten Elijah*
25 *Der Prophet Elijah*
26 *Eliyahu ha-Navi*
27 *Yonah ben Amitai ve-Eliyahu*
28 *Ishim min ha-Mikra*, pp. 235 ff.
29 *Ḥazon ha-Tishbi*
30 'Eliyahu shoel et nafsho la-mut', in *Antologia Tanakhit*, vol. 3 pp. 46–9
31 'Eliyahu ba-Midbar', in ibid., vol. 3, pp. 45–6
32 'Eliyahu', ibid., p. 42
33 A. Me'iri, 'Peridat Eliyahu', ibid., p. 72
34 'Mar'eh Elohim', ibid., pp. 50–2
35 Israel Cohen, *M. Shoham Ḥayyav u-Yeẓirotav*, p. 119
36 *Shirim*, vol. 1, p. 235
37 *Reḥovot ha-Nahar*, p. 284
38 op. cit., vol. 2, pp. 81–6
39 pp. 31–3
40 Described in detail by Eliezer Schweid, 'Yeme Shivah', *Petaḥim*, 1, 1968, pp. 9–23
41 Fully discussed in M. Kasher, *ha-Tekufah ha-Gedolah*

42 D. Flusser, 'Al Zehuto shel ha-Kadosh Barukh Hu', *Petaḥim*, 1, 1968, pp. 37–40

Chapter XII   Elijah, Prototype of the Hero-Archetype

1 See pp. 29ff., 36 above, also J. Campbell, *The Hero with a Thousand Faces*
2 ibid., pp. 162–3
3 M. r. Gen. 33. 4; *Avot de-R. Natan*, ch. 31, version A (p. 91)
4 C. Kerényi, *Hermes der Seelenführer*, pp. 64–5, 98–9, 103, 106–7
5 E. Conze, *Buddhism*, pp. 125 ff.; H. von Glasenapp, *Buddhism*, p. 129; C. Humphreys, *Buddhism*, pp. 158 ff.; A. Watts, *The Way of Zen*, p. 68
6 Robert C. Zaehner, *Hinduism*, pp. 50, 53, 56
7 Glasenapp, op. cit., p. 106; T. Stcherbatsky, *The Conception of Buddhist Nirvana*, pp. 2, 4, 35 ff.; Conze, op. cit., p. 135
8 'Die Psyche und die Wandlung der Wirklichkeitsebenen', in *Eranos-Jahrbuch 1952*, pp. 195 ff.
9 M. r. Exod. 3. 6
10 *Tikkune ha-Zohar*, p. 21a
11 2 Zohar 51b; 3 Zohar 36a
12 2 Zohar 230b
13 BT Berakhot 61a (Rashi); Eruvin 18a (Rashi); M. r. Gen. 8. 1; M. r. Lev. 14. 1; see also E. Benz, *Adam, der Mythos vom Urmenschen*, pp. 14–15; G. Widengreen, *Religionsphänomenologie*, p. 83
14 1 Zohar 91b
15 Especially emphasised by R. Ezra ben Solomon of Gerona, cited from G. Scholem, *Von der mystischen Gestalt der Gottheit*, pp. 58 ff.
16 Ḥ. Vital, *Sefer ha-Likkutim*, p. 13a; see also diagram on p. 104 above
17 *Hartmanns inductive Philosophie im Chassidismus*, p. 118
18 'ha-Bilti Muda ve-Musag Kadmut ha-Sekhel ba-Sifrut ha-Ḥasidit', in *Hagut*, pp. 145 ff.
19 'Archetypische Motive in der chassidischen Mystik', in *Zeitlose Dokumente der Seele*, pp. 138 ff., 202 ff.
20 *ha-Ḥasidut ke-Mistikah*, p. 126
21 'Der schöpferische Mensch und die Wandlung', in *Eranos-Jahrbuch 1954*, p. 51; 'Der mystische Mensch', in *Kulturentwicklung und Religion*, pp. 78, 152; *Zohar Ḥadash* 5a, Rashi's comment on Gen. 1. 27
22 *Likkute Amarim*, p. 22b (44); *Likkutim Yekarim*, p. 22a; *Peri ha-Arez*, p. 21a
23 C. G. Jung, *The Structure and Dynamics of the Psyche*, pp. 67–91; E. Neumann, 'Der schöpferische Mensch und die grosse Erfahrung', in *Eranos-Jahrbuch 1956*, pp. 40–1
24 *Mekhilta de-R. Yishmael*, p. 64a
25 *Enneads*
26 Jacob Boehme, Angelus Silesius, Ruskin, etc.
27 3 Zohar 7b, 232b, 265b
28 *On the Bhagavad Gita*, ch. 6
29 *Cosmic Consciousness*. See also Neumann, 'Die Erfahrung der Einheits-wirklichkeit', in *Eranos-Jahrbuch 1955*

30 J. B. Rhine and J. G. Pratt, *Parapsychology Today*; A. Jaffé, *Geistererschein-ungen und Vorzeichen*; B. Bender, *Parapsychologie*; K. Walker, *The Unconscious Mind*; Richard Cavendish (ed.), *Encyclopedia of The Un-explained*

31 A. S. Eddington, *The Nature of the Physical World*; W. Heisenberg, *The Physicists' Conception of Nature*, p. 9

32 C. G. Jung and W. Pauli, *The Interpretation of Nature and the Psyche*, pp. 151–2. Highly interesting are the description and the photographs of a so-called 'bioplasmatic energy' or 'energy-body', considered as a special kind of vital energy which exists in every living being and plant (S. Ostrander and L. Schroeder, *Psychic Discoveries Behind the Iron Curtain*, pp. 200–36)

33 C. G. Jung, *Aion*, pp. 23 ff.

34 ibid., p. 28

35 ibid., p. 31; *Psychology and Religion: West and East*, p. 363

36 E. Neumann, 'Die Psyche und die Wandlung der Wirklichkeitsebenen', in *Eranos-Jahrbuch 1952*, pp. 210–11

37 'Narzissmus, Automorphismus und Urbeziehung', in *Studien zur analytischen Psychologie C. G. Jungs*, vol. 1, pp. 106 ff.; 'Der mystische Mensch', in *Kulturentwicklung und Religion*, p. 78

38 C. G. Jung, *The Archetypes and the Collective Unconscious*, p. 289; E. Neumann, *The Origins and History of Consciousness*, pp. 397–8; J. Jacobi, *Der Weg zur Individuation*, pp. 25ff.; Jung et al., *Man and his Symbols*, pp. 157–254

39 E. Neumann, 'Der schöpferische Mensch und die grosse Erfahrung', in *Eranos-Jahrbuch 1956*, pp. 54–5

40 C. G. Jung, *Aion*, pp. 8 ff.; E. Neumann, *The Origins and History of Consciousness*, pp. 351–3

41 *Me ha-Shiloah*; see p. 119 above

42 *Dover Ẓedek*, pp. 98–100

43 BT Berakhot 31b; JT Sanhedrin 7. 5; see also p. 48 and n. 33 above

44 BT Yoma 86b

45 *Ẓidkat ha-Ẓaddik*, pts 40, 100, 179

46 Mishnah Berakhot 9. 5, also *Sifre le-Sefer Devarim*, pt 32 (p. 55). This Aggadic explanation is based on the assonance of the Hebrew words 'meod', 'midda', 'mode' ('might', 'measure', 'thank')

47 M. r. Kohelet 3. 15

48 A. Jaffé, *The Myth of Meaning*; E. Neumann, *Depth Psychology and a New Ethic*; P. Pruyser, *A Dynamic Psychology of Religion*, p. 215; see also p. 195 below

49 For *anima* and *animus*, see C. G. Jung, *Aion*, pp. 11 ff.; Emma Jung, *Animus und Anima*; E. Neumann, *The Origins and History of Consciousness*, pp. 353–6; C. Brunner, *Die Anima als Schicksalsproblem des Mannes*; J. Hillman, *Insearch, Psychology and Religion*, ch. 4

50 BT Kiddushin 70a

51 *The Archetypes and the Collective Unconscious*, p. 222

52 ibid., p. 219

53 ibid., p. 35

54 *The Archetypes and the Collective Unconscious*, p. 210
55 ibid., pp. 210-11
56 ibid., pp. 212-13
57 op. cit., pp. 214-15
58 For the relationship between religious and depth-psychological experience, see p. 185. See also G. Adler, *Zur analytischen Psychologie*, pp. 194 ff.

Bibliography

Some Hebrew works are also referred to by title)

General Primary Sources

Mikraot Gedolot, the Hebrew Bible with the Targumim (Aramaic translations) and commentaries by Rashi (R. Solomon Yizhaki), Ramban (R. Moses ben Nahman, Nahmanides), Ibn Ezra, Redak (R. David Kimhi), Ralbag (R. Levi ben Gershon, Gersonides): var. edns

Mishnayot (Mishnah) with commentaries by Obadiah of Bertinoro and *Tosefot Yomtov*: var. edns

Talmud Bavli (Babylonian Talmud) with commentaries by Rashi, *Tosafot*: var. edns

Talmud Jerushalmi (Jerusalem Talmud), var edns

Ha-Zohar shel R. Simeon bar Yohai, Warsaw, 1807

Ha-Zohar im Sulam (trans. and ed. R. J. L. Ashlag), 18 vols, Jerusalem, 1945–53

Zohar Hadash (trans. and ed. R. J. L. Ashlag), 2 vols, Jerusalem, 1954–5

Tikkune ha-Zohar, Warsaw, 1866

Tikkune ha-Zohar im Ma'alot ha-Sulam (trans. and ed. R. I. Z. Brandwein), 3 vols, Tel-Aviv, 1959

The Apocrypha and Pseudepigraphia of the Old Testament (trans. and ed. Robert H. Charles), 2 vols, Oxford 1913

The Septuagint Version of the Old Testament with an English trans. and with various readings and critical notes, London and New York, 1879

The New Testament (revised version)

Die neutestamentlichen Apokryphen und Apokalypsen (ed. E. Hennecke and W. Schneemelcher), 2 vols, Tübingen, 1959, 1964

The Koran (trans. N. J. Dawood), Harmondsworth, 1974

Other Biblical Commentaries, Midrashim, Kabbalist and Hasidic Sources

Aaron, R. of Starosselje, *Avodat ha-Levi*, 2 vols, Warsaw, 1913

Abrarvanel, R. I., *Perush al Neviim Rishonim*, Jerusalem, 1955

——, *Yeshuot Meshiho*, Königsberg, 1862

Aggadat Ester (ed. S. Buber), Krakow, 1897

Albo, R. J., *Sefer ha-Ikkarim* (ed. I. Husik), 4 vols, London and Philadelphia, 1929–30

Arama, R. Isaac, *Akedat Yizhak*, 5 vols, Tel-Aviv, 1961

Avot de-Rabbi Natan (ed. S. Schechter), New York, 1945

Baal Shem Tov (Besht), Letter to R. Gershon of Kutov, Koretz, 1791 (trans. and ed. N. Lamm, *Tradition*, 14(4), 1974)

Bacharach, R. Naphtali, *Emek ha-Melekh*, Amsterdam, 1648

Bate ha-Midrashot (ed. A. Wertheimer), 2 vols, Jerusalem, 1950

Bet ha-Midrash (ed. A. Jellinek), 6 vols, Jerusalem, 1938

Cordovero, R. Moses, *Pardes Rimonim*, Koretz, 1786

—— *Derishat be-Inyane Malakhim*, in R. Margulies, *Malakhe Elyon*, 1st ed. Jerusalem, 1945, appendix

Derekh Hasidim (ed. R. J. Kenig), Jerusalem, 1961

Eleazar ben Judah, R. of Worms, see *Sefer Hokhmat-ha-Nefesh*

Elimelekh, R. of Lizhensk, *Noam Elimelekh*, Lemberg, 1867

Emek ha-Melekh, see Bacharach, R. N.

Ephraim, R. of Sudlikov, *Degel Mahane Efrayim*, Satmar, 1942

Eser Orot (ed. J. Berger), Warsaw, 1913

Gaon of Vilna, R. Elijah, Commentary to *Sifra de-Zeniuta*, with introduction by R. Hayyim of Volozhin, Vilna, 1882

Gikatilla, R. J., *Sha'are Orah*, Zolkiev, 1714

Hayyim, R. of Volozhin, *Nefesh ha-Hayyim*, Bne Berak, 1958

——, *see also* Gaon of Vilna

Ibn Gabbai, R. M., *Avodat ha-Kodesh*, Jerusalem, 1954

'Iggeret Natan ha-Azati al Shabbetai Zevi ve-Hamarato' (ed. G. Scholem), *Kovez al-Yad* (Jerusalem), n.s. 6 (2), 1966, 419–66

Isaiah, R. of Duniwitz, *Or Torah*, Lublin, 1910

Israel, R. of Koznitz, *Avodat Yisrael*, Lemberg, 1875

Jacob Joseph, R. of Pulnoye, *Ben Porat Yosef*, Lemberg, 1866

——, *Ketonet Passim*, New York, 1950

——, *Toldot Ya'akov Yosef*, New York, 1955

——, *Zofnat Paneah*, New York, 1957

Judah he-Hasid, R., *Sefer Hasidim* (ed. J. Wistinetzki and J. Freimann), Frankfurt, 1924

Karo, R. Joseph, *Maggid Mesharim*, Jerusalem, 1967

Kimhi, R. D. (Redak), see Mikraot Gedolot

Kook, R. A. I., *Orot* (ed. R. D. Kahan), Jerusalem, 1961

——, *Orot ha-Kodesh* (ed. R. D. Kahan), 3 vols, Jerusalem, 1950

Leiner, Mordecai Joseph, R. of Izbice, *Me ha-Shiloah*, 2 vols, Lublin, 1922

Likkute Amarim, see Solomon, R. of Lutzk

Likkute Amarim (Sefer Tanya), see Shneor Zalman, R. of Liady

Likkute ha-Shas, see Lurya Ashkenazi, R. J.

Likkute Moharan, see Nahman, R. of Bratzlav

Likkutim mi-Midreshe Shoher Tov, in *Bate ha-Midrashot*, ed. A. Wertheimer

Likkutim Yekarim (ascribed to R. Meshullam of Zhabaraz), Lemberg, 1863

Livai (Löv, Lov), Maharal of Prague, *Nezah Yisrael*, Lemberg, 1866

Lurya Ashkenazi, R. J., *Likkute ha-Shas*, Leghorn, 1790

226

Ma'arekhet ha-Elohut, anon. (ed., with commentary, R. J. Ḥayat), Ferrara, 1558

Maggid Devarav le-Yaakov (or *Likkute Amarim*), see Solomon, R. of Lutzk

Maimonides, R. M., *Mishne Torah*, 4 vols, Berlin, 1880

——, *More Nevukhim* (ed. Yehudah ibn Shemuel), Tel-Aviv, 1935 (trans. *The Guide of the Perplexed*, ed. S. Pines, Chicago, 1963)

Malbim, R. M. L., *Neviim u-Ketuvim*, 3 vols, Vilna, 1912

Margulies, R. Reuben, *Malakhe Elyon*, Jerusalem, 1945

Masekhet Aseret ha-Dibrot, in *Bet ha-Midrash*, ed. A. Jellinek

Masekhet Derekh Erez Rabbah, Tel-Aviv, 1949

Masekhet Derekh Erez Zutta, Vilna, 1872

Mekhilta de-Rabbi Shimon (ed. R. D. Hoffman), Frankfurt, 1905

Mekhilta de-Rabbi Yishmael (ed. M. Ish-Shalom), Vienna, 1870

Menahem Azariah, R. da Fano, *Kanfe Yonah*, Krakow, 1656

——, *Aseret Ma'amarot*, Warsaw, 1894

Menahem Mendel, R. of Lubavitch, *Shir ha-Shirim*, Brooklyn, 1916

——, *Derekh Mizvotekha*, Brooklyn, 1953

Menahem Mendel, R. of Vitebsk, *Peri ha-Arez*, Jerusalem, 1969

Menahem Nahum, R. of Tchernobil, *Sefer Meor Enayim* and *Yismaḥ Lev*, Jerusalem, 1960

Meshullam Fabish, R. of Zharabaz, *Derekh Emet*, Jerusalem, 1970

Midrash Aggadat Bereshit (ed. S. Buber), Krakow, 1902

Midrash Bereshit Rabbati (ed. C. Albeck), Jerusalem, 1940

Midrash ha-Gadol, 5 vols, Jerusalem 1947–75: vol. 1 (ed. R. S. Fisch, 1947)

Midrash Ḥaserot vi-Yterot (ed. A. Marmorstein), London, 1917

Midrash Konen, in *Ozar Midrashim*

Midrash Lekaḥ Tov (ed. S. Buber), Vilna, 1893

Midrash Mishle (ed. S. Buber), Lemberg, 1893

Midrash Rabbah, Jerusalem, 1965: vol. 1, Genesis; vol. 2, Exodus, *Ester rabbah*; vol. 3, Leviticus, *Shir ha-Shirim rabbah*; vol. 4, Numbers, *Rut rabbah*; vol. 5, Deuteronomy, *Ekhah rabbah*, *Kohelet rabbah*

Midrash Shemuel (ed. S. Buber), Krakow, 1893

Midrash Tanḥuma (ed. S. Buber), Vilna, 1884

Midrash Tanḥuma (*Yelamdenu*), 2 vols in 1 book, Jerusalem, 1968 (trans. W. G. Braude, 2 vols, New Haven, 1959)

Midrash Tehillim (*Shoḥer Tov*) (ed. S. Buber), Lemberg, 1891

Midrash Zutta (*Shir ha-Shirim Zutta, Rut Zutta, Ekhah Zutta, Kohelet Zutta*) (ed. S. Buber), Berlin, 1894

Midreshe Geulah (ed. Yehudah ibn Shemuel), Jerusalem, 1954

Mordecai, R. of Tchernobil, *Likkute Torah*, Jerusalem, 1971

Naḥman, R. of Bratzlav, *Likkute Moharan*, New York, 1958

Odeberg, H. (ed. and trans.) *Enock: or the Hebrew Book of Enoch*, Cambridge, 1928

Ozar ha-Geonim (ed. B. M. Levin) 13 vols, Jerusalem, 1928–62

Ozar Midrashim (ed. J. D. Eisenstein) 2 vols, New York, 1915

Pardes Rimonim, see Cordovero, R. Moses

The Pentateuch, with Commentary (ed. R. S. R. Hirsch; trans. I. Levy), 5 vols, London, 1964

Pesikta de-Rab Kahana (trans. W. G. Braude and I. J. Kapstein), Philadelphia and London, 1975

Pesikta de-Rav Kahana (ed. B. Mandelbaum), 2 vols, New York, 1962

Pesikta Rabbati (ed. M. Ish-Shalom), n.p. [Israel], 1963 (trans. W. G. Braude, 2 vols, New Haven and London, 1968)

Pirke de-Rabbi Eliezer, Warsaw, 1852 (trans. G. Friedländer, New York, 1965)

Saadia Gaon, R., *Emunot ve-Deot*, Jerusalem, 1923 (trans. S. Rosenblatt, *The Book of Beliefs and Opinions*, New Haven, 1948)

Seder Eliyahu Rabbah ve-Seder Eliyahu Zutta (ed. with commentary, M. Ish-Shalom), Vienna, 1904; Jerusalem, 1960

Seder Olam Rabbah ha-Shalem (ed. M. Weinstock), 3 vols, Jerusalem, 1915

Sefer ha-Bahir me-ha-Tanna Rabbi Nehunya ben ha-Kanah, anon., Vilna, 1883

Sefer ha-Kanah, anon., Koretz, 1786

Sefer ha-Likkutim, see Vital, R. Hayim

Sefer Hasidim, see Judah he-Hasid, R.

Sefer ha-Peliah, anon., Koretz, 1784

Sefer Hokhmat ha-Nefesh (ascribed to R. Eleazar ben Judah of Worms), Lemberg, 1876

Sefer Tanya, see Shneor Zalman, R. of Liady

Sefer Temunah, anon., Lemberg, 1892

Sefer Yezirah, anon., Jerusalem, 1962

Shneor Zalman, R. of Liady, *Likkute Amarim (Sefer Tanya)*, Tel-Aviv, 1940

Sifra de-Zeniuta, see Gaon of Vilna

Sifre de-Aggadeta (ed. S. Buber), Vienna, 1886

Sifre le-Sefer Bamidbar (ed. M. Ish-Shalom), Vienna, 1864

Sifre le-Sefer Devarim (ed. L. Finkelstein), New York, 1961

Solomon, R. of Lutzk, *Divrat Shelomoh*, Zolkiew, 1848

—— *Likkute Amarim* (or *Maggid Devarav le-Ya'akov*), Satmar, 1905

Steinsalz, R. A., *Hokhmah-Binah-Da'at be-Shitat Habad*, privately printed

——, 'Mashma'ut ha-"Yediah" ba-Tenakh', *Sinai*, 60, 1967

Strack, H. and Billerbeck, P., *Kommentar zum Neuen Testament aus Talmud und Midrasch*, 6 vols in 7 books, Munich, 1922–61

Vital, R. Hayyim, *Ez Hayyim*, 3 vols in 1 book, Warsaw, 1890

——, *Sefer ha-Gilgulim*, Zolkiew, 1779

——, *Sefer ha-Likkutim* (ed. S. W. Ashkenazi), Jerusalem, 1913

——, *Sha'ar ha-Gilgulim*, Jerusalem, 1968

——, *Sha'ar ha-Kavvanot*, Jerusalem, 1873

——, *Sha'are ha-Kedushah*, Warsaw, 1871

Volozhin, R. N. Z. J. (Neziv), *Humash Ha'amek Davar*, 5 vols, Jerusalem, 1970

Yalkut ha-Makhiri le-Sefer Yishayahu (ed. J. Shapira), Jerusalem, 1964

Yalkut Reuveni la-Torah, 2 vols, Warsaw, 1925

Yalkut Shimoni, 2 vols, New York, 1944

Zadok ha-Kohen, R. of Lublin, *Zidkat ha-Zaddik*, Lublin, 1912

——, *Dover Zedek*, New York, 1956

——, *Peri ha-Zaddik*, 5 vols, Jerusalem, 1965

Ze'ev Wolf, R. of Zhitomir, *Or ha-Me'ir*, New York, 1954

Other Sources

Adler, G., *Zur analytischen Psychologie*, Zürich, 1952
Albright, W. F., *Archeology and the Religion of Israel*, Baltimore, 1946
Allport, G., *The Individual and his Religion*, New York, 1961
Alt, A., *Kleine Schriften zur Geschichte des Volkes Israel*, 3 vols, Munich, 1953
Antologia Tanakhit (Biblical Anthology), 3 vols, Tel-Aviv, 1951
Aptowitzer, V., *Die Parteipolitik der Hasmonäer*, Vienna, 1927
——, *Bet ha-Mikdash shel Ma'alah al pi ha-Aggadah*, Jerusalem, 1940
Avida, R. J., *Koso shel Eliyahu ha-Navi*, Jerusalem, 1958
Azulai, R. H., *Ma'arekhet ha-Gedolim (Shem ha-Gedolim*, vol. 1), Warsaw, 1898
Bacharach, J., *Yonah ben Amitai ve-Eliyahu*, Jerusalem, 1959
Bahya ben Joseph ibn Pakuda (trans. and ed. Menahem Mansoor), *The Book of the Direction to the Duties of the Heart*, London, 1973
Bavli, H., 'Eliyahu ba-Midbar', in *Antologia Tanakhit*, vol. 3
Beek, A., *Auf den Wegen und Spuren des Alten Testaments*, Tübingen, 1964
Bender, H., *Parapsychologie*, Bremen, 1970
Benz, E., *Adam, der Mythos vom Urmenschen*, Munich, 1955
Bergmann, J., *Legenden der Juden*, Berlin, 1919
Bergson, H., *The Two Sources of Morality and Religion*, New York, 1957
Bhagavad Gita, On the (trans. and commentary, Maharishi Mahesh), London, 1969
Bousset, W., *The Antichrist Legend*, London, 1896
——, 'Die Religion des Judentums,' in *Handbuch zum Neuen Testament*, no. 21, Tübingen, 1926
Braslawsky, J., 'Me'arot Eliyahu ha-Navi mi-Kahir ad Ḥalab', *Yeda-Am*, 7(25), 1961
Bronner, L., *The Stories of Elijah and Elisha as Polemics against Baal Worship*, Leiden, 1968
Brunner, C., *Die Anima als Schicksalsproblem des Mannes*, Zürich, 1963
Buber, M., *Tales of the Hasidim*, 2 vols, New York, 1947
——, *Eclipse of God*, New York, 1957
——, *Torat ha-Neviim*, Tel-Aviv, 1961
——, *Elija: ein Mysterienspiel*, Heidelberg, 1963
—— (ed. N. Glatzer), *On Judaism*, New York, 1967
——, *Or ha-Ganuz*, Tel-Aviv, 1968
—— and Rosenzweig, F., *Die Schriftwerke*, 4 vols, Cologne and Olten, 1954–70
Bucke, Richard M., *Cosmic Consciousness*, New York, 1960
Campbell, Joseph, *The Hero with a Thousand Faces*, New York, 1956
——, 'The historical development of mythology', in H. A. Murray (ed.), *Myths and Mythmaking*, New York, 1960
Cavendish, Richard (ed.), *Encyclopedia of the Unexplained*, London, 1974
Cohen, Israel, *Ishim min ha-Mikra*, Tel-Aviv, 1958
——, *M. Shoham Ḥayyav u-Yezirotav*, Jerusalem, 1965
Cohn, G. H., *Das Buch Jona im Lichte der biblischen Erzählungskunst*, Amsterdam, 1969
Conze, E., *Buddhism*, London, 1956
Dan, J., *Torat Ḥaside Ashkenaz*, Jerusalem, 1968

Dessler, R. E., 'Koveẓ Ma'amarim', vol. A, London, 1959 (duplicated)
——, *Mikhtav me-Eliyahu*, 3 vols, Bne Berak, 1959–64
Dresnitz, S., *Shivḥe ha-Ari*, Leghorn, 1790
Dreyfuss, G., 'The binding of Isaac: the *Akedah*', *J. Analytical Psychology*, 20 (1), 1975
Dubnow, S., *History of the Jews*, 5 vols, New York, 1971–4
Durkheim, E., *The Elementary Forms of the Religious Life*, Chicago, 1954
Eddington, A. S., *The Nature of the Physical World*, Cambridge, 1932
Eliade, M., *Patterns in Comparative Religion*, London and New York, 1958
Élie le Prophète (Études carmélitaines), 2 vols, Paris, 1956
Encyclopedia of Islam (ed. M. Houtsma *et al.*), 8 vols, Leiden and London, 1913–31
—— (ed. B. Lewis *et al.*), new ed., 3 vols, Leiden and London, 1960–71
Encyclopedia Ivrit, 26 vols, Jerusalem, 1933–74
Encyclopedia Judaica, 16 vols, Jerusalem, 1971
Encyclopedia of Religion and Ethics (ed. J. Hastings), 13 vols, Edinburgh and New York, 1908–26
Encyclopedia talmudit, 17 vols, Tel-Aviv, 1951–73
Fensham, F. C., 'A possible explanation of the name *Ba'al Zevuv*', *Zeitschrift für alttestamentliche Wissenschaft*, 79, 1967
Flavius Josephus (trans. H. St J. Thackeray, R. Marcus and H. Feldman), *The Life; Against Apion; The Jewish War; Antiquities*, 9 vols, London, 1937–53
Flusser, D., 'Melchizedek and the Son of Man', in *Christian News from Israel*, Jerusalem, 1966
——, 'Al Zehuto shel ha-Kadosh Barukh Hu', *Petaḥim*, 1, 1968
——, *Jesus*, New York, 1969
Fohrer, G., *Elias*, Zürich, 1957
Fordham, M., *The Objective Psyche*, London, 1958
Franz, M. L. von, see Jung *et al.*, *Man and his Symbols*
Frazer, J. G., *The Golden Bough*, abridged edn, London, 1963
Friedländer, I., 'Zur Geschichte der Chadirlegende', *Archiv für Religionswissenschaft* (Leipzig), 13, 1910, pp. 92–110
——, 'Alexanders Zug nach der Lebensquelle und die Chadirlegende', ibid., pp. 161–246
——, *Die Chadirlegende und der Alexander Roman*, Leipzig and Berlin, 1913
Fromm, E., *Psychoanalysis and Religion*, New York, 1950
——, *You shall be as Gods*, London, 1967
——, *The Anatomy of Human Destructiveness*, New York, 1973
Frug, S., 'Mar'eh Elohim', in *Antologia Tanakhit*, vol. 3
Gevaryahu, Ḥ., 'Iyunim be-Sefer ha-Melakhim: Eliyahu ha-Navi', Jerusalem, 1963 (duplicated)
Ginzburg, P., 'Eliyahu', in *Antologia Tanakhit*, vol. 3
Ginzburg, S., *R. Moshe Ḥ. Luzzatto u-Vne Doro*, 2 vols, Tel-Aviv, 1937
Glasenapp, H. von, *Buddhism: a Non-Theistic Religion*, London and New York, 1970
Glueck, N., *The River Jordan*, Philadelphia and London, 1946; New York, 1968
Goldziher, I., *Abhandlungen zur arabischen Philologie*, 2 vols, Leiden, 1896, 1899
Goodenough, E., *The Psychology of Religious Experiences*, New York, 1965

Grant, M., *Myths of the Greeks and Romans*, London, 1962
——, *Roman Myths*, London, 1971
Greenberg, U. Ẓ., *Reḥovot ha-Nahar*, Jerusalem, 1951
Gressman, H., *Der Messias*, Göttingen, 1928
Grether, O., *Name und Wort Gottes im Alten Testament*, Giessen, 1934
Guttmann M., *Mafteaḥ ha-Talmud*, Budapest, 1906
Hadari, J., 'Petaḥ shel Eliyahu', *Bi-she'arayikh* (Jerusalem), 9, 1972
Halevy, R. J. E., *Dorot ha-Rishonim: Tekufat ha-Mikra*, Jerusalem, 1939
Handwörterbuch des Islam (ed. A. J. Wensinck and J. Kramers), Leiden, 1941
Haussig, W., *Götter und Mythen im vorderen Orient* (*Wörterbuch der Mythologie*, vol. 1), Stuttgart, 1965
Heinemann, I., *Darke ha-Aggadah*, Jerusalem, 1950
Heisenberg, W., *The Physicists' Conception of Nature*, London, 1956
Heller, B., 'Chadir und der Prophet Elijah', *Monatsschrift für Geschichte und Wissenschaft des Judentums* (Breslau), 81, 1937
Henderson, J. L., 'Ancient myths and modern man', in Jung *et al.*, *Man and his Symbols*
——, and Oakes, Maud, *The Wisdom of the Serpent*, New York, 1963
Heschel, A. J., *Torah min-ha-Shamayim*, 2 vols, London and New York, 1962, 1965
——, *A Passion for Truth*, New York, 1973
Hillman, J., *Insearch, Psychology and Religion*, London, 1967
Hirsch, R. S. R., *Judaism Eternal* (ed. R. I. Grünfeld), 2 vols, London, 1956
——, see also *The Pentateuch*
Horodezki, S. A., (ed.), *Shivḥe ha-Besht*, Tel-Aviv, 1920
——, *Ha-Ḥasidut ve-Ha-Ḥasidim*, 3rd ed., Tel-Aviv, 1951
Humphreys, C., *Buddhism, London*, 1955
Hurwitz, S., 'Archetypische Motive in der chassidischen Mystik', in *Zeitlose Dokumente der Seele*, Zürich, 1952
——, 'Sabbatai Zwi: zur Psychologie der häretischen Kabbala', in *Studien zur analytischen Psychologie C. G. Jungs*, vol. 2, Zürich, 1955, pp. 239–63
——, *Die Gestalt des sterbenden Messias*, Zürich, 1958
Huxley, J., *Religion without Revelation*, New York, 1957
Ibn Gabirol S., *The Kingly Crown* (trans. B. Lewis), London, 1961
Iggeret R. Sherira Gaon (ed. A. Neubauer), Oxford, 1892
Jacob, B., *Im Namen Gottes*, Berlin, 1903
Jacobi, J., *Der Weg zur Individuation*, Zürich, 1965
Jacobs, R. L., *Seeker of Unity*, London, 1966
——, *Hasidic Prayer* London, 1972
Jacobsohn, S., *Binah Ba-Mikra*, Tel-Aviv, 1955
——, *Ḥazon ha-Mikra*, Tel-Aviv, 1959
Jaffé, A., *Geistererscheinungen und Vorzeichen*, Zürich, 1958
——, *The Myth of Meaning*, New York, 1971
James, M. R., *The Lost Apocrypha of the Old Testament*, London, 1936
James, W., *The Varieties of Religious Experience*, New York, 1958
Jashuvi, J., *Der Typengegensatz in der jüdischen Religionsgeschichte*, Zürich, 1934
Jirku, A., *Der Mythos der Kananäer*, Bonn, 1966
Jones, E., *Essays in Applied Psychoanalysis*, London, 1951

Josephus, *see* Flavius Josephus

Jung, C. G., *Aion* (Collected Works (CW), vol. 9(2)), 2nd ed., London, 1968

——, *The Archetypes and the Collective Unconscious* (CW, vol. 9(1)), 2nd ed., 1969

——, *Civilization in Transition*, (CW, vol. 10), 1964

——, *Mysterium Coniunctionis* (CW, vol. 14), 2nd ed., 1970

——, *Psychological Types*, (CW, vol. 6), 1971

——, *Psychology and Alchemy* (CW, vol. 12), 2nd ed., 1968

——, *Psychology and Religion: West and East* (CW, vol. 11), 2nd ed., 1969

——, *The Structure and Dynamics of the Psyche* (CW, vol. 8), 1960

——, *Symbols of Transformation* (CW, vol. 5), 2nd ed., 1967

——, 'Approaching the Unconscious', in *Man and His Symbols*

——, Franz, M. L. von, Henderson, J. L., Jacobi, J. and Jaffé, A., *Man and His Symbols*, London and New York, 1964

——, and Pauli, W., *The Interpretation of Nature and the Psyche*, London, 1955

Jung, Emma, *Animus und Anima*, Zürich, 1967

Justin Martyr, *Dialogue with Trypho*, see Winden, J. C. M. van

Kahan, Jacob, 'Eliyahu shoel et nafsho la-mut', in *Antologia Tanakhit*, vol. 3

——, *Ḥazon ha-Tishbi*, Warsaw, 1920

Kahane, S. Z., 'Eliyahu ha-Navi be-Moẓae Shabbat', *Yeda-Am*, 7(25), 1961

Kasher, R. M., *ha-Tekufah ha-Gedolah*, Jerusalem, 1968

Kaufmann, J., *Toldot ha-Emunah ha-Yisraelit*, 4 vols, 6th ed., Jerusalem and Tel-Aviv, 1964

Kerényi, C., *Hermes der Seelenführer*, Zürich, 1944

——, *The Gods of the Greeks*, London and New York, 1951

——, *The Heroes of the Greeks*, London, 1959

——, *Prometheus: Archetypal Image of Human Existence*, New York, 1963

Keter Malkhut (*The Kingly Crown*), *see* Ibn Gabirol, S.

Kittel, Rudolf, *Die Bücher der Könige* (*Handkommentar zum Alten Testament* (ed. K. Nowack), 3 vols in 14 books), vol. 1, book 5, Göttingen, 1900

Klapholz, J. S., *Sippure Eliyahu ha-Navi*, 2 vols, Tel-Aviv, 1968

Kluger, Rivka Schaerf, *Satan in the Old Testament*, New York, 1967

——, *Psyche and Bible*, New York, 1973

Kohler, K., *Jewish Theology*, New York, 1918

Kohn, S., 'Elijah in der Legende', *Monatsschrift für Geschichte und Wissenschaft des Judentums* (Breslau), 12, 1863

Kopp, C., *Elias und das Christentum auf dem Carmel*, Paderborn, 1929

Kuehn, H., 'Das Problem des Urmonotheismus', Akademie der Wissenschaften und der Literatur, *Abhandlungen der Geistes- und Sozialwissenschaftlichen Klasse*, no. 22, Wiesbaden, 1915

——, *On the Track of Prehistoric Man*, New York, 1961

Lange, I. (ed.), *Perushe ha-Torah* by R. Judah he-Ḥasid, based on MS. Moscow, Günzburg 82, Nat. Univ. Library, Jerusalem, no. 6762

Leibowitz, N., *Iyunim be-Sefer Shemot*, Jerusalem, 1970

Levinsohn, M. W., *Der Prophet Elijah*, New York, 1929

Lexikon der christlichen Ikonographie, 6 vols, Freiburg, 1968–74

Lexikon für Theologie und Kirche, 10 vols, Freiburg, 1957–67

Lidzbarski, M., 'Wer ist Chadir?', *Zeitschrift für Archaeologie*, 2, 1892

Lowie, Robert H., *Primitive Religion*, New York, 1924; London, 1936

Maasseh-Book (ed. M. Gaster), 2 vols, Philadelphia, 1934

Mach, Rudolf, *Der Zaddik in Talmud und Midrash*, Leipzig, 1957

Maitri Upanishad: Second Prapathaka (trans. J. G. Bennett), quoted from K. Walker, *Diagnosis of Man*

Mann, U., *Theogonische Tage*, Stuttgart, 1970

Marcus, A. (Verus), *Hartmann's inductive Philosophie im Chassidismus*, Lemberg, 1889

Marett, Robert, *The Threshold of Religion*, London, 1914

Margaliot, E., *Eliyahu ha-Navi*, Jerusalem, 1960

Me'iri, A., 'Peridat Eliyahu', in *Antologia Tanakhit*, vol. 3

Meyer, Rudolf, *Elias, die Zielsetzung der Erde*, Stuttgart, 1964

Moltmann, J., *Theologie der Hoffnung*, Munich, 1964

Morgenstern, J., *Amos Studies*, 3 vols, Cincinnati, 1941

Mowinckel, S., *Die Erkenntnis Gottes bei den alttestamentlichen Propheten*, Oslo 1941

——, *He That Cometh*, Oxford, 1956

Natan ben Shelomoh, R. (Schapira), *Megale Amukot*, Lvov, 1800

Neumann E., *Depth Psychology and a New Ethic*, London and New York, 1969

——, 'Die Erfahrung der Einheitswirklichkeit', in *Eranos-Jahrbuch 1955*, Zürich, 1956

——, *The Great Mother*, London, 1955; Princeton, N.J., 1972

——, 'Der mystische Mensch', in *Kulturentwicklung und Religion*, Zürich, 1953 (trans. 'Mystical man', in *The Mystic Vision* (Papers from the Eranos-Yearbooks, 5, Princeton, N.J., and London, 1969), pp. 375–415

——, 'Narzissmus, Automorphismus und Urbeziehung', in *Studien zur analytischen Psychologie C. G. Jungs*, vol. 1, Zürich, 1955

——, *The Origins and History of Consciousness*, New York and London, 1954

——, 'Die Psyche und die Wandlung der Wirklichkeitsebenen', in *Eranos-Jahrbuch 1952*, Zürich, 1953

——, 'Der schöpferische Mensch und die grosse Erfahrung', in *Eranos-Jahrbuch 1956*, Zürich, 1957

——, 'Der schöpferische Mensch und die Wandlung', in *Eranos-Jahrbuch 1954*, Zürich, 1955

Newman, L., *The Hasidic Anthology*, New York, 1934

Nigg, W., *Drei grosse Zeichen*, Olten, 1972

Nissim ben Jacob, R., *Ḥibbur yafeh me-ha-yeshuah*, Jerusalem, 1954

Obermann, I., 'Two Elijah stories in Judeo-Arabic transmission', *Hebrew Union College Annual*, 23(1), 1950–1

Ohlmeyer A., *Elias, Fürst der Propheten*, Freiburg, 1962

Ostrander, S. and Schroeder, L., *Psychic Discoveries Behind the Iron Curtain*, New York, 1971

Otto, Rudolf, *The Idea of the Holy*, 2nd ed., New York, 1958

Otto, W. F., *Die Gestalt und das Sein*, Düsseldorf and Cologne, 1955

Patai, Raphael, *Myth and Modern Man*, Englewood Cliffs, N.J., 1972

——, *see also* Rappoport, A. S.

Philo Judaeus, *see* Wolfson, H.

Plotinus, *The Enneads* (trans. S. Mackenna), London, 1962

Preuss, K. T., *Die geistige Kultur der Naturvölker*, Leipzig, 1923
Pruyser, P., *A Dynamic Psychology of Religion*, New York, 1968
Rabinowitz, L. J., 'The tree of Elijah', *Jerusalem Post*, 16 July 1965
Rank, O., *The Art and the Artist*, New York, 1943
——, *The Myth of the Birth of the Hero and other Writings*, New York, 1959
Rappoport, A. S., *Myth and Legend of Ancient Israel*, with Introduction and additional notes by Raphael Patai, 3 vols, New York, rev. ed., 1966
Reallexikon für Antike und Christentum, 10 vols, Stuttgart, 1950–72
Reik, T., *Dogma and Compulsion*, New York, 1951
Rhine, J. B. and Pratt, J. G., *Parapsychology Today*, New York, 1968
Riessler, P., *Altjüdische Schriften ausserhalb der Bibel*, Augsburg, 1928
Robinson, J. A. T., *Elijah, John, Jesus: an Essay in Detection* (New Testament Studies, vol. 4), Cambridge, 1958
Róheim, G., *The Eternal Ones of the Dream*, New York, 1945
Rowley, H. H., *Men of God*, London, 1963
Rudin, J., *Psychotherapie und Religion*, Olten and Freiburg, 1964
Schaerf-Kluger, Rivka, *see* Kluger
Schatz-Uffenheimer, Rivka, 'Autonomia shel ha-Ruah ve-Torat Moshe', *Molad* (Jerusalem), 21, 1961
——, *ha-Hasidut ke-Mistikah* (*Quietistic Elements in Eighteenth-Century Hasidic Thought*), Jerusalem, 1968
Schlatter, H., *Johannes der Täufer*, Basel, 1950
Schmidt, W., *Ursprung der Gottesidee*, 12 vols, Münster, 1926–55; vol. 1, *Eine historisch-kritische und positive Studie*
Scholem, G., 'ha-Bilti Muda ve-Musag Kadmut ha-Sekhel ba-Sifrut ha-Hasidit', in *Hagut*, Jerusalem, 1944
——, *Major Trends in Jewish Mysticism*, New York, 1946; London, 1955
——, *Reshit ha-Kabbalah*, Jerusalem, 1948
——, *Shabbetai Zevi ve-ha-Tenuah ha-Shabbetait*, Tel-Aviv, 1957
——, *Ursprung und Anfänge der Kabbalah*, Berlin, 1962
——, *Von der mystischen Gestalt der Gottheit*, Zürich, 1962
——, *On the Kabbalah and its Symbolism*, London and New York, 1965
——, *Sabbatai Sevi*, London and New York, 1973 (LLJC)
Schütze, J., *Johannes der Täufer*, Zürich, 1967
Schwarzbaum, H., *Studies in Jewish and World Folklore*, Berlin, 1968
Schweid, E., 'Yeme Shivah', *Petahim* (Jerusalem), 1, 1968
Sefer Yuhasin ha-Shalem (ed. H. Freimann), Frankfurt, 1922
Shivhe ha-Besht, see Horodezki, S.A.
Shlonski, A., *Shirim*, 2 vols, Jerusalem, 1971
Shoham, M., *Zor vi-Yrushalayim*, Jerusalem, 1933
Sippure Eliyahu ha-Navi (ed. J. S. Klapholz), 2 vols, Tel-Aviv, 1968
Soloveitchik, R. J., 'The lonely man of faith', *Tradition*, 7(2), 1965
Stcherbatsky, T., *The Conception of Buddhist Nirvana*, London and New York, 1965
Steindorff, G., *Die Apokalypse des Elias*, vol. 2 of *Text und Untersuchungen zur Geschichte der altchristlichen Literatur*, 17 vols, Leipzig, 1899
Steiner, Rudolf, 'Der Prophet Elias im Lichte der Geisteswissenschaft', in *Wendepunkte der Geistesgeschichte*, Dornach, 1922

Thurnwald, Richard, 'Primitive Initiations- und Wiedergeburtsriten', in *Eranos-Jahrbuch 1939*, Zürich, 1940

Tillich, P., *Dynamics of Faith*, New York, 1958

Tishby, J. (ed.), *She'elot u-Teshuvot le-R. Moshe de Leon be-Inyane Kabbalah*, Jerusalem, 1922

——, *Perush ha-Aggadot shel R. Azriel*, Jerusalem, 1945

Uffenheimer, B., *ha-Nevuah ha-Kedumah be-Yisrael*, Jerusalem, 1973

Uffenheimer, Rivka Schatz-, see Schatz-Uffenheimer

Urbach, E., *Hazal: Pirke Emunot ve-Deot*, Jerusalem, 1969

Vollers, K., 'Chidher', *Archiv für Religionswissenschaft* (Leipzig), 12(1), 1909

Vries, B. de, 'Eliyahu ha-Navi ba-Eskhatologia ha-Mikrait', in *Sefer Biram*, Jerusalem, 1947

Walker, K., *The Unconscious Mind*, London, 1961

——, *Diagnosis of Man*, Harmondsworth, 1964

Watts, A., *The Way of Zen*, New York, 1957

Weber, F., *Die Jüdische Theologie auf Grund des Talmud und verwandter Schriften*, Leipzig, 1897

Weiss, J., 'R. Abraham Kalisker's concept of communion with God and men', *Journal of Jewish Studies*, 6, 1955, pp. 87–99

——, 'Spätjüdische Utopie religiöser Freiheit', in *Eranos-Jahrbuch 1962*, Zürich, 1963

Wensinck, A. and Kramers, J., see *Handwörterbuch des Islam*

Werblowsky, R. J. Z., *Lucifer and Prometheus*, London, 1952

——, *Joseph Karo, Lawyer and Mystic*, Oxford, 1962

—— and Bleeker, C. J. (ed.), *Types of Redemption* (International Association for the History of Religions, Supplement 18), Leiden, 1970

Werner, M., *The Formation of Christian Dogma*, London and New York, 1957

Widengreen, G., *Religionsphänomenologie*, Berlin, 1969

Wiesel, E., *The Gates of the Forest*, New York, 1966

Winden, J. C. M. van (ed.), *An Early Christian Philosopher: Justin Martyr's 'Dialogue with Trypho', chapters one to nine*, Leiden, 1971

Wolfson, H. A., *Philo: Foundation of Religious Philosophy*, 2 vols, Cambridge, Mass., 1948

Wormbrand, M., 'Eliyahu ha-Navi ba-Masoret ha-Noẓrit', *Yeda-Am*, 7(25), 1961

Zaehner, Robert C., *Hinduism*, London, 1966

Zion, Robert, *Beiträge zur Geschichte und Legende des Propheten Elijah*, Berlin, 1931

Index

Aaron 33, 65, 101
Aaronide *see* Phinehas
Abba ben Kahana, R. 70
Abihu *see* Nadab
Abraham 24, 69n, 79
Abraham ben David, R. 82
Abraham ben Isaac, R. 82
Abrarvanel, R. Isaac 53n, 202, 204
Absolute Being 179n; *see also* God
Abulafia, R. Abraham 109
Adam: and Elijah 46, 51; and God
    47; new 159; soul 98, 102, 195; *see
    also* sin, original
Adam, book of 93
Adam kadmon (primordial man) 29n,
    98, 100, 104-5, 111, 181
adhesion *see devekut*
Aggadah (legend) 157-8, 164-73,
    187-92; *see also* Elijah; Midrashim;
    Talmud
Aggadists 26, 36-7, 43-77, 126,
    136-40, 149, 177-9
'aha-phenomenon' 189
Ahab, king 4-10, 13-15, 21-4, 46-7,
    96
Ahasver 137n
Ahaziah, king 16, 40, 51
Ahijah the Shilonite 51
AIN (nothingness) 127, 185
Akiva, R. 53

al-Damari 184
al-Khadir (Verdant One) 55n,
    153-9, 179
al-Tabari 152
al-Thalibi 152
Albo, R. Joseph 50n, 73n
Alexandria 140
Ali, caliph 155
Allah 152, 155, 157
Allport, Gordon xi, 199
altar 38, 121, 163
Ambrose, St 145
Amoraim 57, 164
Amram 51
analysis *see* individuation; psychology
Anan, R. 57
Anath (goddess) 10
angel(s): advocate 87; of death
    84n, 95; Elijah as 91, 96, 99-100,
    106-11, 114, 126n, 211; embodi-
    ment 94; and Enoch 41, 97-100,
    106-11; gender of 24-5, 201;
    highest 98; prophet as 34n;
    redeeming 129; *see also* covenant;
    Gabriel; *maggid*; Metatron;
    Michael; Samael; Sandalphon
ANI (I) 127; *see also AIN*
anima 24-5n, 192-3, 223
animal symbolism *see* symbols
anthropology 19, 29, 59, 202

239